THINKING GERMAN TRANSLATION

For details of the Teachers' Handbook and cassette of oral texts please write to:

ROUTLEDGE LTD
ITPS
CHERITON HOUSE
NORTH WAY
ANDOVER
HANTS SP10 5BE

ROUTLEDGE INC.
29 WEST 35TH STREET
NEW YORK
NY 10001
USA

TITLES OF RELATED INTEREST

Thinking Translation: A Course in Translation Method: French to English
Sándor Hervey and Ian Higgins

In Other Words: A Coursebook on Translation
Mona Baker

Redefining Translation
Lance Hewson and Jacky Martin

Translation Studies
Susan Bassnett

The German Language Today
Charles V.J. Russ

The Germanic Languages
Ekkehard König and Johan van der Auwera

The Dialects of Modern German
Charles V.J. Russ, ed.

Colloquial German
Glyn and Dietlinde Hatherall

The Linguistics Encyclopedia
Kirsten Malmkjær, ed.

THINKING GERMAN TRANSLATION

A Course in Translation Method: German to English

Sándor Hervey
Reader in Linguistics, University of St Andrews

Ian Higgins
Senior Lecturer in French, University of St Andrews

Michael Loughridge
Lecturer in German, University of St Andrews

London and New York

First published 1995
by Routledge
11 New Fetter Lane London EC4P 4EE

Simultaneously published in the USA and Canada
by Routledge
29 West 35th Street, New York, NY 10001

Typeset in Times by Michael Mepham, Frome, Somerset
Printed and bound in Great Britain by
T.J. Press (Padstow) Ltd, Padstow, Cornwall

British Library Cataloguing in Publication Data
A catalogue record for this book is available from the British Library

Library of Congress Cataloguing in Publication Data
Hervey, Sándor G.J.
Thinking German Translation: a course in translation method,
German–English/Sándor Hervey, Ian Higgins
and Michael Loughridge
p. cm.
"A teacher's handbook and accompanying cassette
... are also available."
Includes index.
1. German language – Translating into English. I. Higgins, Ian.
II. Loughridge, Michael. III. Title.
PF3498.H46 1995
428′.0231–dc20 95–5794
CIP

ISBN 0–415–11637–6 (hbk)
ISBN 0–415–11638–4 (pbk)

Contents

Acknowledgements

We are very grateful to a number of friends and colleagues who have helped us with specific problems in the preparation of *Thinking German Translation*: Birgit Boes, Sabine Dedenbach, George Goodlad, Sabine Hotho, Dorothy and Gordon Loughridge, Alasdair McClure, John Minchinton, Katharina Riebel, Bärbel Steffens, Dieter Wessels and John Williams. Special thanks go to Malcolm Humble, who has participated in teaching versions of the course at St Andrews, and whose contribution, advice and criticism have been invaluable at a number of stages, right up to reading the text and suggesting improvements. We thank Petra Hervey for her patient assistance in producing the final manuscript. We would also like to thank Claire Trocmé for the thoroughness and good humour with which she guided the text through the editorial minefield. Finally, we acknowledge here the debt we owe to several generations of students who have helped to shape this book by their lively participation in the German Translation Methodology course at St Andrews.

Introduction

This book is a developed version of a tried and tested course in translation methodology for third-year undergraduates in modern languages at the University of St Andrews. The course was first designed for students of French; the French–English version was published by Routledge in 1992 under the title of *Thinking Translation*. However, long before this publication, the French course had proved to be so successful at St Andrews that parallel versions of it were developed for German–English and Spanish–English. These courses are also currently taught at St Andrews.

The present volume is a fully-developed German–English version of the course. While this volume will be found, in many respects, to correspond to the 1992 version of *Thinking Translation*, it is a self-contained, 'parallel' course-book for English-speaking students of German, which contains both major and minor departures from the 1992 version. Some of these departures spring from specific differences between German and French (for instance the 'contrastive topics' in Chapters 16 to 19). Others result from the inevitable process by which ideas are refined through continued application and practice (for instance the section on 'oral genres' in Chapter 11). The most evident departure affecting the structure of the course consists in the inversion of the order in which 'textual levels' are presented. In the 1992 version we opted for what Mona Baker (1992, p. 6) calls a 'top-to-bottom' arrangement: that is to say, textual levels were discussed starting with the broadest and most general level (the 'top') and ending with the level of the smallest, most particular units of language. However, the St Andrews German–English course has always been taught using a 'bottom-to-top' approach (an approach which is, incidentally, Mona Baker's preferred one). Our own experience has confirmed that students explicitly prefer to work from the particular to the general. In the present volume, therefore, we have chosen a 'bottom-to-top' arrangement.

Let us now briefly outline a few basic assumptions that lie at the back of the course structure we are advocating. First, this course is not a disguised version of a 'grammar-and-translation' method of language teaching. Our focus is on how to *translate*, not on how to speak or write German. It is assumed that students already have the considerable linguistic resources in German that they need in order to benefit from the course. We also assume that they have already learned how to use dictionaries and, where appropriate, data-banks. Naturally, in using their linguistic resources to produce good translations, students inevitably extend and improve those resources, and this is an important fringe-benefit.

As we have said, our main interest lies in developing useful translation skills and, generally, in improving *quality* in translation work. In this connection, the point should be made that this quality depends on the translator's having an adequate command of English as much as of German; indeed, Birgit Rommel, head of the Übersetzer- und Dolmetscherschule Zürich, has lamented the lack of mother-tongue training in universities, concluding that: 'Great stress is laid on improving foreign language proficiency, but excellence in the mother-tongue – the translator's target language – is, quite wrongly, taken for granted' (Rommel, 1987, p. 12). As Rommel's comment also suggests, it is normally assumed when training translators that higher quality is achieved when translating into the mother-tongue than into a foreign language; hence the predominance of unidirectional translation, from German into English, in this course.

Second, the course is not intended as a disguised version of translation theory, or of linguistics. 'Theoretical' issues do, of course, arise in it, because translation practice and its deployment of linguistic resources are so complex. However, such issues are not treated out of theoretical interest, but out of direct concern with specific types of problem encountered in translating. That is, our slant is *methodological* and practical – theoretical notions have been freely borrowed from translation theory and linguistics merely with the aim of facilitating and rationalizing methodological problems. Throughout the course, we have provided instant and simple exemplification of each theoretical notion invoked, and linked these notions instantly and directly to practical issues in translation.

Third, the course has a progressive overall structure and thematic organization. After setting out the fundamental issues, options and alternatives of which a translator must be aware, it examines a series of layers that are of textual importance in translation ('upwards' from the nuts and bolts of phonic and graphic details to the generalities of intertextuality and culture). It then moves on, via a series of semantic and stylistic topics (literal meaning, connotation and language variety), to a consideration of textual genres and the demands of translating texts in a range of different genres. If literary genres have, on balance, a higher profile than 'commercial' ones, this is partly offset by the use of non-literary texts of various kinds throughout the course (such as speed translation exercises). In any case, 'commercial' texts tend to present translation difficulties that are far too narrowly specific in subject matter to be suitable for a general course-book on translation method. Our aim has been to produce an integrated, non-specialized approach to the various aspects that need to be discussed in the context of a general methodology of translation. While we cannot claim that this approach is exhaustive, it does have a wide scope and a coherent organization, and it is applicable to translating virtually any type of text likely to be encountered by graduates who go on to translate professionally.

Finally, our claim that the course systematically and progressively builds up a methodical approach to translation should not be taken to mean that we are offering a way of 'mechanizing' the process of translation by providing rules and recipes to be followed. On the contrary, we believe translation to be a highly creative activity in which the translator's personal responsibility is constantly to the forefront. We have, therefore, tried to emphasize throughout the need to recognize options and alternatives, the need for rational discussion, and the need for decision-making. All the material in the course – expository and practical alike – is intended not for silent consumption, but for animated discussion between students and between students and tutor. (In fact, we have found that many of the practicals are best done by students working in small groups and reporting their findings to the class.) Each chapter is, therefore, intended for tutor-student discussion at an early stage in the corresponding practical; this is because we are not trying to inculcate this or that particular theory or method, but simply the general principle that, whatever approach the translator adopts, it should be self-aware and methodical.

While the course we are presenting is a progressively designed whole, it is divided into a series of successive units intended to fit into an academic timetable. Each unit consists of a chapter outlining a set of related notions and problems, and an accompanying practical in which students are given a concrete translation task, working on textual material to which the notions and problems outlined in the chapter are particularly relevant. The first fifteen units are designed to be dealt with progressively, in numerical order. There are, however, four further units, which can be studied at whatever points in the course seem most appropriate to local conditions. These are Chapters 16–19, devoted to four different 'contrastive linguistic' topics. In these four units, the proportion of expository material to practical exercises varies from chapter to chapter.

With the exception of some of the 'contrastive' chapters, each unit needs between 90 minutes' and two hours' class time, and students are also required to prepare in advance for class discussion of the chapter. It is important that each student should have the necessary reference books in class: a monolingual German dictionary, a German–English/English–German dictionary, an English dictionary and an English thesaurus. Some of the practicals will be done at home – sometimes individually, sometimes in groups – and handed in for comment by the tutor. How often this is done will depend on local conditions; in our situation we have found that once a fortnight works well. When an exercise is done at home, this implies that some time should be devoted in the following class to discussion of the issues raised. (Fuller suggestions for teaching and assessment can be found in the *Teachers' Handbook.*)

From consideration of the progressive overall structure of the course and its modular arrangement, it is easy to see how versions of the same course outline can be designed for languages other than French and German. With the exception of the contrastive topics in Chapters 16–19 (which, for each other language, need to be replaced by different contrastive topics dealing with problems that loom large for that language), adapting the course involves the provision of illustrative material for each chapter and of suitable texts for the practicals. The publication of a course-book for Spanish–English along these lines is imminent. A Russian–English version of the course is also on the point of being developed for the Department of Russian at the University of St Andrews.

NB (1) A number of the practicals in the course involve work on texts that are not contained in the present volume, but intended for distribution in class. These texts are found in S. Hervey, I. Higgins and M. Loughridge, *Thinking German Translation: Teachers' Handbook* (Routledge, 1995), which can be obtained from the addresses given on the opening page of this book. (2) The oral texts for use in practicals are available on a cassette: S. Hervey, I. Higgins and M. Loughridge, *Thinking German Translation*, which can also be obtained from the addresses given on the opening page.

1

Preliminaries to translation as a process

There are people who believe that skill in translation cannot be learned and, especially, cannot be taught. Behind this attitude is the assumption that some people are born with a gift of being good translators or interpreters, whereas others simply do not have this knack; in other words, skill in translation is an inborn talent: either you've got it or you haven't.

Up to a point, we would accept this view. No doubt it is true, for instance, that some people take to mathematics or physics, whereas others have little aptitude for such subjects, being more inclined towards the 'humanities'. There is no reason why things should be otherwise for translation; some are 'naturally' good at it, others find it difficult; some enjoy translating and others do not.

The twin assumptions behind this book are that it will help its users acquire proficiency in translation, and that we are addressing ourselves to people who do enjoy translating, even if they are not brilliant at it. Indeed, this assumed element of enjoyment is a vital ingredient in acquiring proficiency as a translator. This, again, is quite normal – elements of enjoyment and job satisfaction play a vital role in any skilled activity that might be pursued as a career, from music to computer technology. Note, however, that when we talk of proficiency in translation we are no longer thinking merely of the basis of natural talent an individual may have, but of the skill and facility that require learning, technique, practice and experience. Ideally, translators should combine their natural talent with acquired skill. The answer to anyone who is sceptical about the formal teaching of translation is twofold: students with a gift for translation invariably find it useful in building their native talent into a fully-developed proficiency; students without a gift for translation invariably acquire some degree of proficiency.

Since this is a course on translation method, it cannot avoid introducing a number of technical terms and methodological notions bordering on the 'theoretical'. (These are set in bold type when they are first explained in the text, and are listed in the Glossary on pp. 228–34.) Our aims are primarily methodological and practical rather than theoretical, but we believe that methods and practices are at their best when underpinned by thoughtful consideration of a rationale behind them. This book is, therefore, only 'theoretical' to the extent that it encourages a thoughtful consideration of the rationale behind solutions to practical problems encountered in the process of translation or in evaluating translations as texts serving particular purposes.

Throughout the course, our aim is to accustom students to making two interrelated sets of decisions. The first set are what we shall call **strategic decisions**. These are general decisions which, ideally, the translator should make before actually starting the translation, in response to such questions as 'what are the salient linguistic characteristics of this text?'; 'what are its principal effects?'; 'what genre does it belong to and what audience is it aimed at?'; 'what are the functions and intended audience of my translation?'; 'what are the implications of these factors?'; and 'which, among all such factors, are the ones that most need to be respected in translating this particular text?'. The other set of decisions may be called **decisions of detail**. These are arrived at in the light of the strategic decisions, but they concern the specific problems of grammar, lexis, and so on, encountered in translating particular expressions in their particular context. We have found that students tend to start by thinking about decisions of detail which they try to make piecemeal without realizing the crucial prior role of strategic decisions. The result tends to be a translation that is 'bitty' and uneven. This is why, in the practicals, students will usually be asked first to consider the strategic problems confronting the translator of a given text, and subsequently to discuss and explain the decisions of detail they have made in translating it. Naturally, they will sometimes find during translating that problems of detail arise which lead them to refine the original strategy, the refined strategy in turn entailing changes to some of the decisions of detail already taken. This is a fact of life in translation, and should be recognized as such, but it is no reason for not elaborating an initial strategy: on the contrary, without the strategy many potential problems go unseen until the reader of the translation trips up over the inconsistencies and the obscurities of detail.

TRANSLATION AS A PROCESS

The aim of this preliminary chapter is to look at translation as a process – that is, to examine carefully what it is that a translator actually does. Before we do this, however, we should note a few basic terms that will be used throughout the course. Defining these now will clarify and simplify further discussion:

Text Any given stretch of speech or writing produced in a given language and assumed to make a coherent, self-contained whole. A minimal text may consist of no more than a single word – for example, 'Prima!' – preceded and followed by a period of silence. A maximal text may run into volumes – for example, Thomas Mann's *Joseph und seine Brüder*.

Source language (SL) The language in which the text requiring translation is couched.
Target language (TL) The language into which the original text is to be translated.
Source text (ST) The text requiring translation.
Target text (TT) The text which is a translation of the ST.

With these terms in mind, the translation process can, in crude terms, be broken down into two types of activity: understanding a ST and formulating a TT. While they are different in kind, these two types of process do not occur successively, but simultaneously; in fact, one may not even realize that one has imperfectly understood the ST until one comes up against a problem in formulating or evaluating a TT. In such a case, one may need to go back to square one, so as to reinterpret and reconstrue the ST in the light of one's new understanding of it (just as a translation strategy may need to be modified in the light of specific, unforeseen problems of detail). In this way, ST interpretation and TT formulation go hand in hand. Nevertheless, for the purposes of discussion, it is useful to think of them as different, mutually separable, processes.

The component processes of translation are not qualitatively different from certain ordinary and familiar processes that all speakers perform in the normal course of their daily lives. In this sense, translation is not an 'extraordinary' process. For a start, comprehension and interpretation of texts are commonplace processes that we all perform whenever we listen to or read a piece of linguistically imparted information. The act of understanding even the simplest message potentially involves all the beliefs, suppositions, inferences and expectations that are the stuff of personal, social and cultural life. Understanding everyday messages is therefore not all that different from what a translator must do when first confronting a ST – and it is certainly no less complicated. It is, however, true that messages may be understood with varying degrees of precision. For instance, suppose that a mother asked her son to get the blue biro from the top left-hand drawer of the bureau, and he responded by giving her a black biro that happened to be handy. She would be justified in thinking that he had not understood her message fully, as he had evidently not paid attention to a number of details in it. Yet he could not be accused of a total lack of comprehension, because he did register and respond to the one salient fact that he had been asked for a biro.

In everyday communication, evidence that a message has been understood may come from appropriate practical response. Another measure of how precisely a message has been understood is appropriate *linguistic* response. Appropriate linguistic response includes such simple things as returning a greeting correctly, giving a satisfactory answer to a question, or filling in a form. While none of these are translation-like processes, they do show that the element of comprehension and interpretation within the translation process involves what can be a perfectly ordinary, everyday activity requiring no special skill or power of intellect, only an average native command of the language used.

There is, however, another kind of ordinary, everyday linguistic response that is rather similar to translation proper. Here is a commonplace example:

BOY:	Ask your Dad if I can take you to the disco tonight.
GIRL:	O.K. (*Exit to find her father*)
	(*to father*) Dad, there's a disco on at the Y.M.C.A. tonight. Can I go?
DAD:	Just a minute. Who's taking you?
GIRL:	Guess who.
DAD:	Oh, I see. And what time does it start?
GIRL:	Eight o'clock – and it finishes at midnight.
DAD:	Right. If you make sure you get your homework done by seven and get what's-his-name to bring you home the moment the thing finishes, you can go. But I want you back here by 12.15 at the latest, and no messing around going round to friends on the way, or whatever it is you lot get up to in the middle of the night. And you come right in and go to bed when you get home, is that clear? No hanging around at the door saying goodnight for hours on end.
GIRL:	O.K., Dad. Thanks. (*Goes back to find Boy*)
BOY:	Well? What did your Dad say?
GIRL:	He says we can go as long as we come straight back at quarter past midnight – and as long as we behave ourselves.

In this commonplace verbal exchange, the girl gives ample evidence of having understood very precisely what her father has said. She does so, not by appropriate practical response, or by making the appropriate reply, but by a process of *interpreting* her father's words (including managing to read skilfully between the lines), and then *reporting the gist* of her father's intended message *in her own words*.

This twofold process is strongly reminiscent of translation proper. Extracting information (by way of comprehension and interpretation) from a given text, and then re-expressing the details of that information in another text using a different form of words is what translators do. We can even distinguish in the example between a ST (the words used by Dad) and a TT (the girl's reply to 'what did your Dad say?'). The only real difference between this example and translation proper is that both ST and TT are in English. We shall follow Jakobson in referring to the reporting or rephrasing of a text in the same language as **intralingual translation** (Jakobson, 1971, pp. 260–6).

In the same article Jakobson also talks of **inter-semiotic translation** (ibid.). This is another commonplace, everyday process, as can be shown in a banal example:

A What does your watch say?
B It says 'five past three'.

Of course, the watch does not actually *say* anything: the words 'five past three' are just a verbal rendering of a message conveyed by the position of the hands. Verbalizing this non-linguistic message is simply a way of *translating*, not from one language to another, but from a non-linguistic communication system to a linguistic one. The common denominator between the two is that they are both 'semiotic systems' (that is, systems for communication), and Jakobson is right to call the process inter-semiotic translation: something we do all the time without even thinking about it. This is another reason, then, for arguing that everybody is a translator of a sort.

Another common process of interpretation that bears a similarity to translation proper is an intra-linguistic process whereby one expands on a particular text and its contents. A good example would be an explanatory commentary on the Lord's Prayer, which might expand and expound the message contained in the single phrase 'Our Father' to read as follows:

> When we pray, we should not pray by ourselves and only ourselves; prayer should always be a corporate activity (compare 'Wherever two or three of you are gathered together...'). This, we may say, is the significance of the word 'our': a first person plural inclusive pronoun. In using the word 'Father', Jesus is suggesting forcefully that one should not think of God as an abstraction, but as a person, and not as a distant, unapproachable one at that, but as a person having some of the attributes associated with a father-figure: head of the household, strict, caring, loving, provident, and so on.

This type of expository interpretation can, as here, easily develop into a full-scale textual exegesis that tries to analyse and explain the implications of a text (perhaps with the addition of cross-references, allusions, footnotes, and so on). This process may not tally with everyone's view of translation, but it does share some common features with translation proper, especially with certain kinds of academic translation: there is a ST which is subjected to comprehension and interpretation, and a TT which is the result of a creative (extended and expository) reformulation of the ST.

The first and third examples above represent two extremes on a continuum of translation-like processes. At one end, the TT expresses only a condensed version of the ST message; we shall call this **gist translation**. At the other end, the TT is far more wordy than the ST, explaining it and elaborating on it; we shall call this **exegetic translation**. Both gist translation and exegetic translation are, of course, matters of degree.

Half-way between these two extremes there is, in principle at least, a process that adds nothing to, and omits nothing from, the message content of the ST, while couching it in terms that are radically different from those of the ST. In *form of expression* ST and TT are quite different, but in *message content* they are as close to one another as possible. We shall call this ideal process **rephrasing**. Thus, we can say that 'Stop!' is a rephrasing of 'red traffic light', and 'yours truly consumed a small quantity of alcohol approximately 60 minutes ago' is a rephrasing of 'I had a little drink about an hour ago'.

The attainability of ideally precise rephrasing is a controversial question that will continue to occupy us in what follows. From the examples just cited, it is clear that precision is a relative matter. 'Stop!' is perhaps a successful inter-semiotic rephrasing of 'red traffic light' (but it omits the associations of danger and the law), while 'yours truly consumed a small quantity of alcohol' is a distinctly less exact (intralingual) rephrasing of 'I had a little drink'. These examples illustrate what is surely a fundamental maxim of translation, namely that rephrasing never allows a *precise reproduction* of the total message content of the ST, because of the very fact that the two forms of expression are different, and difference of form always entails a difference in communicative impact. We shall return to this in Chapter 2, in discussing the concept of translation loss.

So far, then, we have suggested that there are three basic types of translation-like process, defined according to the degree in which the TT abstracts from, adds to, or tries to reproduce faithfully, the details contained in the ST message.

It should be added that there are two important respects in which these three types of process are on an equal footing with one another, as well as with translation proper. First, they all require intelligence, mental effort and linguistic skill; there can be no substitute for a close knowledge of the subject matter and context of the ST, and a careful examination and analysis of its contents. Second, in all three cases, mastery of the TL is a prerequisite. It is salutary to remember that the majority of English mother-tongue applicants for translation posts in the European Commission fail *because of the poor quality of their English* (McCluskey, 1987, p. 17). In a translation course, TL competence needs as close attention as SL competence. There is, after all, not much point in people who do not have the skill to rephrase texts in their native language trying their hand at translation proper into their mother-tongue. Consequently, synopsis-writing, reported speech, intralingual rephrasing and exegesis are excellent exercises for a translator, because they develop one's technique in finding, and choosing between, alternative means of expressing a given message content. That is why the first practical exercise in this course is a piece of intralingual translation in English.

PRACTICAL 1

1.1 Intralingual translation

Assignment

(i) Assess the purpose of the text given below.
(ii) Recast the story in different words, adapting it for a specific purpose and a specific type of audience (define carefully what these are).
(iii) Discuss the textual changes you found it necessary to make, and the reasons for these alterations. (Do this by inserting into your TT a superscript note-

number after each point you intend to discuss, and then discussing the points in order on a fresh sheet of paper. Whenever you annotate your own TTs, this is the system you should use.)

Text

And the LORD said unto Moses, Wherefore criest thou unto me? speak unto the children of Israel, that they go forward:

But lift thou up thy rod, and stretch out thine hand over the sea, and divide it; and the children of Israel shall go on dry ground through the midst of the sea.

[...]

And the Egyptians shall know that I am the LORD, when I have gotten me honour upon Pharaoh, and upon his chariots, and upon his horsemen.

[...]

And Moses stretched out his hand over the sea; and the LORD caused the sea to go back by a strong east wind all that night, and made the sea dry land, and the waters were divided.

And the children of Israel went into the midst of the sea upon the dry ground: and the waters were a wall unto them on their right hand, and on their left.

And the Egyptians pursued, and went in after them to the midst of the sea, even all Pharaoh's horses, his chariots, and his horsemen.

And it came to pass, that in the morning watch the LORD looked unto the host of the Egyptians through the pillar of fire and of the cloud, and troubled the host of the Egyptians,

And took off their chariot wheels, that they drave them heavily: so that the Egyptians said, Let us flee from the face of Israel; for the LORD fighteth for them against the Egyptians.

And the LORD said unto Moses, Stretch out thine hand over the sea, that the waters may come again upon the Egyptians, upon their chariots, and upon their horsemen.

And Moses stretched forth his hand over the sea, and the sea returned to his strength when the morning appeared; and the Egyptians fled against it; and the LORD overthrew the Egyptians in the midst of the sea.

Exodus 14, vv. 15–27, Authorized Version. Extracts from the Authorized Version of the Bible (The King James Bible), the rights in which are vested in the Crown, are reproduced by permission of the Crown's Patentee, Cambridge University Press.

1.2 Gist translation

Assignment
You will be asked to produce a gist translation of a passage given to you in class by your tutor. The tutor will give you any necessary contextual information, and tell you how long you should take over the translation.

2

Preliminaries to translation as a product

As we saw in Chapter 1, translation can be viewed as a process. In this chapter, we shall view it as a product. Here, too, it is useful to start by examining two diametric opposites, in this case two opposed types of translation, one showing extreme SL bias, the other extreme TL bias.

At the extreme of SL bias is **interlineal translation**, where the TT attempts to respect the details of SL grammar by having grammatical units corresponding point for point to every grammatical unit of the ST. Interlineal translation is rare and exists only to fulfil specialized purposes in, say, language teaching, descriptive linguistics, or in certain kinds of ethnographic transcript. Since it is of little practical use to us, we shall not, in fact, give it much consideration, other than to note its position as the furthest degree of SL bias. Interlineal translation is actually an extreme form of the much more common **literal translation**, where the literal meaning of words is taken as if from the dictionary (that is, out of context), but TL grammar is respected. (Literal meaning will be discussed as a topic in Chapter 7.) For our purposes, we shall take literal translation as the practical extreme of SL bias.

At the extreme of TL bias is completely **free translation**, where there is only a global correspondence between the textual units of the ST and those of the TT. The following example contrasts a literal and a free translation of a stock conversation in Chinese between two people who have just been introduced:

	Literal TT		Free TT
A	Sir, are you well?	A	How do you do?
B	Are you well?	B	Pleased to meet you.
A	Sir comes from where?	A	Do you come here often?
B	I come from England.	B	No, this is my first visit.
A	How many persons in your family?	A	Nice weather for the time of year.
B	Wife and five children. And you?	B	Yes, it's been quite warm lately.

The type of extreme freedom seen in the second version is known as **communicative translation**, which is characterized as follows: where, in a given situation (like introducing oneself to a stranger), the ST uses a SL expression standard for that situation, the TT uses a TL expression standard for an analogous target culture situation. This degree of freedom is no more to be recommended as general practice than interlineal translation. (Translators have to use their own judgement about when communicative translation is appropriate.) Communicative translation is, however, mandatory for many culturally conventional formulae that do not allow literal translation. Public notices, proverbs and conversational clichés illustrate this particularly clearly, as in:

Anlieger frei.	Access only.
Man soll den Tag nicht vor dem Abend loben.	Don't count your chickens before they are hatched.
Servus.	Hello.

For further examples, see pp. 24–5 below.

Between the two extremes of literal and free translation, one may imagine an infinite number of degrees, including some sort of a compromise or ideal half-way point between the two. Whether this ideal is actually attainable is the question that lies behind our discussion of 'equivalence' and 'translation loss' below. For the moment, we simply suggest that translations can be usefully judged on a parameter between the two polarities of extreme SL bias and extreme TL bias. Five points on this parameter are schematized in the following diagram adapted from Newmark (1982, p. 39):

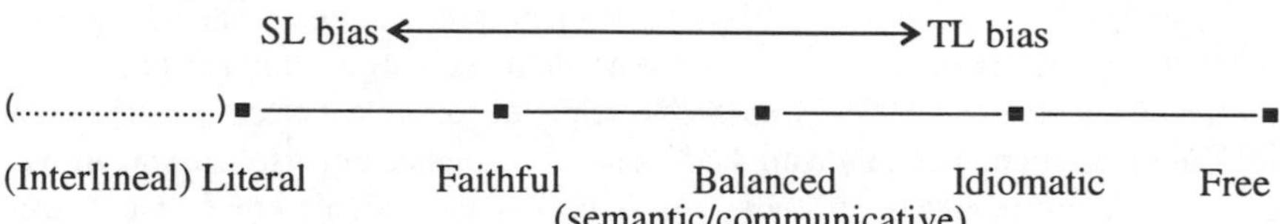

Between the literal and free extremes, the Chinese conversation given above might be rendered at the three intermediate points as follows:

Faithful TT	Balanced TT (semantic/communicative)	Idiomatic TT
A Are you well?	A How do you do?	A How d'you do?
B Are you well?	B How do you do?	B How d'you do?
A Where do you come from?	A Where are you from?	A Where are you from, then?
B I come from England.	B England.	B I'm English.

Faithful TT	Balanced TT (semantic/communicative)	Idiomatic TT
A How big a family do you have?	A Have you any family?	A Any family?
B A wife and five children. And yourself?	B Yes, a wife and five children. Have you?	B Wife and five kids. How about you?

EQUIVALENCE

In characterizing communicative translation, we used the term 'equivalent target culture situation'. Before going any further, we should make it clear what we mean – or rather, what we do not mean – by the terms 'equivalent' and 'equivalence'.

The literature on translation studies has generated a great deal of discussion of what is generally known as *the principle of equivalent effect*.

In so far as 'equivalence' is taken as a synonym of 'sameness' (which is often the case), the concept runs into serious philosophical objections, which we will not go into here. The claim that ST and TT effects and features are 'equivalent' in the sense of 'the same' is in any case unhelpful and misleading for the purposes of translation methodology, for two main reasons.

First, the requirement that the TT should affect its recipients in the same way as the ST does (or did) its original audience raises the difficult problem of how any one particular recipient responds to a text, and of the extent to which texts have constant interpretations even for the same person on two different occasions. Before one could objectively assess textual effects, one would need to have recourse to a fairly detailed and exact theory of psychological effect, a theory capable, among other things, of giving an account of the aesthetic sensations that are often paramount in response to texts. Second, the principle of equivalent effect presumes that the theory can cope not only with the ST and SL audience but also with the impact of a TT on its intended TL audience. Since on both counts one is faced with unrealistic expectations, the temptation for translators is covertly to substitute their own subjective interpretation for the effects of the ST on recipients in general, and also for the anticipated impact of the TT on its intended audience.

It seems obvious, then, that if good translation is defined in terms of 'equivalence', this is not an *objective* equivalence, because the translator remains ultimately the only arbiter of the imagined effects of both the ST and the TT. Under these circumstances, even a relatively objective assessment of 'equivalent effect' is hard to envisage.

More fundamentally still, unlike intralingual translation, translation proper has the task of bridging the cultural gap between monolingual speakers of different languages. The backgrounds, shared knowledge, cultural assumptions and learnt responses of monolingual TL speakers are inevitably culture-bound. Given this fact, SL speakers' responses to the ST are never likely to be replicated exactly by effects on members of a different culture. The notion of cross-cultural 'sameness' of psychological effect is a hopeless ideal. Even a small cultural distance between the ST audience and the TT audience is bound to produce *fundamental* dissimilarity between the effects of the ST and those of the TT – such effects can at best be vaguely similar in a global and limited sense; they can never be 'the same'.

To take a simple example. A translator who decides that the effect of a given ST is to make its audience laugh can replicate that effect by producing a TT that makes its audience laugh. However, claiming 'sameness' of effect in this instance would only be at the expense of a gross reduction of the effects of a text to a single effect. In fact, of course, few texts can be attributed such a monolithic singleness of purpose, and as soon as a ST is acknowledged to have multiple effects, it is unlikely that the TT will be able to replicate them all. (In any case, humour itself is a highly culture-bound phenomenon, which means that even the genuine cross-cultural equivalence of laughter is questionable.)

Another point one must query about the principle of objective equivalent effect concerns the requirement that the TT should replicate the effects of the ST on its *original* audience. This might conceivably be possible for a contemporary ST, but for a work of any appreciable age it may not be feasible, or even desirable. It may not be possible for the translator to determine how audiences responded to the ST when it was first produced. But even if one assumes that such effects can be determined through historical research, one is still faced with a dilemma: should the effects of the TT be matched to those of the ST on its *original* audience, or on a modern audience? The extract from Binding's *Unsterblichkeit* set for translation in Practical 2 is a good example of these problems. Even if it were translated into the English of the 1920s, could one ever know if the TT produced the same effects on an English-speaking readership in the 1990s as the ST did on its post-World War I German readers? The choice between modernizing a TT or making it archaic is fraught with difficulties whatever one decides: on the one hand, the TT may be rendered trivial without the effects it produced on its original audience; on the other, the original cultural impact of the ST may even be incomprehensible, or unpalatable, to a modern TL audience. For example, in the case of a play by Schiller, most people in his Weimar audience would have appreciated the rhetoric for its own sake, as well as the ideas and feelings expressed; but today, few playgoers in Germany – and still fewer in Britain – have enough knowledge of rhetoric to be able to appreciate it as Schiller's original audiences must have done.

In short, we find the principle of equivalent effect, in so far as it implies 'sameness', too vague to be useful in a methodology of translation. At best, a good TT produces a carefully fabricated approximation to some of the manifest properties of the ST. This means that a sound attitude to translation methodology should avoid an absolutist attempt at *maximizing sameness* in things that are crucially different (ST and TT), in favour of a relativist attempt at *minimizing dissimilarities* between things that are clearly understood to be different. Once the latter approach is accepted, there is no objection to using the term 'equivalent' as a shorthand for 'not dissimilar in certain relevant respects'. It is in this everyday sense of the word that we use it in this book.

TRANSLATION LOSS

Our position is best explained in terms of an analogy with engineering. All engineering is based on the premise that the transfer of energy in any mechanical device is necessarily subject to a certain degree of 'energy loss'. A machine that permits energy loss is not a theoretical anomaly in engineering: engineers are not puzzled as to why they have not achieved perpetual motion, and their attention is directed, instead, at trying to design machines with increased efficiency, by reducing energy loss. By analogy, believing in translation equivalence in the sense of 'sameness' encourages translators to believe in the elusive concept of a perfect translation, representing an ideal mean between SL bias and TL bias. But it is far more realistic to start by admitting that the transfer of meaning from ST to TT is necessarily subject to a certain degree of **translation loss**; that is, a TT will always lack certain culturally relevant features that are present in the ST. The analogy with energy loss is, of course, imperfect. While energy loss is a loss *of* energy, translation loss is not a loss *of* translation, but of exact ST–TT correspondence *in* (the process of) translation. Similarly, the very factors that make it impossible to achieve 'sameness' in translation also make it impossible to measure translation loss absolutely and objectively. Nevertheless, once one accepts the concept of inevitable translation loss, a TT that is not a replica of its ST is no longer seen as a theoretical anomaly, and the translator can concentrate on the realistic aim of reducing translation loss, rather than on the unrealistic one of seeking *the* ultimate translation of the ST.

It is important to note that translation loss embraces *any* failure to replicate a ST exactly, whether this involves *losing* features in the TT or *adding* them. Our concept of translation loss is, therefore, not opposed to a concept of translation *gain*; where the TT gains features not present in the ST, this is a form of translation loss. For example, in rendering 'Schleichweg' as 'secret short cut', an obvious translation loss is that the TT lacks the concision of the ST, and its vivid suggestion of furtiveness (even though there is a 'gain' in explicitness); while rendering 'secret short cut' by 'Schleichweg' entails an equally obvious translation loss, in that the TT does not have the explicitness of the ST (even though there is a 'gain' in concision and vividness). Similarly, translating 'Reichstagsabgeordnete' as 'elected members of the German Imperial Parliament' is an instance of translation loss, even though the TT is not only literally exact, but has 'gained' six words *and* makes explicit reference to election and to Germany. A third example exhibits still more sorts of translation loss – the translation of 'Abgasopfer' by 'victims of exhaust fumes'. The German is more concise, but its grammar is a potential source of ambiguity for the unwary; for instance, are exhaust fumes being (metaphorically) offered up by way of sacrifice, or is someone/something (equally metaphorically) falling victim to their harmful effects? In the German case only the context can fully resolve the ambiguity between these two competing metaphors. The grammar of the English expression eliminates all such ambiguity, but it is more cumbersome than the German. As these three examples show, translation loss, in the way we have defined it, is inevitable, even where the TT gains in, say, economy, vividness or avoidance of ambiguity. The challenge to the translator is, therefore, not to eliminate translation loss altogether, but to reduce it by deciding which of the relevant features in the ST it is most important to respect, and which can most legitimately be sacrificed in doing so.

For all translators, but particularly for students, there are two great advantages in the notion that translation loss is inevitable, and that a so-called gain is actually a loss. First, they are relieved of the inhibiting, demoralizing supposition that, if only they were clever enough or lucky enough to find it, the perfect TT is just round the corner; and, second, they are less tempted to try crudely to *outweigh* 'losses' in their TT with a greater volume of 'gains'.

Our approach assumes, then, that the translator's ambition is not an absolutist ambition to maximize sameness, but a relativist one to minimize difference: to look, not for what one is to put into the TT, but for what one might save from the ST, and therefore, to forget the mirage of gain and to concentrate instead on the real benefits of compensation. (We shall discuss compensation in the next chapter.) Once this approach is adopted, the culturally relevant features in the ST will tend to present themselves to the translator in a certain hierarchical order. The most immediately obvious features which may prove impossible to preserve in a TT are 'cultural' in a very general sense, arising from the simple fact of transferring messages from one culture to another – references or allusions to the source culture's history, geography, literature, folklore, and so on. We shall, therefore, discuss such issues in the next chapter. The second step will be to analyse the objectively ostensible formal properties of the ST – syntax, lexis, and so on; we shall suggest a systematic framework for discussing these properties in Chapters 4–6. Subsequent ST features which will inevitably be lacking, or changed, in any TT will have to do with nuances of literal or connotative meaning; yet others will stem from such aspects of language variety as dialect, sociolect and register. We shall be discussing literal and connotative meaning in Chapters 7 and 8 respectively, and questions of language variety in Chapters 9 and 10.

PRACTICAL 2

2.1 Strategic decisions and decisions of detail; translation loss

Assignment

(i) Discuss the strategic problems confronting the translator of the following text, and outline your own strategy for translating it.
(ii) Translate the text into English.

(iii) Explain the significant decisions of detail you made in producing your TT, paying special attention to the question of translation loss.

Contextual information

The passage is from Rudolph G. Binding's 'Unsterblichkeit' (first published in 1921), a 'Novelle' later selected for inclusion in a volume entitled *Deutscher Kitsch* (Killy, 1962). Demeter is the Novelle's central character, and the events narrated in the passage represent the main turning point of the story. (Students are advised to investigate the context of the full 'Unsterblichkeit' text before translating the passage.)

Text

Als sie am Abend mit Gudula zum Strande fuhr, machte sie in der Nähe einer Mole halt, die im spitzen Winkel ins Meer hinauslief und während der Flut überspült wurde. Sie gedachte weit auf ihr entlang zu gehen, um so nahe wie möglich zu der Unendlichkeit vorzudringen. Gudula ließ sie am Wagen zurück, fand sich aber als sie draußen auf der Mole stand nicht eben weit von ihr, da nur eine schmale Wasserzunge, die zwischen der Mole und dem dahinterliegenden Strand hereindrang, sie trennte. Wie am Tag zuvor streifte sie Schuh und Strümpfe ab und ließ sich, die Mole im Rücken, an der nach dem Meere offenen Seite auf dem Sand nieder der hier angeweht war.

Der leichte Wellengang, hier etwas dreister, bespülte und berauschte sie; ihr Blick versenkte sich weit hinaus ins Ferne, Sehnsüchtige; die Welt war hinter ihr verschlossen und sie in unendlicher Weite allein, als plötzlich das Meer beim Küssen ihrer Füße sich veränderte und in eine unheimliche Erregung geriet. Der leise Schlag der Wellen setzte aus; einen Augenblick verharrte die Flut unschlüssig und erstarrt. Dann lief ein Schillern über die Fläche, ein wildes Zittern befiel das Wasser und vor den entsetzten Augen Demeters stand mitten aus der Flut, weit draußen, eine furchtbare Welle auf, hoch und breit, von Schaum gekrönt, und lief mit dunkeln ausgespannten Flügeln geradewegs auf sie zu. Demeter faßte sie in ihren staunenden Blick, ihr Mund stand offen, ihre Finger umkrallten rückwärts greifend erstarrend die rundlichen Steine des Bollwerks. Da stand die Welle vor ihr: hoch aufgereckt. Gudula schrie vom Strande; aber der Schrei verhallte. Die Mole erzitterte, als die Welle am Fuße aufsetzte und mit einem Schwunge die Böschung hinaufsprang. Demeters Hände wurden von den Steinen los hoch über ihren Kopf gerissen, ihr Gewand zerriß in zwei Hälften von oben bis unten, ihr Rücken und Haupt schlugen hart auf den gemauerten Wall. Die Welle ergoß sich, durchdrang, durchfeuchtete, durchblutete sie. Sie rauschte sich in ihre Sinne, packte, erstickte, erwürgte sie. Sie schlug sich in ihren Leib wie mit Fängen und hielt ihn hingestreckt, gefesselt, aufgegeben.

Als das Wasser zurücksank war es, als ob ein Abgrund ihm nachrollte. Aber die Welle kam noch einmal, gesänftigt, mit dem gelasseneren Atem des Meeres zurück. In einer langen zärtlichen Bewegung faßte sie die auf die Mole

Gekreuzigte, hob sie auf und trug sie sanft über den Steindamm hinweg zu dem vor der Flut gesicherten Strand. Dort auf gefeuchteten Sand weich gebettet verließ sie die Welle.

Demeter lag reglos, ihrer Sinne nicht mächtig, mit geschlossenen Augen. Gudula, unvermutet durch den Vorgang in die Nähe ihrer Herrin gelangt, schlich zagend hinzu, sah mit einem Blick daß sie unverletzt war, und bemühte sich um sie. Da richtete sich Demeter langsam halb auf, stützte ihre Hände in den Sand und forschte nach dem Meere hinaus.

'Du hast alles gesehn?' fragte sie matt.

'Alles' sagte Gudula leise.

2.2 Speed translation

Assignment

You will be asked to produce a 300-word newspaper article in English based on a 380-word German ST given to you in class by your tutor. The tutor will tell you how long you have for the exercise. This assignment combines an element of gist translation with an introduction to one of the main demands made of professional translators: working under pressure and at speed.

3

Cultural issues in translation; compromise and compensation

The first part of this chapter brings together, under a single heading, a number of issues directly connected with the fact that translation proper involves not just a transfer of information between two languages, but a transfer from one culture to another. The second part looks at two related translation techniques necessitated by the translation loss attendant on the transfer from one cultural mode of expression to another: compromise and compensation.

CULTURAL TRANSPOSITION

We shall use the general term **cultural transposition** as a cover-term for any degree of departure from purely literal, word-for-word translation that a translator may resort to in an attempt to transfer the contents of a ST into the context of a target culture. That is to say, the various kinds of cultural transposition we are about to discuss are all alternatives to a strictly SL-biased literal translation. Any degree of cultural transposition involves, therefore, the choice of features indigenous to the TL and the target culture in preference to features rooted in the source culture. The result is the minimizing of 'foreign' (that is to say, markedly SL-specific) features in the TT. By suppressing reminders of its SL origins, the TT is to some extent 'naturalized' into the TL and its cultural setting.

The various degrees of cultural transposition can be visualized as points along a scale between the extremes of **exoticism** and **cultural transplantation** :

Exoticism	Cultural borrowing	Calque	Communicative translation	Cultural transplantation

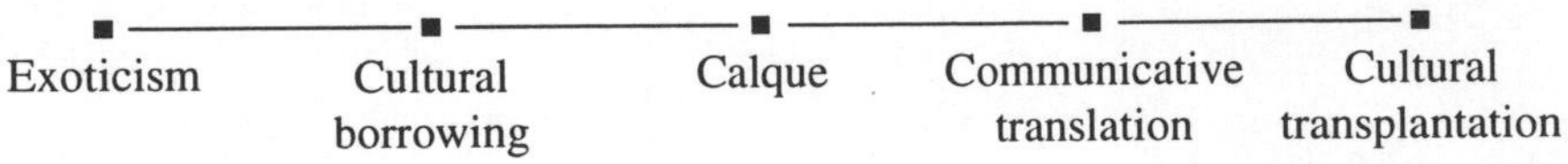

Some of the most straightforward examples of the basic issues involved in cultural transposition are offered by place-names and proper names. Translating names is

not usually a major concern, and certainly does not pose great difficulties for translators, but a brief look at the question will provide a simple introduction to what are often complex problems.

Translating names

In translating a name there are, in principle, at least two alternatives. Either the name can be taken over unchanged from the ST to the TT, or it can be adapted to conform to the phonic/graphic conventions of the TL. The first alternative is tantamount to literal translation, and involves no cultural transposition. It is a form of 'exoticism' in the sense that the foreign name stands out in the TT as a signal of extra-cultural origins. This alternative may be impracticable if, as with Chinese or Russian names, it creates problems of pronounceability and comprehension in an oral TT, or problems of spelling, printing and memorization in a written one. The second alternative, **transliteration**, is less extreme: conversional conventions are used to alter the phonic/graphic shape of the ST name bringing it more in line with TL patterns of pronunciation and spelling. The result is that the transliterated name stands out less clearly as a reminder of foreign and culturally strange elements in the TT. Transliteration is the standard way of coping with, for example, Chinese or Arabic names in English texts.

How a name is transliterated may be entirely up to the translator, if there is no established precedent for transcribing the name in question and no strictly laid down system of transliterational conventions; or it may require following a standard transliteration created by earlier translators. Standard transliteration varies, of course, from language to language. Examples are common in the translation of place-names: 'Wien/Vienna/Vienne'; 'MOCKBA/Moscow/Moskau'; 'Milano/Mailand/Milan', and so on.

Some names are not normally transliterated, but have standard indigenous communicative equivalents in the TL. For example, Flemish 'Luik' = French 'Liège' = German 'Lüttich'; French 'Saint Etienne' = English 'St Stephen' = Hungarian 'Szent István'. Where such conventional communicative equivalents exist, the translator may feel constrained to use them. Not to do so would either display ignorance, or be interpreted as a significant stylistic choice. For example, deliberately using 'Deutschland' instead of 'Germany' in an English TT (for instance, in a translation of P. Celan's 'Todesfuge') would be a form of exoticism, a stylistic device for drawing attention to the German origins of the text.

For some names, particularly place-names, a standard TL equivalent may exist in the form of a **calque**. Here the structure of the TL name imitates that of the SL name, but grammatical slots in it are filled with TL units translating the individual meaningful units of the SL name. For example, 'Black Forest' is a standard calque translation of 'Schwarzwald'. In the absence of a standard calque translation, the option of *creating* a calque may sometimes be open to the translator. For example, in principle at least, in an English translation of a tourist brochure for the Freiburg-im-Breisgau region, the district name 'Kaiserstuhl' might plausibly be rendered as

'Emperor's Seat'. However, calque translations of names must be used with care in order to avoid incongruity; for example, the calque element through which the German title of the recent film of *Cyrano de Bergerac* has been rendered as *Cyrano **von** Bergerac* seems incongruous to those Germans who know Rostand's play as *Cyrano de Bergerac*.

A further alternative in translating names is cultural transplantation. This is the extreme degree of cultural transposition. SL names are replaced by indigenous TL names that are not their referential equivalents, but have similar cultural connotations. For example, in an English translation of 'Mädchen ohne Singular' (a 'humoresque' by Heinrich Spoerl (Rowohlt, 1961) about chorus-girls), the name 'Hildegard Müller' – used in the ST as a stereotypical name for the anonymous chorus-girl – may become, say, 'Betty James'. Cultural transplantation of names is, however, a risky option. For example, if Betty James were portrayed as having lived all her life in Berlin, or as an inveterate addict of coffee and strudel, the effect would be incongruous.

When translating names, one must, therefore, be aware of three things: first, the full range of possible options for translating a particular name; second, the implications of following a particular option (for example, if 'Low Dung Fang' were a character in a novel written in Chinese, an English translator of the novel might want to alter the name sufficiently to avoid its undesirable connotations); and third, all the implications of a choice between exoticism, transliteration, communicative translation and cultural transplantation.

We will now look at issues raised by the various degrees of cultural transposition in more complex units than names.

Exoticism

In general, the extreme options in signalling cultural foreignness in a TT fall into the category of exoticism. A TT translated in a deliberately exotic manner is one which constantly resorts to linguistic and cultural features imported from the ST into the TT with minimal adaptation, and which contains constant reminders of the exotic source culture and its cultural strangeness. Of course, this may be one of the TT's chief attractions, as with some translations of Icelandic sagas or Arabic poetry that deliberately trade on exoticism. However, such a TT has an impact on TL audiences which the ST could never have on a SL audience, for whom the text has none of the features of an alien culture. As a strategic option, exoticism needs to be carefully handled: there is always a danger that audiences will find the TT's eccentricities more irritating than charming. Furthermore, if a culturally distant exotic TT is to be understood, many of the terms used in it may need to be explained; yet the constant intrusion of glosses, footnotes and academic explanations of exotic features in a TT is likely to reduce its attractiveness. This may present a serious dilemma for the translator.

Cultural transplantation

At the opposite end of the scale from exoticism is cultural transplantation, whose extreme forms are hardly to be recognized as translations at all, but are more like adaptations – the wholesale transplanting of the entire setting of the ST, resulting in the text being completely reinvented in an indigenous target culture setting. Examples include James Bridie's *Storm in a Teacup* (a transplantation of Bruno Frank's *Sturm im Wasserglas* (1930) into an entirely Scottish setting, staged in London in 1936), and the transplantation of Rostand's *Cyrano de Bergerac* into the film *Roxanne*. These are not different in kind from the intralingual adaptation of *Romeo and Juliet* into the musical *West Side Story*, or of Shaw's *Pygmalion* into *My Fair Lady*. As these examples show, cultural transplantation on this scale can produce highly successful texts, but it is not normal translation practice. However, on certain points of detail – as long as they do not have knock-on effects that make the TT incongruous – cultural transplantation may be considered as a serious option; a notable, if not entirely successful, example is James Joyce's (1901) translation of Gerhart Hauptmann's *Vor Sonnenaufgang* into an Irish idiom (Perkins, 1978).

By and large, normal, middle-of-the-road translation practice avoids both wholesale exoticism and wholesale cultural transplantation. In attempting to avoid the two extremes, the translator may have to consider the alternatives lying between them on the scale given on p. 20.

Cultural borrowing

The first alternative is to transfer a ST expression verbatim into the TT. This process is termed **cultural borrowing**. The translator will resort to it when it proves impossible to find a suitable indigenous expression in the TL for translating the ST expression. '*Weltanschauung*' is an example: first attested in English in 1868, it is defined in the OED as 'a philosophy of life; a conception of the world'.

A vital condition for the success of cultural borrowing in a TT is that the textual context of the TT should make the meaning of the borrowed expression clear. Cultural borrowing will be most frequent in texts on history, or philosophy, or on social, political or anthropological matters, where the simplest solution is to give a definition of terms like 'glasnost', 'perestroika', 'Ausgleich', 'Reichstag', or 'Gastarbeiter', and then to use the original SL word in the TT.

Of course, cultural borrowing only presents translators with an open and free choice in cases where previous translation practice has not already set up a precedent for the verbatim borrowing of the ST expression. The Saussurean linguistic terms '*langue*' and '*parole*' are good examples of this issue. The option of translating 'langue' and 'parole' as 'language' and 'speaking' does exist, but the fact that specialist English texts frequently resort to the borrowed terms '*langue*' and '*parole*' in the precise linguistic sense prejudices the issue in favour of borrowing. Furthermore, where terms with SL origins have already passed into common usage in the TL without significant change of meaning, thus constituting standard conventional equivalents of the original SL terms borrowed, the translator may not be faced with a significant decision at all. So, for example, such expressions as '*Lebensraum*', '*Weltanschauung*', '*joie de vivre*', '*savoir-faire*', 'kindergarten', 'schnapps', 'bonsai', 'totem' or 'taboo' can be treated as standard conventional equivalents of the corresponding foreign expressions from which they originate. Unless special considerations of style can be invoked, there is little reason not to render such terms verbatim in an English TT. On occasion it may even seem perverse not to do so.

Communicative translation

In contrast with cultural borrowing, the translator may opt for communicative translation. As we saw briefly in Chapter 2 (p. 13), this is often mandatory for culturally conventional formulae where a literal rendering would be inappropriate.

For example, many proverbs, idioms and clichés have readily identifiable communicative equivalents in the TL. Only special contextual reasons can justify opting against a standard communicative translation in such cases. Otherwise the result is likely to be a piece of ludicrous translationese, as in the deliberately comic rendering 'Es ist. Ist es nicht?' (in *Asterix bei den Briten)* calqued on 'Il est, n'est-il pas?' (in *Astérix chez les Bretons;* Goscinny and Uderzo, 1966, *pass.*), which is, in turn, calqued on English 'It is, isn't it?'. The translator has virtually no freedom of choice in rendering stock institutionalized phrases like the following: 'Vorsicht, bissiger Hund/Beware of the dog/Chien méchant'; 'Einbahnstraße/One way/Sens unique'; 'Notwehr/Self-defence/Légitime défense'. Similarly, only for reasons of blatant exoticism, or (again) for special contextual reasons, could one avoid a communicative translation of 'die Katze im Sack kaufen' as 'to buy a pig in a poke', or of 'mausetot' as 'dead as a doornail'. The very fact that the ST uses a set phrase or idiom is usually part and parcel of its stylistic effect, and if the TT does not use corresponding TL set phrases or idioms this stylistic effect will be lost.

However, it often happens that set phrases in the ST do not have readily identifiable communicative TL equivalents. In such cases, the translator has a genuine choice between a literal rendering and some kind of attempt at communicative translation. Assuming that a communicative translation is strategically appropriate in the context, it can only be achieved by rendering the situational impact of the ST phrase in question with a TT expression that, while not a cliché, is nevertheless plausible in the context defined by the TT. An example of this choice and its implications can be drawn from translating a Hungarian ST into English. (We choose Hungarian because it is unfamiliar to most readers, and therefore capable of giving a genuinely exotic impression.) Waking on the first morning of the holiday, the children are disappointed to find that it is raining heavily. Their mother comforts them with a proverb, suggesting that it will soon clear up: 'Nem baj! Reggeli vendég nem maradandó'. Compare these three translations of her words:

Literal: 'No problem! The morning guest never stays long.'

Communicative equivalent: 'Never mind! Sun before seven, rain before eleven.'

Communicative paraphrase: 'Never mind! It'll soon stop raining.'

The only possible advantage of the literal translation is its exoticism, but this advantage is cancelled by two things: the obscurity of the TT, and its lack of contextual plausibility. If there were good reason for preserving the exoticism, one could mitigate these disadvantages by obliquely signalling in the TT that the mother is using what is, for TL readers, an exotic proverb: 'Never mind! You know the saying: the morning guest never stays long.'

The communicative equivalent has the advantage of rendering proverb for proverb. However, in the circumstances, the communicative equivalent is incongruous – what the narrative context requires is 'rain before seven, sun before eleven', but this is not a universally recognized form of the English proverb.

The communicative paraphrase has the advantage of being idiomatic and plausible in the TT – it is the kind of thing the children's mother might plausibly say in English in the situation. It has the disadvantage of losing the stylistic flavour of 'speaking in proverbs' (which might be an important feature of the way the mother speaks).

Which solution is deemed best will naturally depend on contextual factors outside the scope of this example. Nevertheless, the example illustrates very well the alternatives in cultural transposition, including the one we have yet to discuss, namely calque.

Calque

'The morning guest never stays long' is a calque, an expression that consists of TL words and respects TL syntax, but is unidiomatic in the TL because it is modelled on the structure of a SL expression. In essence, then, calque is a form of literal translation. A bad calque imitates ST structure to the point of being ungrammatical in the TL; a good calque manages to compromise between imitating a ST structure and not offending against the grammar of the TL.

Calquing may also be seen as a form of cultural borrowing, although, instead of verbatim borrowing of expressions, only the model of SL grammatical structures is borrowed. For example, if ST 'Sturm und Drang' is rendered in the TT as '*Sturm und Drang*', that is cultural borrowing proper, whereas TT 'Storm and Stress' is a calque. Like cultural borrowing proper, and for similar reasons, translation by creating calques does occur in practice. Furthermore, as also happens with cultural borrowing proper, some originally calqued expressions become standard TL cultural equivalents of their SL originals. Examples are German 'Vier-Sterne-General' calqued on American English 'four star general'; English 'world-view', calqued on German 'Weltanschauung' (also existing as a verbatim borrowing, as we have seen); French 'jardin d'enfants', calqued on German 'Kindergarten' and American

English 'ants in the pants' calqued (by popular etymology) on German 'Angst in den Hosen'.

Clearly, there are certain dangers in using calque as a translation device. The major one is that the meaning of calqued phrases may not be clear in the TT. In the worst cases, calques are not even recognizable for what they are, but are merely puzzling bits of gibberish for the reader or listener. This is why, in our Hungarian example, we suggested using a device like 'you know the saying' as a means of signalling the calquing process in the TT. But, of course, it is not sufficient for the TT to make it clear that a particular phrase is an intentional calque. The meaning of the calqued phrase must also be transparent in the TT context. The most successful calques need no explanation; less successful ones may need to be explained, perhaps in a footnote or a glossary.

Like all forms of cross-cultural borrowing, calque exhibits a certain degree of exoticism, bringing into the TT a flavour of the cultural foreignness and strangeness of the source culture. Consequently, it should generally be avoided in texts where exoticism is strategically inappropriate, such as an instruction manual, whose prime function is to give clear and explicit information. In any text, one should also definitely avoid unintentional calquing resulting from too slavish a simulation of the grammatical structures of the ST. At best, such calques will give the TT an unidiomatic flavour as in 'before our oldest pollution victims most close their eyes', calqued on 'vor unseren ältesten Abgasopfern verschließen die meisten ihre Augen'. At worst, the TT may become effectively ungrammatical, as is the sentence 'In case all the other species will be studied, hints on a function-related use of song types will be obtained', presumably calqued on 'Falls alle anderen Arten untersucht werden, werden sich Hinweise auf einen funktionsverwandten Gebrauch von Gesangtypen ergeben'.

In brief summary of the discussion so far: where standard communicative equivalents exist for a ST expression, the translator should give these first preference, and only reject them if there are particular reasons for doing so. Where standard communicative equivalents are lacking, and also a particular ST concept is alien to the target culture, preference should be given to cultural borrowing, *unless* there are particular reasons against it.

The emphasis in the preceding paragraph on solutions being preferable unless certain conditions militate against them draws attention to the need to balance one set of considerations against another. This is, indeed, a general feature of the translation process, and remarking on it in the context of a choice between literal translation, communicative translation, cultural transplantation, and so on brings us to a discussion of compromises made necessary by this feature.

COMPROMISE AND COMPENSATION

Throughout this course, it will be obvious that translation is fraught with compromise. Compromise in translation means reconciling oneself to the fact that, while one would like to do full justice to the 'richness' of the ST, one's final TT inevitably suffers from various translation losses. Often one allows these losses unhesitatingly. For instance, a translator of prose (particularly in the commercial sector) may without any qualms sacrifice the phonic and prosodic properties of a ST in order to make its literal meaning perfectly clear, while a translator of verse (e.g. song lyrics) may equally happily sacrifice much of the ST's literal meaning in order to achieve certain desired metric and phonic effects. These are just two examples of the many kinds of compromise translators make every day.

Compromises should be the result of deliberate decisions taken in the light not only of what latitudes are allowed by the SL and TL respectively, but also of all the factors that can play a determining role in translation: the nature of the ST, its relationship to SL audiences, the purpose of the TT, its putative audience, and so forth. Only then can the translator have a firm grasp of which aspects of the ST can be sacrificed with the least detriment to the effectiveness of the TT, both as a rendering of the ST and as a TL text in its own right. Much of the material in this book will in fact draw attention, in both principle and practice, to the different kinds of compromise suggested – perhaps even dictated – by different types of text.

The issue of undesirable, yet inevitable, translation losses raises a special problem for the translator. The problem consists in knowing that the loss of certain features sacrificed in translation does have detrimental effects on the quality of the TT, but seeing no way of avoiding these unacceptable compromises. So, for instance, 'cake' is admittedly far from being an exact translation of the literal meaning of 'Gugelhupf'; it lacks the association with the characteristic shape of a 'Gugelhupf' which is so much part of the meaning of the word. Nevertheless, translating 'Gugelhupf' as 'cake' may be an acceptable compromise if the ST merely makes casual mention of it. However, this is less acceptable if the shape of a 'Gugelhupf' is mentioned in the ST and the author seems to be deliberately conjuring up a mental image of that shape. And such a compromise is quite unacceptable if 'gugelhupfförmig' is the sole means by which the configuration of a hill is described in the ST, as in the Musil passage in Practical 15: in this case, 'shaped like a cake' is an unsatisfactory rendering.

It is when faced with apparently inevitable, yet unacceptable, compromises that translators may feel the need to resort to techniques referred to as **compensation** – that is, techniques of making up for the loss of important ST features through replicating ST effects approximately in the TT by means other than those used in the ST. For methodological purposes it is useful to distinguish four different aspects of compensation (while remembering that these aspects frequently occur together).

Compensation in kind

The first aspect we shall call **compensation in kind**. This refers to making up for one type of textual effect in the ST by another type in the TT. One area where compensation in kind is often needed is in the differences between 'gender' in German and English. The contrast in German between masculine and feminine forms of nominalized past participles is one that frequently causes problems. There is an example of this in the text by Rudolf Binding, used in Practical 2. Here the contrast between the textually explicit '*die* Gekreuzigte' and the textually unnamed '*der* Gekreuzigte' is of undoubted importance in the ST: the effect of the combination between an allusion to Christ and use of feminine gender is greatly to increase the emotional charge, through endowing the fate suffered by the female protagonist with a quasi-religious, mystical significance.

The formation of English verb-based nominals does not in itself permit the expressive power which this ST derives from the contrast between feminine and masculine gender. The option of rendering 'die Gekreuzigte' as 'the crucified one' is (besides being unidiomatic) incapable of recreating the tension between feminine and masculine gender which characterizes the ST; it represents an unacceptable translation loss. One way of overcoming this lack might be to compensate in kind, by translating 'die Gekreuzigte' as 'the crucified *woman*'.

Compensation in kind can be further illustrated by three of its most typical forms. First, explicit meanings in the ST may be compensated for by implicit meanings in the TT. In the following example from the lyrics of the Brecht/Weill song 'Surabaya Johnny', the ST 'Sixpencebett' explicitly denotes the cheap price of the accommodation shared by the protagonist and her lover, while TT 'flophouse' indirectly connotes cheapness:

Eines Morgens in einem Sixpencebett Werd' ich donnern hören die See...	One fine morning I'll wake in some flophouse To the thundering roar of the sea...

(Brecht, 1993, p. 346)

Second, connotative meanings in the ST may be compensated for by literal meanings in the TT. Here is a simple example:

Die Kugeln gehen durch ihn durch Doch aus den Löchern fließt Bei Franz Villon nicht Blut heraus Nur Rotwein sich ergießt...	The bullets pass right through Villon And off the Wall they whine But from their holes there comes no blood Just gallons of red wine...

(*Wolf Biermann: Poems and Ballads*, translated by Steve Gooch, 1977, pp. 86–7)

In the ST the notion of liberal quantities of red wine is not explicitly mentioned but merely implied by the connotative meaning of 'sich ergießt' (which suggests a copious flow, not just a mere trickle). This implicit meaning is lost in the TT's use of 'comes' to render at one stroke both 'fließt' and 'gießt'. The loss of this connotation is compensated for by inserting the explicit reference to 'gallons'. (We shall discuss literal and connotative meaning as such in Chapters 7 and 8.)

Third, where, for example, the humour of the ST hinges on the comic use of calque, the TT may have to derive its humour from other sources, such as a play on words. Successful examples of this sort of compensation in kind abound in the

Astérix books; compare, for instance, *Astérix chez les Bretons* with *Asterix bei den Briten*:

OBELIX: Nous aurions dû emporter quelques vivres.	OBELIX: Wir hätten ein paar Lebensmittel mitnehmen sollen!
JOLITORAX: Bonté gracieuse!	TEEFAX: Gute Güte!
(Goscinny and Uderzo, 1966)	(Goscinny and Uderzo, 1971)

In the ST, the humour of 'bonté gracieuse' hinges on the fact that it is a facetious calque on English 'goodness gracious'; in the German TT, instead of coining a facetious calque, the translator has attempted to achieve a humorous effect through a play on the words 'gute' and 'Güte'.

Compensation in place

Compensation in place consists in making up for the loss of a particular effect found at a given place in the ST by creating a corresponding effect at an earlier or later place in the TT. A simple example of compensation in place is that of compensating for a comic effect in the ST by constructing a similar comic effect at a different place in the TT, as in *Asterix bei den Briten*:

JOLITORAX: Justement cousin Astérix il nous faut de la *magique potion* pour combattre les *romaines armées*.	TEEFAX: Genau, Vetter Asterix, wir brauchen den magischen Trank, *um zu schlagen* die römischen Armeen.
(Goscinny and Uderzo, 1966; our italics)	(Goscinny and Uderzo, 1971; our italics)

The ST comic effect depends on the inversion of grammatical order between adjective and noun, which is different for French and English. Such a device is not feasible in German, which, in this respect, follows the same order as English. However, a similar comic inversion can be achieved in German by imitating the English syntactic order of predicate followed by direct object. This is the compensation device the translator has used in the German TT.

Compensation in place is also needed in translating the following ST:

Que**r** du**r**ch Eu**r**opa von Westen nach Osten
Rüttert und **rattert** die Bahnmelodie.
Gil**t** es die Seligkei**t** schnelle**r** zu kos**t**en?
Komm**t** e**r** zu spä**t** an im Himmelslogis?
FortfortfortFortfortfort drehn sich **d**ie **Räder**
Rasen**d d**ahin auf **d**em Schienengeä**der**,
Rauch ist **der** Bestie ver**schwindender Schw**eif,
Schaffne**rpfiff**, Lokomotivenge**pfeif**.
(D. von Liliencron, 'Der Blitzzug', 1911, p. 237)

Here the element of sound symbolism that is so central to the poem as a whole is reinforced by alliterations and assonances which concentrate particularly, on the one hand, on the sounds [r], [t] and [d], and, on the other, on [f], [pf] and **[ʃ]**. This phonetic reinforcement cannot be precisely, and equally intensively, replicated in an English TT because the key words do not alliterate in the required ways. The following TT attempts at least partly to compensate for this by using phonetic reinforcement distributed in different places from where it occurs in the ST:

Right ac**r**oss Eu**r**ope in eastern di**r**ection
Rumbling and **ratt**ling the **t**une of the **tr**ain.
Af**t**er a fo**ret**as**te** of blissful salvation
Will it **t**urn up too la**t**e **at** heaven's domain?

On**w**ardsandon**w**ards the **wh**eels keep on **t**urning
Rushing ahead on a**rt**e**r**ial **r**ails
Smoke **f**orms a **tr**ain **wh**ich is **gr**adually **f**ading,
Whistle of **g**uard, as the engine **w**ails.

(unpublished translation by Malcolm Humble)

Compensation by merging

The technique of compensation by merging is to condense ST features carried over a relatively long stretch of text (say, a complex phrase or a compound word) into a relatively short stretch of the TT (say, a simple phrase or a single word). In some cases, compensation by merging is the only way to strike a fair balance between doing justice to the literal meaning of a piece of ST and constructing an idiomatic TT, as in this example:

Und wesentlich häufiger *Busse und Bahnen* nutzen

An accurate literal translation of the italicized words would have to take into consideration that the modes of transport referred to include buses, trolleybuses, trams and trains; but the resulting TT phrase would be far too long-winded and ponderous to be suitable. The semantic contents of the ST expression are rendered accurately, and in a more streamlined fashion, through compensation by merging:

And make much greater use of *public transport*

Another example is furnished by Spoerl's earlier mentioned essay 'Mädchen ohne Singular' (Spoerl, 1961, p. 112):

Mister Tiller war *Menschenkenner*, *Männerkenner* (our italics)

Mr Tiller was a connoisseur of ***man***kind

The ST effect involves a play, made in a thoroughly 'male chauvinist' context, on the gender-neutral sense of 'Menschen' and the explicitly masculine gender of 'Männer', with the implication that what Mr Tiller understood was *men* in particular, not *human nature* in general. To try and render this effect by, say, a phrase like 'Mr Tiller was a connoisseur of human nature; of men' would be to lose the transparent ambivalence on which the ST trades, as well as to destroy the crispness with which the opposition between 'Menschen' and 'Männer' is presented in the ST. In English, the single word 'man' already has the requisite gender-ambivalence built into it, while something of the crispness of the opposition can be achieved through merging the two senses into the one word 'mankind' and, somewhat archly, highlighting the item 'man'. In other words, compensation by merging seems to be a neat solution in this instance; though it relies heavily, of course, on the specific context of gender relations.

Compensation by splitting

Compensation by splitting may be resorted to, if the context allows, where there is no single TL word that covers the same range of meaning as a given ST word. A simple example is furnished by the German word 'Bahnen', which, for literal exactitude, has to be translated as 'trains and trams' (or 'trams and trains'). The following example is more complex, but no less typical:

Rund um Todtnau ist die Welt *noch* in Ordnung (our italics)

This piece of ST is the title of a section in a glossy tourist guide (*HB Bildatlas Südlicher Schwarzwald,* published in 1985). The problem element in translating it is the italicized 'noch'; such attempted renderings as 'all's still well with the world in Todtnau', 'all's well with the world still in Todtnau', 'all's well with the world in Todtnau still', besides being stilted and inelegant, seem to miss the central persuasive message of the caption: Todtnau remains unspoilt. This message can be encapsulated into a TT caption by expanding the sense of 'noch' into 'still unspoilt'. One way of translating the sentence would therefore be to use compensation by splitting:

All's well with the world in *still unspoilt* Todtnau

As well as illustrating compensation by splitting, this TT is also an example of compensation in kind: the ST's implicitly connoted notion of the unspoilt landscape of Todtnau is rendered in the TT by literal means through the explicit addition of the word 'unspoilt'. We will not pursue this any further, because what is involved is the question of literal versus connotative meaning, and these questions are not addressed until Chapters 7 and 8. Suffice it to say that the TT exhibits the substitution of literal meaning for connotative meaning.

The four types of compensation discussed above can, of course, take many different forms; and, as our last example indicates, it also often happens that a single case of compensation belongs to more than one category at the same time. Good examples of multiple compensation will be found in the texts set for analysis in Practical 3.

We conclude with a word of caution: while compensation exercises the translator's ingenuity, the effort it requires should not be wasted on textually unimportant features. The aim is to reduce some of the more serious and undesirable translation losses that necessarily result from the fundamental structural and cultural differences between SL and TL.

PRACTICAL 3

3.1 Cultural transposition; compensation

Assignment

(i) Discuss the strategic problems confronting the translator of the following text, and outline your own strategy for translating it.
(ii) Translate the text into English.
(iii) Explain the main decisions of detail you made in producing your TT.

Contextual information
The text appears as a full-page advertisement (in colour) in the January 1991 issue of a lavishly produced glossy German magazine entitled *Geo*. The magazine features mainly articles of a popular anthropological and geographical nature, fully illustrated with exotic photography. The advertisement is sponsored by the Verband Deutscher Verkehrsunternehmen and the Deutsche Bundesbahn.

Text

EUROCOM

Vor unseren ältesten Abgasopfern verschließen die meisten ihre Augen.

Die steigende Schadstoffbelastung in unseren Innenstädten nimmt nicht nur den Menschen den Atem. Auch die steinernen Zeugen der Vergangenheit, die seit Jahrhunderten Wind und Wetter trotzen konnten, kapitulieren angesichts der Luftverschmutzung. Und die wird trotz Katalysator zum größten Teil von Auto-Abgasen verursacht. Was können wir also tun?

Wir alle müssen umdenken und lernen, unsere Verkehrsmittel sinnvoller und überlegter zu gebrauchen. Und wesentlich häufiger Busse und Bahnen nutzen – so wie es täglich 18 Millionen Fahrgäste tun. Denn Busse und Bahnen sind die saubersten motorisierten Verkehrsmittel überhaupt.

Je mehr Menschen umdenken, desto besser für uns alle. Denn die Denkmäler in unseren Städten sollen auch in Zukunft eine Zukunft haben.

Wir nicht.

ZEIT ZUM UMDENKEN
BUSSE & BAHNEN

Eine Initiative des Verbandes Deutscher Verkehrsunternehmen und der Deutschen Bundesbahn.

Reprinted by kind permission; a motive of the national advertising drive of the Verband Deutscher Verkehrsunternehmen and the Deutsche Bundesbahn, Cologne 1991.

3.2 Compensation

Assignment

Working in groups, analyse the various cases of cultural transposition and of compensation in the following TT. Give your own version where you can improve on the TT.

Contextual information

The poem is by Wolf Biermann, East German singer–songwriter whose critical political songs made him a thorn in the flesh of the government of the GDR throughout the 1960s and 1970s. In 1976, while he was performing in West Germany, Biermann was stripped of his citizenship by the East German authorities. In spite of being banned from the media, Biermann's critical, acid and often somewhat vulgar 'Hetzlieder' (provocative songs), proclaiming his own personal communism and his opposition to hypocrisy, meanness and degradation, continued to penetrate every corner of German culture. While 'Kunststück' is one of his lighter pieces, it is characteristic in its blend of politics with a celebration of a love of life and of the common man. The translation is by Steve Gooch.

Source text

KUNSTSTÜCK

Wenn ich mal heiß bin
Wenn ich mal heiß bin
  lang ich mir ne Wolke runter
  und wring sie über mir aus.
Kalte Dusche.
        Kunststück.

Wenn ich mal kalt bin
Wenn ich mal kalt bin
  lang ich mir die Sonne runter
  und steck sie mir ins Jackett.
Kleiner Ofen.
        Kunststück.

Wenn ich bei ihr bin
Wenn ich bei ihr bin
  schwimmen Wolken mit uns runter
  rollt die Sonne gleich mit.
Das ist Liebe.
        Kunststück.

Target text

PIECE A CAKE

When I get hot, son
When I get hot, son
  I reach up and grab a cloud
  and wring it out over me.
Ice-cold shower.
        Piece a cake.

When I get cold, son
When I get cold, son
  I reach up and grab the sun
  and pop it under my coat.
Little oven.
        Piece a cake.

When I'm with her, son
When I'm with her, son
  clouds come floating down, son, with us
  and the sun comes down too.
That's love for you.
        Piece a cake.

Wenn ich mal müd bin	When I get tired, son
Wenn ich mal müd bin	When I get tired, son
lang ich mir den lieben Gott runter	I reach up and grab the dear Lord
und er singt mir was vor.	so he'll sing me a song.
Engel weinen.	Angels weeping.
Kunststück.	Piece a cake.
Wenn ich mal voll bin	When I get pissed, son
Wenn ich mal voll bin	When I get pissed, son
geh ich kurz zum Teufel runter	I nip down to see the devil
und spendier Stalin ein Bier.	and buy old Stalin a beer.
Armer Alter.	Poor old bugger.
Nebbich.	Nebbish.
Wenn ich mal tot bin	When I am dead, son
Wenn ich mal tot bin	When I am dead, son
werd ich Grenzer und bewache	I'll be keeping an eye on the border
die Grenz zwischen Himmel und Höll.	the border of heaven and hell.
Ausweis bitte!	Passports ready!
Kunststück.	Piece a cake.

Reprinted from *Wolf Biermann: Poems and Ballads*, translated by Steve Gooch (London: Pluto Press, 1977, pp. 70–3) and by kind permission from Wolf Biermann, *Alle Lieder* © 1991 by Verlag Kiepenheuer & Witsch Köln.

3.3 Cultural transposition; compensation

Assignment

You will be given a text in class by your tutor. Working in groups:

(i) Discuss the strategic problems confronting the translator of the following ST, and say what your own strategy would be.

(ii) In the light of your findings in (i), translate the text into English, paying particular attention to cultural transposition and compensation.

Contextual information

The text is part of a glossy information brochure published for distribution to commuters in the Frankfurt region by the Frankfurter Verkehrsverbund (FVV) in 1978. The purpose of the brochure was to introduce, explain and promote the (then new) integrated regional transport system, and, in particular, the newly installed ticket machines that have been in use since.

4

The formal properties of texts: phonic/graphic and prosodic problems in translating

If the challenge of translation is not to replicate a ST in the TL but rather to reduce translation loss, the immediate problem that arises after the general cultural issues have been assessed is that of the ST's objectively ostensible formal properties. There are, doubtless, insurmountable problems in establishing objectively what the ostensible properties of a text are, but it can at least be said that whatever effects, meanings and reactions are triggered by a text must originate from features objectively *present in it*. It is, therefore, necessary for the translator to look at the text as a linguistic object.

THE FORMAL PROPERTIES OF TEXTS

In trying to assess the formal properties of texts, one can usefully turn to some fundamental notions in linguistics. There is no need for a detailed incursion into linguistic theory, but linguistics does offer a hierarchically ordered series of systematically isolated and complementary *levels* on which the formal properties of texts can be located for the purposes of a methodical discussion.

It is true of any text that there are various points on which it could have been different. For instance, where there is an allusion to the Bible, there might have been a quotation from Shakespeare; or where there is a question mark there might have been an exclamation mark (compare 'Was he drinking?' and 'Was he drinking!'); or where the text has a letter 'c' there might have been a letter 'r' (compare 'It's cutting time for tea-roses' and 'It's rutting time for tea-cosies'). All these points of detail, no matter how large or small, where a text could have been different (that is, where it could have been *another* text) can be designated **textual**

variables. It is these textual variables that the series of levels defined in linguistics makes it possible to identify.

Taking the linguistic levels one at a time has two main advantages. First, looking at textual variables on an organized series of isolated levels enables one to see which textual variables are important in the ST and which are less important. As we have seen, some of the ST features that fall prey to translation loss may not be worth the effort of compensation. It is, therefore, excellent strategy to decide which of the textual variables are indispensable, and which can be ignored, for the purpose of formulating a good TT. (In general, as we shall see, the more prominently a particular textual variable contributes to triggering effects and meanings of a text, and the more it coincides in this with other textual variables with related meanings and effects, the more important it is.)

Second, one can assess a TT, whether one's own or somebody else's, by isolating and comparing the formal variables of both ST and TT. This enables the translator to identify what textual variables of the ST are absent from the TT, and vice versa. That is, although translation loss is by definition not ultimately quantifiable, it is possible to make a relatively precise accounting of translation losses on each level. This also permits a more self-aware and methodical way of evaluating TTs and of reducing details of translation loss.

We propose six levels of textual variables, hierarchically arranged from lowest to highest, in the sense that each level is, as it were, built on top of the previous one. Naturally, other schemes could have been offered, but arguing about alternative theoretical frameworks would involve a deeper plunge into linguistic theory than is useful for our purposes. In this chapter and the next two, we shall work our way up through the levels, showing what kinds of textual variable can be found on each, and how they may function in a text. Together, the six levels constitute a kind of 'filter' through which the translator can pass a text to determine what levels and formal properties are important in it and most need to be respected in the TT. Surprising as it may seem at this early stage, this method does not imply a plodding or piecemeal approach to texts: applying this filter (and others) quickly becomes automatic and very effective in translation practice. (A schematic representation of all the filters we are suggesting can be found on p. 227.)

THE PHONIC/GRAPHIC LEVEL

The most basic level of textual variables is the **phonic/graphic level**. Taking a text on this level means looking at it as a sequence of sound segments (or *phonemes*) if it is an oral text, or as a sequence of letters (or *graphemes*) if it is a written one. Although phonemes and graphemes are different things, they are on the same level of textual variables: phonemes are to oral texts as graphemes are to written ones. To help keep this in mind, we shall refer to the 'phonic/graphic level' regardless of whether the text in question is an oral one or a written one.

Every text is a unique configuration of phonemes/graphemes, these configurations being restricted by, among other things, the conventions of a particular language. This is why, in general, no text in a given language can reproduce exactly the same sequence of sound segments/letters as any text in another language. Occasional coincidences apart (which may be cited as curiosities, such as the sequence 'I VITELLI DEI ROMANI SONO BELLI' which can be read alternatively, and with two completely different meanings, in either Latin or Italian: as 'Go, Vitellus, to the martial sound of the god of Rome', or as 'the calves of the Romans are beautiful', respectively), ST and TT will always consist of markedly different sequences. This automatically constitutes a source of inevitable translation loss. The real question for the translator, however, is whether this loss matters at all. Could we not simply put it down as a necessary consequence of the transition from one language to another, and forget about it?

The suggestion that the translator should not bother with the sound/letter sequences in texts echoes Lewis Carroll's jocular translation maxim: 'Take care of the sense and the sounds will take care of themselves'. We may give two initial answers to this maxim. First, some translators have been known to pay special attention to re-creating phonic/graphic effects of the ST, at times even to the detriment of the sense. Second, some texts would lose much of their point (and meaning) if deprived of their special phonic/graphic properties.

As a matter of fact, even in the most ordinary, prosaic text one may come across problems of translation that have to do specifically with the phonic/graphic level. The transcription of names is a prime example. When looking, in the last chapter, at the possibilities for cultural transposition of names, we noted that it is a matter of conventional equivalence that accounts for the translation of German 'Wien' as English 'Vienna', Russian 'MOCKBA' as English 'Moscow', and so on. Equally conventional is the standard English transliteration 'Mao Tse Tung'. This transliteration in fact occasions a phonic distortion (from [mɒwdʒduŋ] to [mɒwtsit'uŋ]), which does not much matter even to the few people who are aware of it. On the other hand, if 'Blue Mist' were the international brand name of a perfume, one might well be reluctant, for word-associative reasons, to retain this brand name when advertising the product in Germany.

As these examples show, a measure of phonic/graphic inventiveness and decision-making may be involved in the process of translation. These resources are, of course, called upon to a much greater degree in translating a ST that makes important and self-conscious use of phonic/graphic variables for *special effects*. We mean by such special effects the patterned use of phonic/graphic features in order to create or – more usually – to reinforce a thematic motif or mood within a text.

The simplest example of such special effects is onomatopoeia. Onomatopoeia is either directly *iconic* – that is, the phonic form of a word impressionistically imitates a sound which is the referent of the word – or *iconically motivated* – that is, the phonic form of the word imitates a sound associated with the referent of the word (for example, 'cuckoo'). If it has a thematically important function, onomatopoeia may require care in translation. Some examples are straightforward, of course, as in those instances where German 'Krach' is appropriately rendered by 'crash', which presents little difficulty or translation loss. Others, while still straightforward, are potentially more problematic, as in the conventional translation of German 'Brummen' into English 'buzzing', where there is slightly more phonic translation loss and that loss could conceivably be significant in certain contexts.

Cross-cultural variations in onomatopoeia are common – compare, for example, German 'patsch!' with English 'splash!'. What is more, many SL onomatopoeic words do not have one-to-one TL counterparts. For instance, 'squeak' may be rendered in German as 'quieken' (if a mouse is making the noise) or as 'knarren' (if it is a badly oiled door, or wheel); German 'pfeifen' may be rendered as 'whistle', 'hiss' or 'wheeze', depending on who or what is making the noise and in what circumstances; similarly, German 'patsch!' may translate alternatively as 'smack!', 'pop!' or 'splash!'. In these and many other cases the range of reference of the SL word does not coincide exactly with that of its nearest TL counterpart. These types of cross-cultural difference are phonic in nature, and are in themselves potential sources of translation problems.

Onomatopoeia may cause more of a translation problem where the nearest semantic equivalents to an onomatopoeic SL word in the TL are not onomatopoeic. For instance, German 'Uhu' is onomatopoeic, but its English rendering as 'great horned owl' is clearly not onomatopoeic. To the extent that the very fact of onomatopoeia is an effect contributing to textual meaning, its loss in the TT is a translation loss that the translator may regret.

Other translation difficulties may be caused by onomatopoeia where cross-cultural differences arise on a grammatical as well as the phonic/graphic level. Words like 'bimbam!', 'wauwau!' and 'ticktack!' are onomatopoeia at its most basic: sound-imitative interjections, not onomatopoeic nouns. 'Kuckuck' is a noun, but it is still onomatopoeic; translating it as 'cuckoo' involves little translation loss. Translating German 'Zirpe' as 'cicada', on the other hand, involves more translation loss, which could be significant in certain contexts. Some onomatopoeic words, however, can be used both as interjections and as nouns or verbs; for example, in spoken German the interjections 'patsch' and 'krach' can double as nouns, while their English counterparts, 'splash' and 'crash' (or 'crack') are even more grammatically versatile (nouns or verbs). Where such onomatopoeic counterparts exist, translation loss is limited to minor losses on the phonic/graphic level. Take, however, a hypothetical case where 'she climbed the stairs slowly, her footsteps clacking on the marble' is to be translated into German. The onomatopoeic 'clacking' is a verbal unit in the ST, which, on purely phonic grounds, one might be tempted to render by the onomatopoeic German verbal unit 'klappernd', were it not for the fact that the meaning of 'klappern' is totally inappropriate to this context (it normally denotes a rattling sound or the chattering of teeth). Consequently, the option of translating the ST as 'sie stieg langsam die Treppe hinauf mit auf dem Marmor klapperndem Schritt', which preserves onomatopoeia and involves minimum translation loss on the phonic/graphic level, creates considerably more loss on the level of literal meaning. In fact, 'klappernd' neither denotes nor imitates the appropriate sound of *slow* footsteps on a marble staircase: instead, the

TT is iconic of a rapid rattling noise, which creates an incongruity of meaning within the text. It is avoiding this incongruity that makes 'mit... klingendem Schritt' (with ringing steps) preferable as a rendering of 'footsteps clacking', even though in this TT the appropriate element of sound imitation is virtually lost. Loss in onomatopoeic effect could be compensated for in yet another version of the TT in which 'mit... klingendem Schritt' is replaced by 'mit... schallendem Schritt' (with echoing steps). This TT lacks onomatopoeia and gives a literally imprecise rendering of 'clacking', but it adds its own phonic effect (consisting in a recurrence of [ʃ] sounds) that helps to underline the repetitive aspect of the noise. (We have here, incidentally, a good example of compensation in kind, as discussed in Chapter 3.) This recurrence of [ʃ], however, has its own disadvantages – it may interfere with the literal meaning by phonically suggesting the sound of shuffling footsteps rather than slow resounding ones. The example typifies a common translation problem: that of a single thematic clue combining with onomatopoeia or the recurrence of phonic/graphic variables to give unwanted connotative force to a TT expression.

Even something as simple as onomatopoeia, then, may need attention in translating. The same is true, in fact, of any type of word-play that hinges on phonic/graphic similarities between expressions with different meanings. For example, the more obviously a pun or a spoonerism is not accidental or incidental in the ST, the more it is in need of translating. A major strategic decision will then be whether to seek appropriate puns or spoonerisms for the TT, or whether to resort to some form of compensation. Typical problems of this kind will be found in Practicals 4 and 8.

A more frequently encountered area of phonic/graphic special effects is alliteration and assonance. We define **alliteration** as the recurrence of the same sound/letter or sound/letter cluster at the beginning of words (for example, '**m**any **m**ighty **m**idgets') and **assonance** as the recurrence, within words, of the same sound/letter or sound/letter cluster (for example, 'their cr**a**f**t**y hi**st**ory-m**ast**er's b**a**th**t**ub'). It is important to remember a vital difference between alliteration/assonance and onomatopoeia. Alliteration and assonance do not involve an imitation of sounds (unless they happen to coincide with onomatopoeia, as would be the case in 'ten tall clocks tock'). We have already seen something of how alliteration and assonance work, in the stanza from 'Der Blitzzug' discussed in Chapter 3, and we shall see a further example in the Hebrew text discussed in Chapter 5. As we shall see, the crucial associative feature in the pattern underlying that text is the X-Z-R phonic/graphic root (involving a combination of alliteration and assonance). Every time this root recurs in the text, it coincides with a vital moment in the narrative, so that it very soon acquires emphatic force, underlining crucial narrative and thematic points. A major strategic decision for the translator of this story arises on the phonic/graphic level, but affecting also the grammatical level (as we shall see in more detail in Chapter 5). This decision is whether to create a corresponding pattern of lexical items in the TT for underlining crucial points in the narrative and, if so, whether to make systematic phonic/graphic recurrences the hub of that TT pattern.

This example makes clear why the problems raised by phonic/graphic special effects can be so intractable. It is common to find that the literal sense and the mood of a text are reinforced by some of the phonic qualities of the text (so-called 'sound symbolism'). This makes it all the easier to forget the contribution of the reader/listener's subjectivity to the textual effect. This subjective input is relatively minor in the case of onomatopoeia, but it is greater in texts like the Hebrew story where the pattern of phonic/graphic special effects may easily be overlooked by the casual or unsophisticated reader, and greater still where alliteration and assonance are more varied and objectively less obtrusive. The important thing to keep in mind is that, onomatopoeia aside, the sound-symbolic effect of words is not intrinsic to them, but operates in conjunction with their literal and connotative meanings in the context.

For example, the sound [R] does not, in and of itself, suggest the wild and dramatic starkness of jagged rocks with the waves crashing against them, or the sound of a train rushing through the night, or the imminent danger of derailment and death. Yet it may be said to suggest the first of these things in the opening line of Heine's poem 'Es **r**agt ins Mee**r** de**r** **R**unenstein' (Heine, 1978, p. 479). And it may be said to carry the other connotations in Liliencron's 'Der Blitzzug' (see Chapter 3, p. 29): the first, in stanza 1 of the poem:

Fo**r**tfo**r**tfo**r**tFo**r**tfo**r**tfo**r**t d**r**ehn sich die **R**äde**r**
Rasend dahin auf dem Schienengeäde**r**

the second, at a turning point in the text, where the mood suddenly changes to menace and a sense of imminent disaster:

Fo**r**tfo**r**tfo**r**tFo**r**tfo**r**tfo**r**t, steht an de**r** Ku**r**ve,
Steht da de**r** Tod mit de**r** Bombe zum Wu**r**fe?

In each case, [R] draws its suggestive power from four things in particular: first, the lexical meanings of the words in which it occurs; second, the lexical meanings of the words associated with those in which it occurs; third, other phonetic qualities of both those groups of words; and, fourth, the many other types of connotative meaning at work in these texts, as in any other. (We shall discuss connotative meaning as such in Chapter 8.)

In these three examples, sound symbolism clearly has such an important textual role that to translate the texts without some attempt at producing appropriate sound-symbolic effects in the TT would be to incur severe translation loss. The more a text depends for its very existence on the interplay of onomatopoeia, alliteration and assonance, the more true this is – and the more difficult the translator's task becomes, because, as our examples show, sound symbolism is not only largely language-specific, but a very subjective matter as well.

By far the most widespread textual effects arising from the use of phonic/graphic variables involve the exploitation of *recurrences*. Apart from alliteration and assonance, rhyme is the most obvious example. When such recurrences are organized into recognizable patterns on a large scale, for example in a regularly repeated rhyme scheme, they are clearly not accidental or incidental. At this point, the translator is forced to take the resulting phonic/graphic special effects into serious consideration. However, this does not mean that one is obliged, or even well-advised, to reproduce the exact patterns of recurrence found in the ST. In fact, opinions are divided among translators of verse about the extent to which even such obvious devices as rhyme scheme should be reproduced in the TT. In English, for example, blank verse is a widespread genre with at least as high a prestige as rhyming verse, so that there is often a case for translating rhyming STs from other languages into blank verse in English. In the end, this is a decision for individual translators to make in individual cases; often the genre of the ST and the availability of TL genres as 'models' will be crucial factors in the decision. (We shall consider at length the importance of genre as a factor in translation in Chapter 11.)

We can conclude so far that the phonic/graphic level of textual variables *may* merit the translator's attention, and that translation losses on this level *may* be serious. There is no suggestion here that attention to sounds should be to the detriment of sense; on the contrary, it is where ignoring the contribution of phonic/graphic features would damage the sense of the text that they are considered important.

There is, however, a style of translation that actually more or less reverses the maxim quoted from Lewis Carroll; that is, it concentrates on taking care of the sounds and allows the sense to emerge as a kind of vaguely suggested impression. This technique is generally known as **phonemic translation**. An extraordinary example, whose authors seem to take their method perfectly seriously, is a translation of Catullus' poetry by Celia and Louis Zukovsky. Here is part of one poem, followed by (i) the phonemic translation and (ii) a literal prose translation:

Ille mi par esse deo videtur,
Ille, si fas est, superare divos,
qui sedens adversus identidem te
        spectat et audit
dulce ridentem, misero quod omnis
eripit sensus mihi; [...]

(i) He'll hie me, par *is* he? the God divide her,
he'll hie, see fastest, superior deity,
quiz – sitting adverse identity – mate, in-
        spect it and audit –
you'll care ridden then, misery holds omens,
air rip the senses from me; [...]

(Catullus, 1969, poem 51)

(ii) He seems to me to be equal to a god, he seems to me,
if it is lawful, to surpass the gods, who, sitting
opposite to you, keeps looking at you and hearing you
sweetly laugh; but this tears away all my senses,
wretch that I am.

We shall not dwell on this example, beyond saying that it perfectly illustrates the technique of phonemic translation: to imitate as closely as possible the actual phonic sequence of the ST, while suggesting in a vague and impressionistic way something of its literal content.

As a matter of fact, it is difficult, if not impossible, for a TT to retain a close similarity to the actual phonic sequences of the ST and still retain anything more than a tenuous connection with any kind of coherent meaning, let alone the meaning of the ST. This difficulty is ensured by the classic 'arbitrariness' of languages, not to mention the language-specific and contextual factors which, as we have seen in discussing onomatopoeia, alliteration and assonance, make phonic effect such a relative and subjective matter.

An entertaining illustration of the way phonic imitation in a TT renders the sense of the ST unrecognizable is John Hulme's *Mörder Guss Reims*, which consists in a playful imitation of English nursery rhymes. Here, for example, the text of 'Humpty-Dumpty' is reproduced as

Um die Dumm' die Saturn Aval;
Um die Dumm' die Ader Grät' fahl.
Alter ging's Ohr säss und Alter ging's mähen.
Kuh denn 'putt' um Dieter Gitter er gähn.
(John Hulme, 1981, p. 34)

While providing an entertaining pastiche, *Mörder Guss Reims* does not really count as phonemic translation proper: there is no attempt at all to render anything of the literal meaning of the ST. What we have here is a form of pastiche which consists in the phonic imitation of a well-known text used for humorous purposes.

Although phonemic translation cannot be recommended as a technique for serious translation of sensible texts, there are texts that are not intended to be sensible in the original and which qualify as suitable objects for a degree of phonemic translation. Nonsense rhymes, like Lewis Carroll's 'Jabberwocky', are a good example. Here, by way of illustration, is a sample of a German TT of 'Jabberwocky':

DER JAMMERWOCH	JABBERWOCKY
Es brillig war. Die schlichten Toven	'Twas brillig, and the slithy toves
Wirrten und wimmelten in Waben;	Did gyre and gimble in the wabe:
Und aller-mümsige Burggoven	All mimsy were the borogoves,
Die mohmen Räth' ausgraben.	And the mome raths outgrabe.

Finally, though they are less common than sound symbolism, special effects may also be contrived through the spatial layout of written texts. Such cases illustrate the potential importance of specifically graphic textual variables. An obvious example is the acrostic, a text in which, say, reading the first letter of each line spells out, vertically, a hidden word. Another is concrete poetry, where the visual form of the text is used to convey meaning. A simple example of this, and one which would pose no translation problems in English, is R. Döhl's 'Apfel':

Reproduced by kind permission of the author. Originally part of a triptych 'Apfel/Birne/Blatt', copyright © R. Döhl 1965.

The Gottfried Kleiner text in Practical 4 is also a good example; just as onomatopoeia is iconic phonically, this text – like much concrete poetry – is iconic graphically, imitating visually what it represents linguistically.

THE PROSODIC LEVEL

On the **prosodic level**, utterances count as 'metrically' structured stretches, within which syllables have varying degrees of prominence according to accent, stress and emphasis, varying melodic qualities in terms of pitch modulation, and varying qualities of rhythm, length and tempo. Groups of syllables may, on this level, form *contrastive* prosodic patterns (for example, the alternation of a short, staccato, fast section with a long, slow, smooth one), or *recurrent* ones, or both.

In texts not designed to be read aloud, such prosodic patterns, if they are discernible at all, are relatively unlikely to have any textual importance. However, in texts intended for oral performance (or intended to evoke oral performance), such as plays, speeches, poetry or songs, prosodic features can have a considerable theme-reinforcing and mood-creating function. In texts where prosodic special effects play a vital role, the translator may have to pay special attention to the prosodic level of the TT. A humorous example is found in Goscinny and Uderzo (1965), where an Alexandrian says 'Je suis, mon cher ami, très heureux de te voir', and this flowery greeting, which has the classical metric properties of an alexandrine (2 + 4/3 + 3 syllables), is explained by someone else with the observation 'C'EST UN ALEXANDRIN' (He's an Alexandrian/That's an alexandrine).

In most cases, it is not possible to construct a TT that both sounds natural in the TL and reproduces in exact detail the metric structure of the ST. This is because languages often function in fundamentally different ways from one another on the prosodic level, just as they do on the phonic/graphic level. However, in this respect translating from German to English, or vice versa, constitutes a somewhat privileged case as compared to, say, translating between French and English or Spanish and English. The reason is that the prosodic structures of English and German differ less radically than those of many other pairs of European languages.

In English, patterns of accent are distributed idiosyncratically over the syllables of words, with each polysyllabic word having one maximally prominent, and a number of less prominent, syllables in a certain configuration – for example, '^{1}un^{2}na^{1}tu^{1}ral^{0}ly' (the numbers denoting a greater or lesser degree of stress on the syllable to which they are prefixed). Only by knowing the word can one be sure what its prosodic pattern is; that is, accent patterns in a group of words are tied to the identity of the individual words. This is known as *free word-accent*.

While many other languages differ radically from English by having a *fixed word-accent* (as opposed to a *moveable word-accent*), German is also characterized by free word-accent, with every word having its own accentual pattern of prominent and less prominent syllables – for example, '^{1}be ^{2}rech ^{1}ne ^{1}te' (calculated). Clearly, the similarities between English and German prosodic structures make it substantially easier to match the prosodic special effects of a German ST with those of an English TT, or vice versa.

RHYTHM IN ENGLISH AND GERMAN VERSE

We have seen that on the phonic/graphic level, translators of verse often have to pay special attention to patterns of recurrence in a text. The same is true on the prosodic level. Fortunately, the differences between German and English do not usually constitute a problem in this respect; both languages function in terms of stressed and unstressed syllables. We shall deal here in elementary terms with the question of rhythmic structure, which is the main feature of the patterned use of recurrences on the prosodic level. (It does not, however, exhaust the entire field of prosody, since it ignores tempo and melodic pitch, which may also constitute vital textual variables in an oral text.) We shall not discuss free verse, which would need too detailed a study for the purposes of this course. However, in so far as free verse is defined by its difference from fixed-form verse, our analysis will help translators isolate the relevant features of STs in free verse.

In translating verse, one strategic decision that needs to be made is on the prosodic level: assuming (and this is a big assumption) that the TT is to be in verse, should it attempt to copy the rhythms of the ST? (Copying German rhythms in an English TT is relatively easy, witness the extract from the translation of 'Blitzzug' on p. 30.) This decision regarding rhythm will depend ultimately on the textual function of rhythm in the ST, and on whether copying it in the TT would lead to unacceptable translation loss on other levels.

In discussing one's decision, it is useful to have a basic terminology for describing rhythms. The elementary terms illustrated below will permit both precision and concision. To take first an example we have already seen, Liliencron's 'Blitzzug' is predominantly *dactylic* in rhythm; that is, it has an overriding pattern consisting of one stressed syllable followed by two unstressed ones. Each such group is called a *dactyl*, and can be represented as /˘˘. So, for the purposes of analysis, the first line of the poem can be notated as follows:

/ ˘ ˘ / ˘ ˘ / ˘ ˘ / ˘
Quer durch Europa von Westen nach Osten

A variant of this pattern is *anapestic* rhythm, where two unstressed syllables are followed by one stressed syllable. Such a group is called an *anapest*, represented as ˘ ˘ /. Here is an example, notated using the same simple system:

˘ ˘ / ˘ ˘ / ˘ ˘ / ˘ ˘ / ˘ ˘ / ˘
Und ihr Leben ist immer ein ewiges Gehen und Kommen.

Very commonly, there is only *one* unstressed syllable grouped with a stressed one. Such a pattern is either *trochaic* (a succession of *trochees*: /˘) or *iambic* (a succession of *iambs*: ˘/). Here is a notated line consisting of five trochees:

/ ˘ / ˘ / ˘ / ˘ / ˘
Fertig schon zur Abfahrt steht der Wagen,

and a line consisting of four iambs:

˘ / ˘ / ˘ / ˘ /
Im Nebel ruhet noch die Welt.

These rhythmic patterns are also commonly found in English:

˘ ˘ / ˘ ˘ / ˘ ˘ / ˘ ˘ /
(1) Anapestic: With a leap and a bound the swift anapests throng.

/ ˘ ˘ / ˘ ˘ / ˘ ˘ / ˘
(2) Dactylic: Right across Europe in eastern direction

/ ˘ / ˘ / ˘ / ˘
(3) Trochaic: Present mirth brings present laughter

˘ / ˘ / ˘ / ˘ / ˘ /
(4) Iambic: The curfew tolls the knell of parting day.

Naturally, in both English and German, following a single rhythmic pattern without variation would quickly become tedious. Hence the sort of variation typified in lines 1 and 6 of Wordsworth's 'Composed upon Westminster Bridge':

(˘ /) (/ /)
/ ˘ ˘ / ˘ ˘ ˘ / ˘ /
Earth has not anything to show more fair

/ / ᴗ / / ᴗ ᴗ / ᴗ /
Ships, towers, domes, theatres and temples lie.

Like the rest of the poem, these lines may be described as iambic, because their rhythm is predominantly iambic; but within this overriding pattern there is considerable variation. (Similarly, in the examples given above, there are typical slight variations in the German dactylic and anapestic lines and the English trochaic and dactylic lines.) In German, the picture is more fluid still, in that some of the greatest German poets have developed their own adaptations of ancient Greek and Latin verse forms, sometimes combining them with the patterns illustrated above. There is also, in German, a flexible form of verse characterized by having an irregular distribution of unstressed syllables around stressed ones: such rhythms are known as *freie Rhythmen*. Their closest English equivalent is strong-stress metre, in which all or most of the lines have equal numbers of stressed syllables, but the number of unstressed syllables is irregular.

As these observations suggest, true metrical analysis and scansion in English, and even more so in German, are a far more complex and subtle issue than our simple notation of rhythm. However, for the purposes of an introduction to translation methodology, only three things are required: a simple method of identifying and notating rhythmic recurrences and variations; a way of assessing their expressive function in the ST; and a means of deciding, in the light of these things, what TL verse form (if any) to adopt. Translators who become proficient enough in these skills to want to specialize in verse translation are recommended to consult the books by Malof (1970) and Wagenknecht (1981) listed in the bibliography.

PRACTICAL 4

4.1 The formal properties of texts

Assignment

(i) With particular reference to its salient formal properties, discuss the strategic problems confronting the translator of the following text, and outline your own strategy for translating it.
(ii) Translate the text into English.
(iii) Explain the main decisions of detail you made in producing your TT.

Contextual information

The passage is taken from Thomas Mann, *Der Tod in Venedig*, first published in 1912, and contains part of the description of a sunrise in Venice seen through the eyes of von Aschenbach, the central character of the Novelle. The lead-up to this description, starting with his early awakening 'ums erste Morgengrauen', is heavily loaded with references and allusions to figures from Greek mythology. The reference in this passage to 'der Bläulichgelockte' (the God with the purple locks) is to Poseidon.

Text

> Aber der Tag, der so feurig-festlich begann, war im ganzen seltsam gehoben und mythisch verwandelt. Woher kam und stammte der Hauch, der auf einmal so sanft und bedeutend, höherer Einflüsterung gleich, Schläfe und Ohr umspielte? Weiße Federwölkchen standen in verbreiteten Scharen am Himmel gleich weidenden Herden der Götter. Stärkerer Wind erhob sich, und die Rosse Poseidons liefen, sich bäumend, daher, Stiere auch wohl, dem Bläulichgelockten gehörig, welche mit Brüllen anrennend die Hörner senkten. Zwischen dem Felsengeröll des entfernteren Strandes jedoch hüpften die Wellen empor als springende Ziegen. Eine heilig entstellte Welt voll panischen Lebens schloß den Berückten ein, und sein Herz träumte zarte Fabeln.

Reprinted from Thomas Mann, *Der Tod in Venedig* (Fischer-Bücherei, Frankfurt: Lizenzausgabe des S. Fischer-Verlages, 1954, p. 55), by permission of S. Fischer Verlag GmbH, Frankfurt am Main.

4.2 The formal properties of texts; graphic

Assignment

Working in groups:

(i) Assess the salient formal properties – especially on the *graphic* level of textual variables – of the following text, discuss the strategic problems confronting the translator and outline your own strategy for translating it.

(ii) In the light of your findings in (i), translate the text with due attention to graphic detail.

Contextual information

'Die Bäume des HErrn' is reprinted in *Epochen der deutschen Lyrik, Vol. 5 (1700–1770)* edited by J. Stenzel and published in 1969, originally from Gottfried Kleiner's *Garten-Lust im Winter* (1732). The poem's intended devotional function is set in context by Kleiner's explanatory title. The quotation from Psalm 104 at the foot of the diagram is the title of the poem; lines 29 to 1 are intended to be read in that order, upwards. (The line numbering is by the editor of *Epochen der deutschen Lyrik*.)

steh.
Früchte
und dort voll
hinnen geh,
Biß ich von
O mach mich grün,
O laß mich blühn,
Bewässert gutt.
Dein mildes Blutt
Die deine Liebe sucht.
Und pflantz in mich die Frucht,
In meinem Hertzen selbst den Platz,
Bereite Dir, Du Seelen-Schatz!
Ach nihm mich mir, und gieb mich Dir!
Als Du, *mein JESU*, meine Zier!
Soll Niemand seyn, und Niemand werden,
Mein Alles, dort, und hier auf Erden,
Mein auserkohrnes GOTTES-Lamm /
Mein schönster Himmels-Bräutigam /
Mein Seelen-Ruhm /
Mein Eigenthum /
Mein Port,
Mein Hort,
Mein Theil,
Mein Heil,
Mein Steig,
Mein Zweig,
Mein Raum,
Mein Baum,

Die Bäume des HErrn stehen voll Saffts / wie die Cedern
Libanon / die Er gepflantzet hat.
Ps. 104/16.

4.3 The formal properties of texts

Assignment

Working in groups:

(i) With particular reference to the phonic/graphic and prosodic levels of textual variables, discuss the strategic problems confronting the translator of the following text, and outline your own strategy for translating it.
(ii) Translate the text into English.
(iii) Explain the main decisions of detail you made in producing your TT.

Contextual information

Bertolt Brecht's 'Großer Dankchoral' (1927) is a pastiche with a serious, and highly cynical, satirical purpose. It is a parody modelled on a clearly recognizable German hymn, whose English version is one of the best-known items in the repertoire of Christians in Britain.

Text

Großer Dankchoral

1
Lobet die Nacht und die Finsternis, die euch umfangen!
Kommet zuhauf
Schaut in den Himmel hinauf:
Schon ist der Tag euch vergangen.

2
Lobet das Gras und die Tiere, die neben euch leben und sterben!
Sehet, wie ihr
Lebet das Gras und das Tier
Und es muß auch mit euch sterben.

3
Lobet den Baum, der aus Aas aufwächst jauchzend zum Himmel!
Lobet das Aas
Lobet den Baum, der es fraß
Aber auch lobet den Himmel.

4
Lobet von Herzen das schlechte Gedächtnis des Himmels!
Und daß er nicht
Weiß euren Nam' noch Gesicht
Niemand weiß, daß ihr noch da seid.

5

Lobet die Kälte, die Finsternis und das Verderben!
Schauet hinan:
Es kommet nicht auf euch an
Und ihr könnt unbesorgt sterben.

5

The formal properties of texts: grammatical and lexical issues in translation

The level of textual variables considered in this chapter is the **grammatical level**. It is useful to divide the contents of this level into two areas: first, grammatical arrangement of meaningful linguistic units into larger units (complex words and syntactic constructions); second, the actual meaningful linguistic units that figure in constructions (in particular, words).

A great deal of the explicit literal meaning of a text is carried by the configuration of words and phrases. Therefore part of interpreting any text consists in construing the literal meaning conveyed by its grammatical structure. (Literal meaning as such will be discussed in Chapter 7.) Furthermore, a TT has normally to be constructed by putting words into meaningful grammatical configurations according to the conventions and structures of the TL, and using the lexical means available in the TL. Consequently, translators can never ignore the level of grammatical variables in either the ST or the TT. Let us look at the question of grammatical arrangement first.

GRAMMATICAL ARRANGEMENT

Under this heading we subsume two main types of grammatical structure: first, the patterns by which complex and compound words are formed – that is, affixation/inflection, compounding and word-derivation; second, the successive patterns whereby words are linked to form phrases, and phrases can be linked to form yet more complex phrases.

It is important to remember that these structural patterns differ from language to language. Even where apparent cross-linguistic similarities occur, they are often misleading, the structural equivalent of *faux amis*. The following pairs illustrate this point:

überblicken	oversee, get a full view
übersehen	overlook, fail to see
überhören	fail to hear
versprechen	promise
ich habe mich versprochen	I made a slip of the tongue
das sehe ich ein	I quite see that (*not* I look/see into it)

In fact, much of what one might be tempted to call the 'ethos' of a typical German, French, or classical Chinese text is simply a reflection of preponderant grammatical structures specific to these languages. Thus, to take an obvious example, the potential for complex word-formations such as 'Autobahnbrücke' or 'Ungeziefervertilgungsanstalt' is typical of German, and is often absent in other languages. This implies that, for example, a translator into English cannot in principle replicate 'Autobahnbrücke' as a compound word, but must resort to syntactic means, probably using the complex phrase 'motorway bridge', or perhaps 'bridge over the motorway'. A similar solution would apply to 'Ungeziefervertilgungsanstalt', probably best rendered by the phrase 'pest control office'. While there is a notable tendency for English (under American influence) to move closer to German in the formation of compound words, such as 'failsafe', 'foolproof', 'roadblock', or 'childcare', a large proportion of German compound words can only be rendered syntactically. (Another obvious instance of grammatical differences between German and English is the characteristic difference in word order, which we have already seen exploited for comic purposes in the example of compensation in place from *Asterix bei den Briten*, in Chapter 3.)

The extent to which grammatical differences between languages can cause major translation loss is dramatically illustrated from 'exotic' languages, for instance from a comparison of English with Chinese. In a normal predicative phrase in Chinese, there are three particularly troublesome grammatical features. First, neither subject nor object need be explicitly singular or plural. Second, there is no definite or indefinite article for either subject or object. Third, there may be no indication of a tense or mood for the predicate. Since all these features are obligatorily present in predicative phrases in English, the Chinese phrase 'rén mǎi shū' (interlineally rendered as 'man buy book') has no exact literal counterpart in English, but has to be rendered, according to what is most plausible in the context, as one of the following combinations:

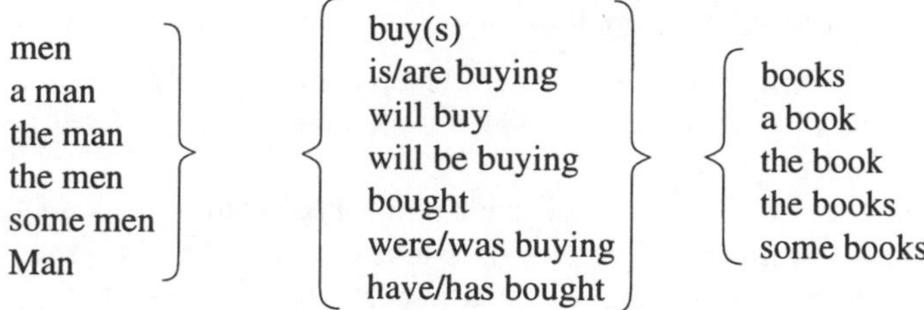

Because English syntax is so different from Chinese, the phrase 'rén măi shū' can only be translated if one explicitly specifies in the TT certain details not expressed in the ST – that is, at the cost of considerable, but inevitable, translation loss (as defined in Chapter 2).

Wherever the grammatical structures of the ST cannot be matched by analogous structures in the TT, the translator is faced with the prospect of major translation losses. The problems that may be caused by this are not necessarily serious, but they are complex and many, which means that we can only touch on them briefly here. (Such problems are illustrated in more detail in Chapters 16–19.)

The need for circumlocution in a TT is one of the commonest of these problems. For example, the simple everyday word 'kolkhoz' in Russian may have to be rendered in English by the circumlocution 'state-owned co-operative farm'. This is an obvious case of translation loss, a neat and compact piece of ST corresponding to a relatively complex and long-winded TT. What may be less obvious is that the converse case of rendering a complex ST word by a simple word in the TT, or a complex ST phrase by a single word, is just as much a translation loss, because the grammatical proportions of the ST are not adhered to in the TT. For example, translating German 'Ausflug' by 'trip', or English 'curd cheese' by German 'Quark', both entail translation loss in terms of grammatical structure. These examples show how, as a rule, *semantic* considerations override considerations of *grammatical* translation loss, priority being given almost automatically to the *mot juste* and to constructing grammatically well-formed TL sentences.

Nevertheless, translators should be aware of grammatical differences between SL and TL, and aware of them as potential sources of translation loss, for there are exceptions to the 'rule' mentioned above, namely STs with salient textual properties manifestly resulting from the manipulation of grammatical structure. Take, for example, this opening sentence from a business letter in English:

> We acknowledge receipt of your letter of 6 April.

This is a more likely formula than 'We have received the letter you sent on 6 April' or 'Thank you for the letter you sent on 6 April'. In putting the sentence into German, the translator should not aim at the simplest, most everyday grammatical structure capable of rendering the literal message of the ST, but should take into consideration the respective effects of 'formality' required in English and German business letters:

Wir bestätigen hiermit den Eingang Ihres Schreibens vom 6. April.

This is more likely in formal German business letters than, say, 'Wir bestätigen hiermit, daß wir Ihren Brief vom 6. April erhalten haben', let alone 'Ihr Brief vom 6. April ist angekommen'.

As this example shows, a great deal depends on nuances within the particular TL genre, an issue to which we shall return in Chapters 11–14.

Grammatical structure may assume particular importance in literary translation. A prestigious author's hallmark may partly consist in characteristic grammatical structuring. For example, Kafka's style is noted for the extreme streamlining of his syntax, Thomas Mann's for its extreme syntactic complexity. By way of example, here is a relatively short construction from Thomas Mann's *Der Tod in Venedig*:

> Mehrmals, wenn hinter Venedig die Sonne sank, saß er auf einer Bank im Park, um Tadzio zuzuschauen, der sich, weiß gekleidet und farbig gegürtet, auf dem gewalzten Kiesplatz mit Ballspiel vergnügte, und Hyakinthos war es, den er zu sehen glaubte und der sterben mußte, weil zwei Götter ihn liebten.
>
> (Th. Mann, 1954, p. 55)

Thomas Mann's intricate elaboration of syntactic structure typically contains numerous co-ordinated phrases, as well as layers of phrases embedded in phrases. To reduce it to a series of small, easily digestible English sentences would be possible, but inappropriate; the resulting TT would fail to convey the feel of Thomas Mann's style to TL readers. The following version is just such a failure:

> Sometimes he would sit on a park bench as the sun set behind Venice. There he would watch Tadzio disporting himself at playing ball on the rolled gravel. Tadzio was clad in white and wore a brightly coloured sash. Yet it was not Tadzio he saw, but Hyacinthus, who had to die because two gods loved him.

A more suitable TT would need to be fairly complex and elaborate syntactically. Here, for discussion in class, is the Lowe-Porter translation:

> When the sun was going down behind Venice, he would sometimes sit on a bench in the park and watch Tadzio, white-clad, with gay-coloured sash, at play there on the rolled gravel with his ball; and at such times it was not Tadzio whom he saw, but Hyacinthus, doomed to die because two gods were rivals for his love.
>
> (Th. Mann, 1955, p. 56)

There is another reason why translators must keep a close eye on grammatical structure – contrasts and recurrences in syntactic patterning can be used as devices creating special textual effects. A simple example is seen in the well-known children's rhyme about magpies:

> One for sorrow,
> Two for joy,
> Three for a girl,

Four for a boy,
Five for silver,
Six for gold,
Seven for a secret that's never been told.

The grammatical patterns underlying this rhyme can be schematized as follows:

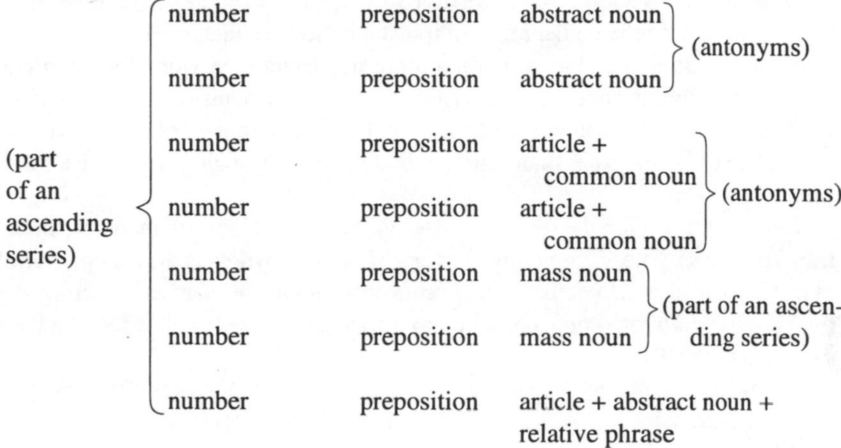

To translate this rhyme into another language, one would have to give careful consideration to the grammatical patterning as schematized above, because the loss of its effects would deprive the text of much of its point – in effect, the structural scheme would be the basis for formulating a TT.

Much less blatantly playful texts, such as rhetorical speeches, may make similar use of devices based on syntactic patterns of contrast and recurrence. In such cases, it would be a serious stylistic error not to recognize the textual importance of these grammatical devices, and a potentially serious translation loss not to try to reconstruct them in the TT. There are also literary texts that amount to a kind of virtuoso performance in syntactic density and complexity; this is a major consideration in translating the Andersch text in Practical 5.

WORDS

For reasons of educational bias (for instance, the paramount use that students make of dictionaries and lexically arranged encyclopaedias), people are far more directly aware of individual words than of other units and structures of language. In particular, mentioning 'meaning' or the semantic properties of languages (and therefore also of texts) tends to evoke first and foremost the level of individual words. Yet meanings are certainly not exclusively concentrated in words individually listed in isolation in dictionaries. Any text shows that the combination of words (and their use in contexts) creates meanings that they do not possess in isolation, and even meanings that are not wholly predictable from the literal senses of the words combined.

As our multi-level approach to textual variables indicates, lexical translation losses (such as want of an exact translation for a particular word) are just one kind of translation loss among many. There is no *a priori* reason, as long as the overall sense of the ST is successfully conveyed by the TT, why they should be given a heavier weighting than other kinds of translation loss. In fact, as we saw in Chapter 3, communicative translation is often more important than word-for-word correspondences. For instance, 'man kann nie wissen' can be plausibly translated in most modern contexts as 'you never can tell', not as 'one can never know'; even then, the choice of 'you' rather than 'one', 'a body', or even 'a girl' would be entirely a matter of context.

Lexical translation losses, then, are no more avoidable than other kinds of translation loss. Exact synonymy between SL and TL words is the exception rather than the rule, and problems arising from this should be neither maximized nor minimized, but treated on a par with other translation losses that affect the overall meaning of the TT.

Comparing the lexical meanings of words across languages underlines the fact that lexical translation losses are as likely to result from 'particularization' (where the TT word has a narrower meaning than the ST word) as from 'generalization' (where the TT has a wider meaning than the ST word). So, for example, translating, in a given context, German 'geistig' as 'spiritual', rather than as 'mental' or 'intellectual', is an inevitable particularization, because one has to choose one of these three TL words, but each has a narrower range of reference than German 'geistig'. Conversely, translating 'er hat 'nen Revolver!' as 'he's got a gun!' is a case of generalization, because 'gun' can also mean 'Pistole', 'Gewehr' and 'Kanone' – that is, it has a wider range of reference than 'Revolver'. The translation problems arising from particularization and generalization are very common, and we shall return to them in Chapter 7.

Another reason why, in ordinary language, no TL word is ever likely to replicate precisely the 'meaning' of a given SL word is that, in each language, words form idiosyncratic associations with sets of other words. Such associations may hold by virtue of the forms of words, as in the homonymic association between 'crane' (bird) and 'crane' (machine); or by virtue of the literal meanings of the words, as with the associations of relative value in the series 'gold', 'silver' and 'bronze'; or by virtue of culture-bound prejudices and assumptions, as in the association of 'law and order' (or 'brutality') with 'police'. The exact associative overtones of words in the overall context of a ST are often difficult enough to pinpoint, but it is even more difficult, if not impossible, to find TL words that will, over and above conveying an appropriate literal meaning, also produce exactly the right associative overtones in the context of the TT. This is another source of lexical translation loss, and another potential dilemma between choosing literal meaning at the expense of associative overtones, or vice versa. We shall return to these questions in Chapter 8.

Series of words can be distributed in contrastive and recurrent patterns that signal or reinforce the thematic development of the text. In the rhyme about magpies on pp. 56–7, there are a number of examples of the patterned use of lexical sets over an entire text. In Aphek and Tobin (1988), the term **word system** is used to denote this phenomenon. A word system is a pattern (within a text) of words having an associative common denominator, a pattern which 'nurtures the theme and message of the text with greater intensity' (Aphek and Tobin, 1988, p. 3). Aphek and Tobin illustrate their concept of theme-reinforcing word systems from texts in Hebrew. In Hebrew, words consist of consonantal roots with variable vocalic fillers. Thus, for instance, the word 'XaZiR' ('pig') has the basic consonantal root 'X-Z-R' (an example earlier alluded to in Chapter 4, p. 41). All words with the same consonantal root are perceived in Hebrew as belonging to a single associative set. (This is mainly because of the system of writing, in which vocalic fillers may be omitted.) There is therefore a strongly bonded associative lexical set based on the 'X-Z-R' root, members of which may form a word system distributed over a text in a way that reinforces the theme and message of the text. Aphek and Tobin discern an 'X-Z-R' word system in a twentieth-century Hebrew short story entitled 'The Lady and the Pedlar', in which 'X-Z-R' words are systematically found at various key points in the narrative:

> A Jewish pedlar *makes his rounds* (me XaZeR al ptaxim) in villages.
>
> He meets a gentile woman and he *bows before her repeatedly* (XoZeRet vehishtaxava).
>
> He takes out and *replaces* (maXZiR) his merchandise, but she *goes back* (XoZeRet) indoors.
>
> The man begins to *court* (meXaZeR) the woman and becomes her lover. He forgets to live according to Jewish customs (for example, he eats pork).
>
> Eventually it transpires that the woman is a vampire, and, in a climactic argument, she laughs at the pedlar and calls him a *pig* (XaZiR).
>
> As a turning point in the story, the man returns (XoZeR) to the forest, *returns* (laXZOR) to his religion and *repents* (XoZeR betshuva).
>
> Returning (XoZeR) to the house, he finds that the woman has stabbed herself with his knife. She dies.
>
> The pedlar *resumes his rounds* (XiZeR ve-X-XiZeR) *crying* (maXRiZ) his wares *repeatedly* (XoZeR ve-maXRuZ; note the final inversion of X-Z-R to X-R-Z).

The example speaks for itself. The pattern of 'X-Z-R' (and 'X-R-Z') words coincides with salient points in the narrative, thus marking and reinforcing them. It also highlights the important thematic points in the interplay between abandoning Jewish religious observance, eating pork, being a metaphorical pig in the eyes of the vampire woman and eventual repentance. These points are more tightly bound together by the 'X-Z-R' word system than they would be by the mere narrative sequence of the text.

This example shows that it is worth scanning certain types of text for theme-reinforcing word systems (such as a series of thematic key words, or phonetic patterns, or an extended metaphor), because such things may be important textual devices. Where a word system is found in the ST, the construction of some analogous word system in the TT may be desirable; if so, this will be a strong factor influencing the translator's lexical choices. In the case of Aphek and Tobin's example, the word system in question hinges on a phonic/graphic common denominator which is highly specific to Hebrew; constructing a similar phonic/graphic word system seems virtually impossible in an English TT. Two of the translator's first strategic decisions will, therefore, be how much priority to give to this type of pattern, and how to construct an appropriate word system in the TT.

PRACTICAL 5

5.1 The formal properties of texts

Assignment

(i) Examine carefully the syntax of the passage below, discuss the strategic problems confronting the translator and outline your own strategy for translating it.
(ii) Translate lines 10–21 (from 'Blickte man' to the end) into English.
(iii) Explain the main decisions of detail you made in producing your TT.
(iv) After discussion of the translations, your tutor may give you a published TT for analysis and discussion in class.

Contextual information

The passage is taken from Thomas Mann's Novelle *Der Tod in Venedig*, first published in 1912. The 'Schriftsteller' whose works the passage discusses is Gustav von Aschenbach, the central fictional character of the Novelle. He has already been characterized as a writer of very considerable artistic and intellectual stature. It has been emphasized that the prevalent ethos of his writings is one of gritted-teeth morality ('sein Lieblingswort war "Durchhalten"', p. 14). The 'literary-biographical' section of the Novelle from which the excerpt is taken follows an initial narrative section in which von Aschenbach experiences an irrationally triggered, disturbing and alluring vision of distant and unhealthy places.

Text

Über den neuen, in mannigfach individuellen Erscheinungen wiederkehrenden Heldentyp, den dieser Schriftsteller bevorzugte, hatte schon frühzeitig ein kluger Zergliederer geschrieben: daß er die Konzeption 'einer intellektuellen und jünglinghaften Männlichkeit' sei, 'die in stolzer Scham die Zähne aufeinanderbeißt und ruhig dasteht, während ihr die Schwerter und Speere durch den Leib gehen'. Das war schön, geistreich und exakt, trotz seiner scheinbar allzu passivischen Prägung. Denn Haltung im Schicksal, Anmut in der Qual bedeutet nicht nur ein Dulden; sie ist eine aktive Leistung, ein positiver Triumph, und die Sebastian-Gestalt ist das schönste Sinnbild, wenn nicht der Kunst überhaupt, so doch gewiß der in Rede stehenden Kunst. Blickte man hinein in diese erzählte Welt, sah man: die elegante Selbstbeherrschung, die bis zum letzten Augenblick eine innere Unterhöhlung, den biologischen Verfall vor den Augen der Welt verbirgt; die gelbe, sinnlich benachteiligte Häßlichkeit, die es vermag, ihre schwelende Brunst zur reinen Flamme zu entfachen, ja, sich zur Herrschaft im Reiche der Schönheit aufzuschwingen; die bleiche Ohnmacht, welche aus den glühenden Tiefen des Geistes die Kraft holt, ein ganzes übermütiges Volk zu Füßen des Kreuzes, zu *ihren* Füßen niederzuwerfen; die liebenswürdige Haltung im leeren und strengen Dienste der Form; das falsche, gefährliche Leben, die rasch entnervende Sehnsucht und Kunst des geborenen Betrügers: betrachtete man all dies Schicksal und wieviel gleichartiges noch, so konnte man zweifeln, ob es überhaupt einen anderen Heroismus gäbe als denjenigen der Schwäche.

5.2 The formal properties of texts

Assignment

Working in groups:

(i) With particular reference to its salient grammatical properties, discuss the strategic problems confronting the translator of the following text and outline your own strategy for translating it.
(ii) Translate the text into English.
(iii) Explain the main decisions of detail you made in producing your TT.

Contextual information

The passage opens the second paragraph of 'Mit dem Chef nach Chenonceaux' (1957/8), a short story by Alfred Andersch (1914–1980). The story has opened with the businessman Herr Schmitz mistakenly ordering a 'Terrine du Chef' for the chauffeur Jeschke on the grounds that he will want soup for a starter. Doktor Honig has no French either.

Text

Jeschke, hager und schwärzlich, sicherlich überzeugter Kartoffelesser, musterte finster die Platte, gab aber nach einigen Versuchen zu, die Leberwurst sei ausgezeichnet, was angesichts seiner sonstigen Schweigsamkeit bemerkenswert war und Herrn Schmitz veranlaßte, seinen Appetit nicht weiter zu zähmen und sich Proben aus Jeschke's Hors d'œuvre zu fischen; er forderte auch den Doktor auf, Jeschke zu entlasten, aber Honig zog es vor, seine Weinbergschnecken abzuwarten und, bis sie kamen, den beiden Männern zuzusehen: dem steif aufgerichteten dürren Jeschke, der keinen Knopf seiner grauen Livreejacke öffnete und mit der Gabel von oben her im Aufschnitt stockerte, und dem in gesundes, festes Fett verpackten Herrn Schmitz, der halb über seinem Teller lag und es fertigbrachte, zu reden, fast unablässig und dabei ganz gescheit zu reden, und dennoch intensiv und genießerisch zu essen, nicht etwa wie ein dicker Mann – auf eine so einfache Formel war er nicht zu bringen –, sondern ein Mann, der sich viele Jahre hindurch sorgfältig und nur vom Besten ernährt hatte, was, wie der Doktor überlegte, etwas ganz anderes ist als ein Mann, der sich vollfrißt.

Alfred Andersch, 'Mit dem Chef nach Chenonceaux'. Alfred Andersch, *Gesammelte Erzählungen*

6

The formal properties of texts: sentential, inter-sentential and intertextual issues in translating

There will be three levels of textual variables considered in this chapter: the sentential level, the discourse level and the intertextual level. These levels, which are successively higher in the hierarchy of levels outlined in Chapter 4, will complete our discussion of textual variables.

THE SENTENTIAL LEVEL

The next higher level of textual variables above the grammatical level is the **sentential level,** on which sentences are considered. By 'sentence' we mean a particular type of linguistic unit that is a complete, self-contained and ready-made vehicle for actual communication: nothing more needs to be added to it before it can be uttered in concrete situations. So, for example, the starter's one-word command 'Go!' or the exclamation 'What bliss!' are sentences. Words and phrases are mere abstractions from sentences, abstractions stripped of practical communicative purpose, intonation and other features that make sentences genuine vehicles of linguistic utterance.

For the nature of the textual variables on the sentential level to be grasped, a distinction must be drawn between spoken and written texts, since spoken languages and written languages differ sharply on this level.

A spoken text counts on the sentential level as a sequence of sentences, each with a built-in communicative purpose conveyed by one or more such features as *intonation* (for example, the rising pitch that signals a question in English and German); *sequential focus* (for example, the word order of 'Him I don't like', which shifts the emphasis on to the object of the sentence); or illocutionary particles (for example, the colloquial German question-forming particle 'gell?', or the particle 'leider', which has the force of qualifying a statement as an expression of regret – in other words, an illocutionary particle tells the listener how to take an utterance). These features do not fit into syntax proper; their function, and 'meaning', consists in marking sentences for particular communicative purposes, and is quite different from the function of syntactic units. Compare, for instance:

> '*Immer* ist er neugierig' (where 'immer' has a *syntactic* function) versus
> '*Jedoch* ist er neugierig' (where 'jedoch' has a *sentential* function)

Compare also the different functions and different identities of 'schon' in

> 'Er ist *schon* da' (where 'schon' has an adverbial *syntactic* function)

with

> 'So sag' *schon*!' (where 'schon' has a *sentential* function of conveying impatience).

As we know, a number of different sentences, marked for different purposes, can be created purely through intonation:

> 'The salt' (with falling intonation: *statement*)
> 'The salt' (with rising intonation: *question*)
> 'The salt' (with fall-rise intonation: *emphatic query*)
> 'The salt' (with high, level intonation: *command)*

Similar effects can be achieved by a combination of intonation and other features with a sentential function:

> 'That's the salt' (falling intonation: *statement)*
> 'Surely that's the salt' (illocutionary particle + fall-rise intonation: *question*)
> 'Is that the salt' (inverted sequence + fall-rise intonation: *question*)
> 'That's the salt, isn't it' (fall-rise intonation + illocutionary particle: *question*)
> 'The salt, please' (falling intonation + illocutionary particle: *request)*
> 'The salt, damn it' (fall-rise intonation + illocutionary particle: *peremptory command)*

The breakdown of a spoken text to its constituent sentences, as indicated by intonation contours, can be vitally important in determining its impact in terms of practical communication. Compare for instance:

> 'Yes, please pass the salt' (with a single-sentence intonation)
> 'Yes. Please pass the salt' (with a fall and a pause after 'yes')
> 'Yes, please. Pass the salt' (with a rise on 'please' followed by a pause)
> 'Yes. Please. Pass the salt' (uttered as three sentences)

As these examples suggest, the sentential level of oral languages is extremely rich, with fine shades of intonation distinguishing sentences with subtly different nuances. A lot of these refinements tend to disappear in written texts, as a result of the relatively impoverished sentential level in writing systems. Notably, the only ways of conveying intonation in writing are punctuation and typography, which offer far fewer alternatives than the rich nuances of speech. Failing that, the writer has to fall back on explicit information about how particular sentences are spoken, by adding such comments as 'she exclaimed in surprise', 'she said angrily', and so on.

In translating both oral and written texts, then, the sentential level of language demands particular care, so that important nuances of meaning are not missed. Fortunately, sequential focus and illocutionary particles can be represented in written texts, but they are often problematic all the same. For instance, the impact of 'mal' as an illocutionary particle in 'Kommen Sie mal herein' is not easily rendered in a written English TT (the translation of German illocutionary particles is notoriously difficult, and will form the subject matter of the contrastive topic in Chapter 16): the translator must choose from various alternatives including 'Come *in*', 'Come on in', 'Come in a moment/minute' and 'Just come in, won't you?' Even more difficult is how to convey the intonational nuancing of a TT sentence like 'It makes no difference to me', depending on which of the following STs it is meant to render:

'Es macht mir gar nichts aus' (with gradually falling intonation: *statement*)
'Es macht mir gar nichts aus' (with rising intonation: *indignant question*)
'Es macht mir gar nichts aus' (with intonation and loudness rising sharply as far as 'gar': *indignant denial*)
'Mir macht's gar nichts aus' (with emphasis on 'mir': *emphatic statement*)
'Mir macht's aber gar nichts aus' (with emphasis on 'gar': *disclaimer*)
'Mir macht's eigentlich gar nichts aus' (with shrug of shoulder: *indifference*)

Languages vary significantly in the sentence-marking features they possess and the way they use them. The frequent use of a wide variety of illocutionary particles (see Chapter 16) is particularly characteristic of German; most of these particles, as for example 'doch', 'aber', 'mal', or 'auch', have no exact English counterparts and are a source of considerable difficulties in translation. There are also differences between English, German and French punctuation, for instance in the use of colons and semi-colons.

Sentence markers are capable of self-conscious, patterned uses as devices contributing to the thematic development of the overall text in which they are distributed. For instance, a dialogue containing persistent recurrences of sentential 'Well... um' may highlight the tentativeness and uncertainty typical of a particular character in a novel or play. Recurrences of 'innit, eh?', or German 'was?' (potential features of sociolect or social register, see Chapters 9 and 10), may have a similar function in the characterization of another protagonist. Or a philosophical argument may be constructed by the regular textual alternation of question and answer. In less obvious cases than these, the progression of a textual theme may be supported or underlined by a patterned progression between sentence types. This can be an effective dramatic device in an introspective monologue or soliloquy. Thus, for instance, the famous eighty-line monologue in Schiller's *Wallensteins Tod* is structured on a pattern of rhetorical questions and answers. The incidence of rhetorical questions – initially a torrent – falls away rapidly as the amplitude of Wallenstein's commentary grows. In this way, the pattern of sentence types contributes to the transition which this remarkable monologue accomplishes: for the protagonist, from upset to relative poise, from victim to challenger; for the dramatic perspective, from tactics and the moment to contemplation and the long term.

Clearly, where the translator finds a correlation in the ST between thematic motifs and patterned use of sentential features, the features are probably not accidental or incidental to the meaning, but devices instrumental in creating it. In such cases, it is more or less incumbent on the translator to use appropriate sentential features of the TL as devices enhancing the theme in the TT. Not to do so would be to court unacceptable translation loss.

THE DISCOURSE LEVEL

We now move up one step, to the **discourse level**. The textual variables considered here are the features that distinguish a cohesive and coherent textual flow from a random sequence of unrelated sentences. This level is concerned both with relations between sentences and with relations between larger units: paragraphs, stanzas, chapters, volumes, and so on.

Looking at individual sentences in discourse reveals that they often contain 'markers' signalling how sentences relate to one another, markers whose main role is to give a text a transparent inter-sentential organization. Compare, for instance, these two texts:

> I was getting hungry. I went downstairs. I knew the kitchen was on the ground floor. I was pretty sure that the kitchen must be on the ground floor. I don't know why I was so sure, but I was. I didn't expect to find the kitchen so easily. I made myself a sandwich.
>
> I was getting hungry. *So* I went downstairs. *Well...* I knew the kitchen was on the ground floor. *I mean*, I was pretty sure *it* must be *there*. *Actually*, I don't know why I was so sure, but I was. *Still*, I didn't expect to find it so easily. *Anyway*, I made myself a sandwich.

The first text is so devoid of inter-sentential connectives that, if it hangs together at all – that is, if it is *cogent* at all – this is only thanks to the underlying chronological narrative structure. In the second text, however, a rational 'train of thought' is restored by filling in the discourse-connectives (in italics) missing from the first text, which act as markers of a transparent inter-sentential structure. Some of the markers are rather like illocutionary particles, while others are instances of **anaphora** – that is, the replacement of previously used words and phrases by elements such as pronouns or adverbs that refer back to them; here, the anaphoric elements are 'it' (replacing 'the kitchen') and 'there' (replacing 'on the ground floor'). The place of these markers is in individual sentences, but their function would seem to be outside them: an inter-sentential function relating sentences to one another.

As for the larger units of texts mentioned earlier, there are, in written texts at least, some very obvious textual variables whose function is to form parts of a text into clearly recognizable units, and to indicate something about how they are interrelated. Devices like titles, paragraphs, sub-headings, cross-references, and so on are typical examples. While such devices may often cause no problems in translating, they may on occasion be subject to cross-cultural differences (we have already seen examples of this in Practical 3.3; further examples will be found in Chapter 14); translators are well advised not to take them too much for granted.

Cogency

The degree to which a text hangs together is known as its **cogency**. The considerable recent research into what it is that makes texts cogent suggests that there may be tacit, yet to some extent conventional, strategies and constraints that regulate cogency. It also suggests that, in so far as they can be isolated, these strategies and constraints are specific to textual genres (see especially Chapters 11 and 12) and vary from culture to culture. This would indicate that rational discourse is not a universal concept identical for all language-users in all communities, but a culture-specific and context-specific concept. Assuming this to be the case, translators must be aware of two things.

First, the SL may have different standards of cogency from the TL. Second, what counts for normal, rational cogency in texts of a certain type in one culture may give the appearance of lack of cogency or excessive fussiness to members of another culture, so that a TT that reproduced point-for-point the discourse structure of the ST, and did not reorganize it in the light of the TL, might appear stilted, poorly organized or over-marked to a TL audience. So, for instance, it is more common in German than in English for texts to be explicitly structured by punctuation and by the use of connectives ('also', 'auch', 'denn', 'zwar', 'trotzdem', and so on) that signpost the logical relationships between sentences. Consequently, an English TT that uses explicit connectives to reproduce all those found in a German ST is likely to seem tediously over-marked in discourse structure, and therefore stilted, pedantic, or patronizing. This piece of dialogue is a simple example:

– Bei Kafka kommt das öfter vor.
– Ich hab' eben Kafka gemeint.

In an oral TT, the 'eben' would probably be rendered not with a connective, but either by voice stress and intonation:

– You often get that in Kafka.
– I was *thinking* of Kafka.

or by intonation and sentential focus:

– You often get that in Kafka.
– It was Kafka I had in mind.

In a written TT, one might well render 'eben' with a connective: 'I was indeed thinking of Kafka'. The decision will be heavily influenced by the genre of the ST and of the TT – in a novel, italics would probably be used rather than the connective, and in a play one might even consider the alternative 'That's *exactly* who I was thinking about'; but in an academic text, or if the character in the play were a pompous type, the connective 'indeed' would be more appropriate. As this example shows, one cannot lay down a rigid rule for translating connectives. Nevertheless, in the case of emphasis, one can say that English readily uses voice stress or italics where German is more likely to use discourse connectives. This difference between German and English is observable even in quite formal written texts.

Cohesion and coherence

Halliday and Hasan (1976) make a useful distinction between two aspects of cogency in discourse: cohesion and coherence.

Cohesion refers to the transparent linking of sentences (and larger sections of texts) by the use of explicit discourse connectives like 'then', 'so', 'however', and so on. If correctly used, these act as 'signposts' in following the thread of discourse running through the text. Discourse connectives need careful attention in translating, not just because they are more liberally used in some languages than in others, but because they can be *faux amis* (for instance, 'auch', often wrongly rendered as 'too' where the appropriate rendering would be 'even').

As the example of going down to the kitchen suggested, another common way of signalling explicit cohesion is to use anaphora. It is clear from that example that not using anaphora can make for an absurdly stilted, disjointed text. However, rules of anaphora differ from language to language. This implies that translators should follow the anaphoric norms of the TL, rather than slavishly reproducing ST anaphora. Translating from German, this is vividly illustrated by the anaphoric element 'dessen/deren'. For example, 'Es war ein alter Landauer, dessen Kutscher einen altmodischen Filzhut trug' is better rendered as 'It was an old landau with a driver who wore an old-fashioned felt hat' than as 'It was an old landau whose driver wore an old-fashioned felt hat'; and 'das Essigfaß, dessen Hahn langsam tropfte' is better rendered as 'the vinegar barrel, its spigot dripping slowly' than as 'the vinegar barrel, the spigot of which was dripping slowly'. Preserving the ST anaphora in such cases tends to be at the cost of producing unidiomatic calques.

Coherence is a more difficult concept than cohesion, because it is, by definition, not explicitly marked in a text, but is rather a question of tacit thematic development running through the text. Coherence is best illustrated by contrast with cohesion. Here, first, is an example of a *cohesive* text (units responsible for the explicit cohesion are italicized):

The oneness of the human species does not demand the arbitrary reduction of

> diversity to unity; *it* only *demands* that it should be possible to pass from one particularity to another, *and that* no effort should be spared in order to elaborate a common language in which each *particularity* can be adequately described.

If we systematically strip this text of all the units on which its explicitly marked cohesion rests, the resultant text, while no longer explicitly cohesive, remains nevertheless *coherent* in terms of its thematic development:

> The oneness of the human species does not demand the arbitrary reduction of diversity to unity. All that is necessary is that it should be possible to pass from one particularity to another. No effort should be spared in order to elaborate a common language in which each individual experience can be adequately described.

While coherence is clearly culture-specific in some respects, it may also vary significantly according to subject matter or textual genre. The coherence of a TT has, by and large, to be judged in TL terms, and must not be ignored by the translator.

THE INTERTEXTUAL LEVEL

The topmost level of textual variables is the **intertextual level**: the level of external relations between a particular text and other texts within a given culture. No text exists in total isolation from other texts. Even an extremely innovative text cannot fail to form part of an overall body of literature by which the impact and originality of individual texts is coloured and defined. The originality of Joyce's *Ulysses*, for instance, is measured and defined by reference to a whole body of literature from Homer onwards, including the most unoriginal of works.

The inevitable relationship any text bears to its neighbours in the SL culture can cause translators notable problems. If the ST is an utterly 'average' specimen of an established SL genre, the translator may feel obliged to produce a similarly unoriginal TT. Formulating a TT that is as unoriginal in the TL as the ST is in the SL has its own difficulties, obliging the translator to identify a TL genre that closely matches the genre of the ST. Such matching is, at best, approximate, and may sometimes be unattainable. The same is true, *a fortiori*, of STs that are predominantly original. For instance, in the context of translating Scottish lyrical poetry into German, Brentano may be as close a German counterpart to Burns as any, but in terms of current prestige and common knowledge, a better counterpart would be Heine. Conversely, there seem to be no immediately identifiable poetic and musical counterparts to Brecht's operas in English – certainly none that enjoy the same renown.

If the ST is stylistically innovative, it may be appropriate, where circumstances permit, to formulate a TT that is just as innovative in the TL. Alternatively, it may be necessary to allow the originality of the ST to be lost in translation, for example in the case of technical or scientific texts, where the subject matter and thematic content outweigh considerations of style. There are, however, academic texts (Husserl's writings, for instance) where the style and the thematic content together form an indissoluble whole. In such cases, translation cannot do full justice to the ST without trying to re-create the innovative nature of the ST. Whatever the text, these are all matters for strategic evaluation and decision by the translator.

Texts are also in significant relationship with other texts if they directly invoke, by allusion or quotation, parts of other well-known texts, such as Goethe, or the Bible. The Liliencron poem 'Der Blitzzug' (cited in Chapter 3, p. 29 and Chapter 4, p. 42) contains an example in the line 'Dämmerung senkt sich allmählich wie Gaze', which directly echoes the opening of Goethe's late poem 'Dämmrung senkte sich'. The translator must always be on the look-out for such echoes. What to do with them depends on the circumstances. Some cases will simply necessitate finding the appropriate TL passages and integrating them into the TT (although in the case of the Bible or ancient classics, thought will have to be given to which version to choose). In yet other cases, the echoes are too abstruse or unimportant from the point of view of a TL audience to be worth building into the TT.

We shall return to the problem of allusion, with examples, on pp. 93–5.

Another significant mode of intertextuality is imitation. An entire text may be designed specifically as an imitation of another text or texts, as in pastiche or parody. (An example of this is Brecht's 'Großer Dankchoral' used in Practical 4.3.) Alternatively, sections of a text may deliberately imitate different texts or genres – an example is David Lodge's *The British Museum is Falling Down*, in which each chapter parodies a different author. Here the overall effect is of a text contrived as a mixture of styles that recall the various genres from which they are copied. (We shall return to this question in Chapter 11.) This aspect of intertextuality has to be borne in mind, because there are STs that can only be fully appreciated if one is aware that they use the device of imitating other texts or genres. Furthermore, to recreate this device in the TT, the translator must be familiar with target culture genres, and have the skill to imitate them.

PRACTICAL 6

6.1 The formal properties of texts; discourse and intertextuality

Assignment

(i) Discuss the strategic problems confronting the translator of the ST below.
(ii) Translate lines 1–20 of the poem (to 'wir trinken dich abends'), paying special attention to its textual and intertextual properties.
(iii) Explain the main decisions of detail you made in producing your TT.

Contextual information

Paul Celan is the pseudonym of Paul Antschel, who was born in 1920 in Czernowitz, Romania and died in 1970. His homeland became part of the Soviet Union in 1940 and was then occupied by the Germans. His Jewish origins meant ghetto and forced labour for him and disappearance to concentration camps for his parents. According to one critic (Siegbert Prawer), 'Todesfuge' occupies the place in Celan's work that 'Guernica' does in Picasso's, and, like 'Guernica', confounds those who would divorce modern art from actuality. Leonard Forster, in a 1971 edition, described 'Todesfuge' as probably the most famous poem written in German since 1945.

Text

Todesfuge

Schwarze Milch der Frühe wir trinken sie abends
wir trinken sie mittags und morgens wir trinken sie nachts
wir trinken und trinken
wir schaufeln ein Grab in den Lüften da liegt man nicht eng
Ein Mann wohnt im Haus der spielt mit den Schlangen der schreibt
der schreibt wenn es dunkelt nach Deutschland dein goldenes Haar Margarete
er schreibt es und tritt vor das Haus und es blitzen die Sterne er pfeift seine Rüden herbei
er pfeift seine Juden hervor läßt schaufeln ein Grab in der Erde
er befiehlt uns spielt auf nun zum Tanz

Schwarze Milch der Frühe wir trinken dich nachts
wir trinken dich morgens und mittags wir trinken dich abends
wir trinken und trinken
Ein Mann wohnt im Haus der spielt mit den Schlangen der schreibt
der schreibt wenn es dunkelt nach Deutschland dein goldenes Haar Margarete
Dein aschenes Haar Sulamith wir schaufeln ein Grab in den Lüften da liegt man nicht eng
Er ruft stecht tiefer ins Erdreich ihr einen ihr andern singet und spielt
er greift nach dem Eisen im Gurt er schwingts seine Augen sind blau
stecht tiefer die Spaten ihr einen ihr andern spielt weiter zum Tanz auf

Schwarze Milch der Frühe wir trinken dich nachts
wir trinken dich mittags und morgens wir trinken dich abends

wir trinken und trinken
ein Mann wohnt im Haus dein goldenes Haar Margarete
dein aschenes Haar Sulamith er spielt mit den Schlangen

Er ruft spielt süßer den Tod der Tod ist ein Meister aus Deutschland
er ruft streicht dunkler die Geigen dann steigt ihr als Rauch in die Luft
dann habt ihr ein Grab in den Wolken da liegt man nicht eng

Schwarze Milch der Frühe wir trinken dich nachts
wir trinken dich mittags der Tod ist ein Meister aus Deutschland
wir trinken dich abends und morgens wir trinken und trinken
der Tod ist ein Meister aus Deutschland sein Auge ist blau
er trifft dich mit bleierner Kugel er trifft dich genau
ein Mann wohnt im Haus dein goldenes Haar Margarete
er hetzt seine Rüden auf uns er schenkt uns ein Grab in der Luft
er spielt mit den Schlangen und träumet der Tod ist ein Meister aus Deutschland

dein goldenes Haar Margarete
dein aschenes Haar Sulamith

6.2 The formal properties of texts; sentential and discourse levels

Assignment

Working in groups:

(i) Discuss the strategic problems confronting the translator of the following text, paying careful attention to the sentential and inter-sentential means by which the links between successive ideas are indicated.
(ii) Translate the second paragraph of the text (from 'Es sei zunächst...'), paying special attention to cohesion markers.
(iii) Explain the main decisions of detail you made in producing your TT.

Contextual information

The passage comes from a standard (now superseded) textbook by L. Ryan (in the Metzler *Realienbücher* series) on the life and work of the poet Hölderlin. The words in quotation marks are quoted from Hölderlin's own critical theory.

Text

Die Arbeit am *Empedokles* trieb die Klärung dichtungstheoretischer Fragen, die Hölderlin in Homburg besonders angelegen waren, weit voran. Er hat eine Reihe von Aufsatzentwürfen hinterlassen, die zwar allgemeine Fragen der Philosophie, der Ästhetik und der Poetik behandeln, ihre hauptsächliche Bedeutung aber für die Hölderlin-Forschung in ihrer Beziehung zu Hölderlins eigenem Werk haben: sie halten gleichsam den Prozeß der Selbstreflexion des Dichters fest. In ihrer Sprache wie in ihrer deduktiven Begriffsführung verraten diese Aufsätze ihre idealistische Herkunft: sie setzen die schon längst im Gang befindliche Auseinandersetzung Hölderlins mit der Philosophie des Idealismus fort und markieren dabei den konsequenten Ausbau eines eigenen Standpunkts. Gleichzeitig stehen sie in enger Verbindung mit seiner Dichtung, bezeugen also das handwerkliche Wissen des formbewußten Dichters; und sie verkörpern ferner sein an der Kunstübung der Antike orientiertes Bestreben, auch der 'umherirrenden' neueren Kunst zu jenem 'durch und durch bestimmten und überdachten Gang' zu verhelfen, der den 'alten Kunstwerken' eigen war. Die Schwierigkeit und Komplexität der Entwürfe, die größtenteils nicht für den Druck redigiert wurden und die nur mühevoll erschlossen werden können, verbietet in diesem Rahmen eine einläßliche Behandlung, doch sollen einige leitende Gesichtspunkte herausgehoben werden.

Es sei zunächst ein Wort zur Frage des Verhältnisses von Dichtung und Philosophie gestattet, die bei Hölderlin oft Anlaß zu Mißverständnissen gegeben hat. Hölderlins philosophische Ausführungen ernst nehmen, heißt nicht, seine dichterische Potenz in Zweifel stellen und seine Dichtungen auf philosophische Aussagen reduzieren, die man lieber gleich in ihrer theoretischen Formulierung aufsuchen möchte. Ordnet man hingegen seine Philosophie der Dichtung unter, so darf das nicht zu dem Schluß verführen, er dilettiere in der Philosophie auf spielerisch unsystematische Weise. Das Verhältnis der beiden Bereiche hat er selber dahingehend bestimmt, daß das in der Philosophie 'Unvereinbare' 'am Ende auch wieder... in der geheimnisvollen Quelle der Dichtung' zusammenläuft; entsprechend wird in der ganzen Anlage des Hyperion-Romans die ursprüngliche und sich immer neu bezeugende Einheit der Natur dem Bewußtsein übergeordnet.

7

Literal meaning and translation problems

In Chapter 2 we raised objections to using the concept of 'equivalence' in assessing the relationship between a ST and a corresponding TT. This is because it does not seem helpful to say that good translation produces a TT that has 'the same meaning' as the corresponding ST, when such a claim rests on the comparison of two virtually imponderable and indeterminable qualities. The term 'meaning' is especially elastic and indeterminate when applied to an entire text. At one end of the scale, the 'meaning' of a text might designate its putative socio-cultural significance, importance and impact – a historian might define the meaning of *Mein Kampf* in such terms. At the other end of the scale, the 'meaning' might designate the personal, private and emotional impact the text has on a unique individual at a unique point in time – say, the impact of *Mein Kampf* on a German bride presented with a copy of it at her wedding in 1938. Between these two extremes lie many shades of shared conventional meaning intrinsic to the text because of its internal structure and explicit contents, and the relation these bear to the semantic conventions and tendencies of the SL in its ordinary, everyday usage.

Meanings in a text that are fully supported by ordinary semantic conventions (such as the lexical convention that 'window' refers to a particular kind of aperture in a wall or roof) are normally known as **literal** (or 'cognitive') **meanings**. In the case of words, it is this basic literal meaning that is given in dictionary definitions. However, even the dictionary definition of a word, which is meant to crystallize precisely that range of 'things' that a particular word can denote in everyday usage, is not without its problems. This is because the intuitive understanding that native language-users have of the literal meanings of individual words does itself tend to be rather fluid. That is, a dictionary definition imposes, by abstraction and crystallization of a 'core' meaning, a rigidity of meaning that words do not often show in reality. In addition, once words are put into different contexts, their literal meanings become even more flexible. These two facts make it infinitely difficult to pin down the precise literal meaning of any text of any complexity. This difficulty is still further compounded by the fact that literal meanings supported by a consensus of semantic conventions are not the only types of meaning that can function in a text and nuance its interpretations. As we shall see in Chapter 8, there are various connotative tendencies – not sufficiently cut and dried to qualify as conventional meanings accepted by consensus – which can play an important role in how a text is to be interpreted and translated.

SYNONYMY

Although the apparent fixity of literal meaning is something of an illusion, a narrow concept of 'semantic equivalence' is still useful as a measure of correspondence between the literal meanings of isolated linguistic expressions (words or phrases) figuring in texts. If one is prepared to isolate such expressions, one can talk about semantic equivalence as a possible, and fairly objective, relationship between linguistic items that have identical literal meanings (such as 'viper' and 'adder', or 'bachelor' and 'unmarried man'). In what follows, we shall discuss ways of comparing degrees of correspondence in literal meaning between STs and TTs, and our discussion will presuppose the type of semantic equivalence defined here.

We make one further basic supposition: that literal meaning is a matter of *categories* into which, through a complex interplay of inclusion and exclusion, a language divides the totality of communicable experience. So, for example, the literal meaning of the word 'page' does not consist in the fact that one can use the word to denote the object you are staring at as you read this. It consists rather in the fact that all over the world (in past, present and future) one may find 'similar' objects each of which is *included in* the category of 'page', as well as, of course, countless other objects that are *excluded from* it. To define a literal meaning, then, is to specify the 'range' covered by a word or phrase in such a way that one knows what items are included in that range or category and what items are excluded from it. The most useful way to visualize literal meanings is by thinking of them as circles, because in this way we can represent intersections between categories, and thus reflect overlaps in literal meaning between different expressions. In exploring correspondence in literal meaning, it is particularly the intersections between categories that are significant; they provide, as it were, a measure of semantic equivalence.

Comparisons of literal meaning made possible by considering overlaps between categories, and visualized as intersections between circles, are usually drawn between linguistic expressions in the same language. They allow, in the semantic description of a language, for an assessment of types and degrees of semantic correspondence between items (for example, lexical items). There is, however, no reason why analogous comparisons may not be made between expressions from two or more different languages, as a way of assessing and representing types and degrees of cross-linguistic semantic equivalence.

Thus, for instance, the expressions 'my mother's father' and 'my maternal grandfather' may be represented as two separate circles. The two ranges of literal meaning, however, coincide perfectly. This can be visualized as moving the two circles on top of each other and finding that they cover one another exactly, as in Figure 7.1:

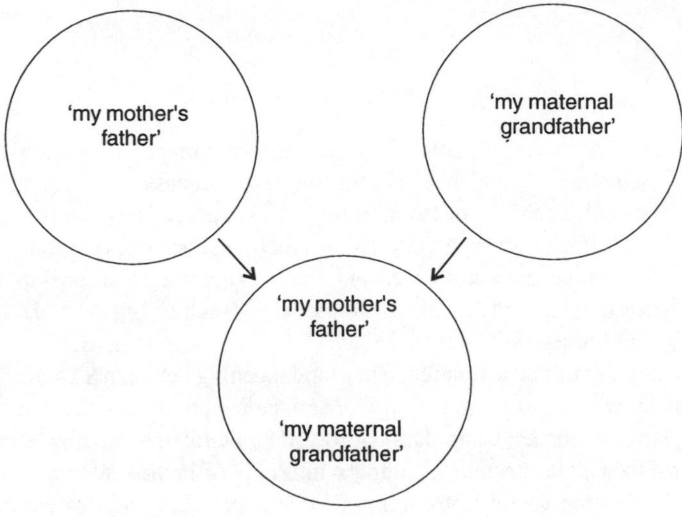

Figure 7.1

Both in general and in every specific instance of use, 'my mother's father' and 'my maternal grandfather' include and exclude exactly the same referents; that is, their literal meanings are identical in range. This exemplifies the strongest form of semantic equivalence: full **synonymy**.

Just as alternative expressions in the same language may be full synonyms, so, in principle at least, there may be full synonymy across two different languages. As one might expect, the closer the SL and the TL are in the way they process and categorize speakers' experience of the world, the more likely it is that there will be full cross-linguistic synonyms between the two languages. Thus, one can fairly confidently say that 'bitte, ein Glas Wein' and 'a glass of wine, please' cover exactly the same range of situations, and are, therefore, fully synonymous in their literal meanings, as is seen in Figure 7.2:

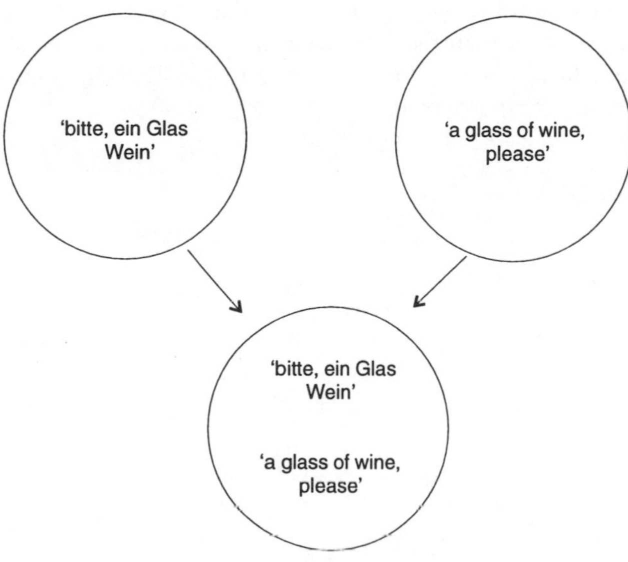

Figure 7.2

HYPERONYMY–HYPONYMY

Unfortunately, full cross-linguistic synonymy is more the exception than the rule, even between historically and culturally related languages. More often than not, the so-called 'nearest equivalent' for translating the literal meaning of a ST expression falls short of being a full TL synonym. Compare, for example, 'Das Kind öffnet das Fenster' with 'The child opens the window'. It is at least possible that the German phrase refers to a progressive event reported by the speaker. This would have to be expressed in English by 'The child *is opening* the window'. That is, 'Das Kind öffnet das Fenster' and 'The child opens the window' are not full synonyms, but have non-identical ranges of literal meaning. There is a common element between the two phrases, but the German covers a wider range of situations, a range that is covered by at least two different expressions in English. This can be shown diagrammatically, as in Figure 7.3:

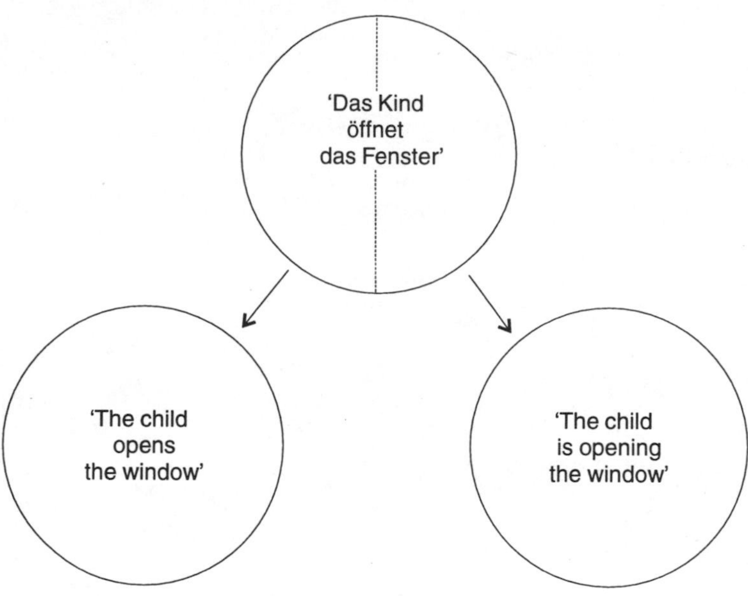

Figure 7.3

The type of relationship between these two phrases can also be instanced within a single language. For example, 'There's a window broken' and 'There's a dormer broken' have a common element of literal meaning, but show a discrepancy in the fact that 'There's a window broken' covers a wider range of situations, including in its literal meaning situations that are excluded from 'There's a dormer broken'

– such as 'There's a skylight broken', 'There's a casement broken', and so on. This is seen diagrammatically in Figure 7.4:

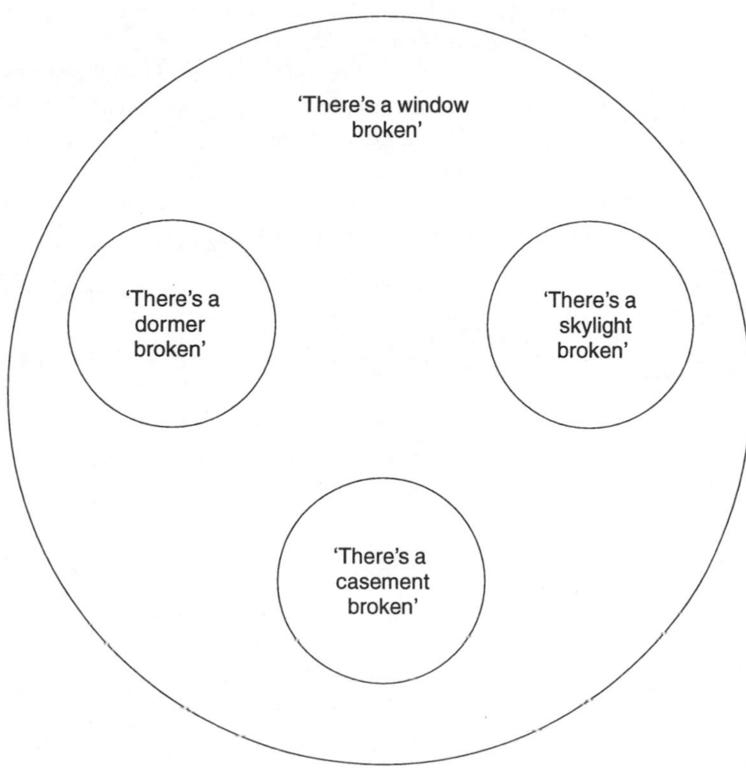

Figure 7.4

The relationship between 'There's a window broken' and 'There's a dormer broken' is known as **hyperonymy–hyponymy**. The expression with the wider, less specific, range of literal meaning is a *hyperonym* of the one with the narrower and more specific literal meaning. Conversely, the narrower one is a *hyponym* of the wider one. So, 'There's a window broken' is a hyperonym of each of the other three phases, while these are hyponyms of 'There's a window broken'. Similarly, 'Das Kind öffnet das Fenster' is a hyperonym of both 'The child opens the window' and 'The child is opening the window', while these two are hyponyms of the German expression.

Hyperonymy–hyponymy is so widespread in any given language that one can say that the entire fabric of linguistic reference is built up on such relationships. Take, for example, some of the alternative ways in which one can refer to an object

– say, a particular biro. If there is need to particularize, one can use a phrase with a fairly narrow and specific meaning, such as 'the black biro in my hand'. If such detail is unnecessary and one wants to generalize, one can call it 'a writing implement', 'an implement', 'an object' or, even more vaguely, just 'something'.

It is in the very essence of the richness of all languages that they offer a whole set of different expressions, each with a different range of inclusiveness, for designating any object, any situation, anything whatsoever. Thus the series 'the black biro in my hand', 'a biro', 'a writing implement', 'an implement', 'an object', 'something' is a series organized on the basis of successively larger, wider inclusiveness – that is, on the basis of hyperonymy–hyponymy. The series can be visualized as a set of increasingly large concentric circles, larger circles representing hyperonyms, smaller ones hyponyms, as follows:

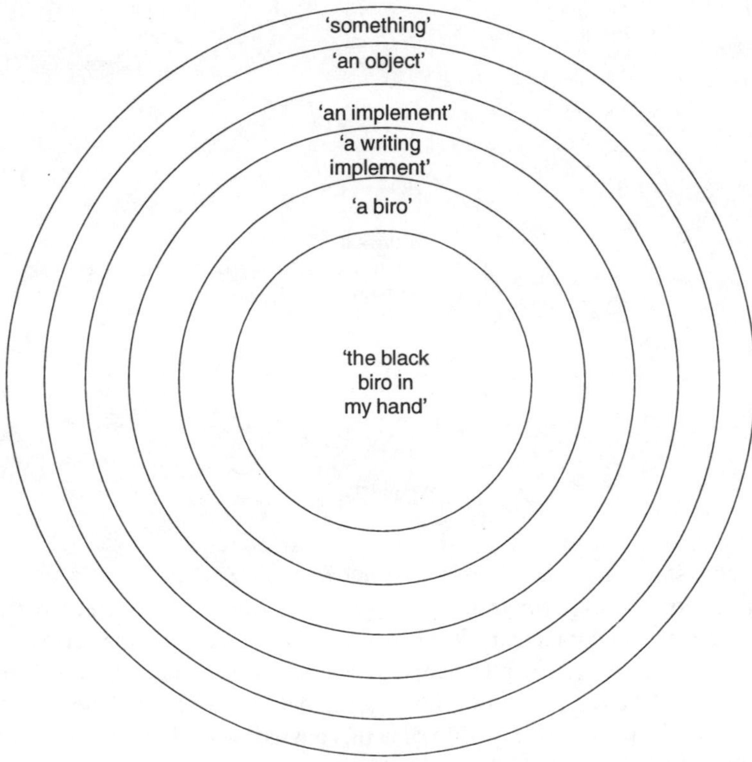

Figure 7.5

As this example shows, the same external reality can be described in an indefinite number of ways, depending on how precise or vague one needs to be.

By its very nature, translation is concerned with rephrasing, and in particular with rephrasing so as to preserve to best advantage the integrity of a ST message, including its degree of precision or vagueness. Therefore, the fact that both a hyperonym and a hyponym can serve for conveying a given message is of great importance to translation practice. It means that, as soon as one acknowledges that there is no full TL synonym for a particular ST expression (for example, 'Das Kind öffnet das Fenster'), one must start looking for an appropriate TL hyperonym or hyponym. In fact, translators do this automatically, which is why they may see 'The child opens the window' as the 'nearest' semantic equivalent to 'Das Kind öffnet das Fenster'; but they do not always do it carefully or successfully. For example, in most contexts 'How long shall I boil the eggs?' is effectively translated as 'Wie lange soll ich die Eier kochen?'. Yet the German expression is wider and less specific in literal meaning than the English one, since 'kochen' could also mean 'fry', 'poach', and so on. In other words, a SL hyponym may be unhesitatingly translated by a TL hyperonym as its nearest semantic equivalent, as shown in the diagram:

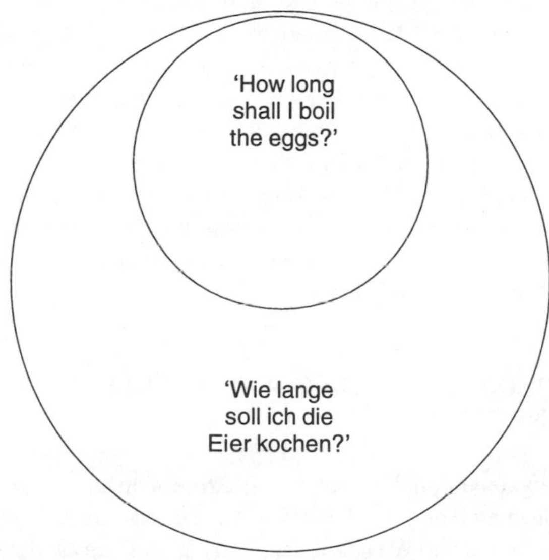

Figure 7.6

Conversely, translating 'That's my cousin' into contemporary German necessarily implies choosing between 'Das ist mein Cousin' and 'Das ist meine Kusine'. Each of the German phrases excludes people of one sex, and is therefore narrower and more specific in literal meaning than the English phrase. Either case is an example of translating a SL hyperonym by a TL hyponym. This can be represented thus:

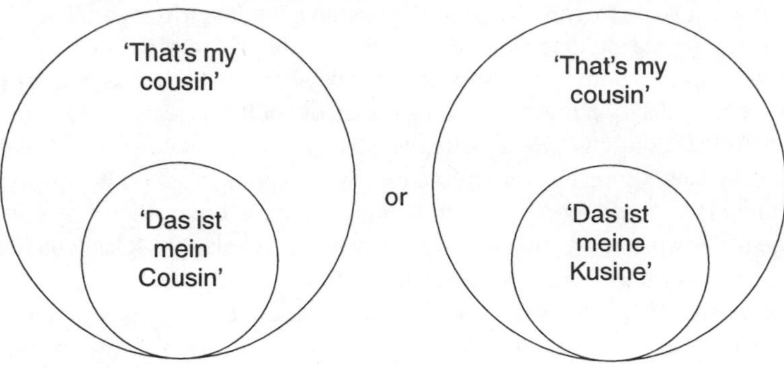

Figure 7.7

In the absence of plausible synonyms, translating by a hyperonym or a hyponym is standard practice and entirely unremarkable. Indeed, choosing a hyperonym or hyponym where a synonym does exist may actually be the mark of a good translation. For instance, the terms 'Schwert' and 'Degen' are sufficiently distinct to be used with discrimination even in a swashbuckling German narrative; yet in English, specifying 'rapier' or 'foil', rather than simply using the generic term 'sword', would usually be unduly pedantic. In all but a technical context, the hyperonym 'sword' is the appropriate translation. It is, then, only when using a TL hyperonym or hyponym is unnecessary, or unnecessarily extreme, or misleading, that a TT can be criticized on this basis.

PARTICULARIZING TRANSLATION AND GENERALIZING TRANSLATION

Translating by a hyponym implies that the TT expression has a narrower and more specific literal meaning than the ST expression. That is, the TT gives *particulars* that are not given by the ST. We shall therefore call this **particularizing translation**, or **particularization** for short. Thus, in our earlier example, 'Das ist meine Kusine' is a particularizing translation of 'That's my cousin'.

Conversely, translating by a hyperonym implies that the TT expression has a wider and less specific literal meaning than the ST expression. That is, the TT is more *general*, omitting details that are given by the ST. We shall call this **generalizing translation**, or **generalization** for short. Our earlier example of translating 'Degen' as 'sword' is a case of generalizing translation.

Particularization and generalization both naturally imply a degree of translation loss as we defined it in Chapter 2 – detail is either added to, or omitted from, the ST meaning. However, neither the addition nor the omission of detail is necessarily a matter for criticism, or even comment, in evaluating a TT. We outline here a set of criteria under which particularizing and generalizing translation are acceptable or unacceptable.

Particularizing translation is acceptable on two conditions: first, that the TL offers no suitable alternative; second, that the added detail is implicit in the ST and fits in with the overall context of the ST. For instance, translating the title of Liliencron's 'Der Blitzzug' as 'Lightning Express', rather than as 'Lightning Train', accords better with the context of the poem.

Particularizing translation is *not* acceptable where one or more of the following three conditions hold: first, if the TL does offer suitable alternatives to the addition of unnecessary detail; second, if the added detail creates discrepancies in the TT; third, if the added detail constitutes a misinterpretation of the overall context of the ST. As an example, one may take Schopenhauer's sentence 'Denn dieselbe Gehirnfunktion, welche, während des Schlafes, eine vollkommen objektive, anschauliche, ja handgreifliche Welt hervorzaubert, muß eben so viel Antheil an der Darstellung der objektiven Welt des Wachens haben'. Rendering 'Gehirnfunktion' as 'cerebral/brain function' instead of 'mental activity' or 'activity of the mind' would be unacceptable in this context for all three reasons.

Generalizing translation is acceptable on two conditions: first, that the TL offers no suitable alternative; second, that the omitted detail either is clear and can be recovered from the overall context of the TT, or is unimportant to the ST. For example, in the context of the Rudolf Binding passage in Practical 2 (p. 18), translating 'Wasserzunge' as 'stretch of water' occasions a harmless, insignificant translation loss.

Generalizing translation is not acceptable where one or more of the following three conditions hold: first, if the omitted details are important to the ST; second, if the TL does offer suitable alternatives to the omission of this detail; third, if the omitted detail is not compensated for elsewhere in the TT, and cannot be recovered from the overall context of the TT. Thus, to return to an earlier example, translating 'Degen' simply by 'sword' in a sporting manual describing the rules of fencing, as distinct from a novel, occasions unacceptable translation loss.

PARTIALLY OVERLAPPING TRANSLATION

As well as particularizing and generalizing translation, there is another type of semantic near-equivalence. This is more easily illustrated in phrases than in single words. Take the phrase 'The teacher treated brother and sister differently'. 'Der Lehrer hat die Geschwister unterschiedlich behandelt' is a plausible literal rendering into German. Yet in the English phrase it is not explicitly specified that the teacher was male, whereas this is made explicit in the German TT. In respect to the gender of the teacher, the German TT *particularizes* (just as it would have done in specifying 'Lehrerin'). Conversely, in the English phrase the gender difference between the two siblings is specified unambiguously, whereas the German TT leaves this ambiguous: the German TT *generalizes* here, in that 'Geschwister' is a gender-neutral term, more or less equivalent in its literal meaning to 'siblings'.

In other words, this TT combines particularization with generalization, *adding* a detail not found in the ST and *omitting* a detail that is given in the ST. This is best visualized as two partially overlapping circles:

'The teacher
treated brother
and sister
differently'
'Der Lehrer hat
die Geschwister
unterschiedlich
behandelt'

Figure 7.8

This type of case is a further category of degree in the translation of literal meaning: along with synonymic, particularizing and generalizing translation, there is **partially overlapping translation**, or **overlapping translation** for short. The concept of overlapping translation applies less obviously, but more importantly, in the case of individual words (as distinct from phrases). For example, if in translating 'we had mutton for dinner' one were to render 'mutton' as 'Lamm', this would constitute a case of overlapping translation: the German keeps the reference to 'sheep', but it *loses* explicit reference to 'meat' and *adds* the detail that the animal was young.

Once again, overlapping translation may or may not involve comment when one is evaluating a TT. The conditions under which it is acceptable and the criteria for criticizing it are similar to those for particularization and generalization. Overlapping translation is acceptable on two conditions: first, if the TL offers no suitable alternatives; second, if the *omitted* detail is either unimportant or can be recovered from the overall TT context, and the *added* detail is implicit in, or at least not contradictory to, the overall ST context. For example, in most contexts 'Slept well?' is the most accurate idiomatic rendering of 'Ausgeschlafen?', but it does *add* (by making explicit) the quality of sleep, and *lose* (by making implicit) the sufficiency of sleep explicit in the ST.

Overlapping translation is not acceptable when one or more of the following three conditions hold: first, if the omitted detail is important to the ST but cannot be recovered from the overall context of the TT; second, if the added detail creates discrepancies in the TT; third, if the TL does offer suitable alternatives to avoiding either the omissions or the additions or both. For an example, see the translation of 'Schönheitssinn' by 'sense of beauty' on p. 87, and our comments on p. 86.

PRACTICAL 7

7.1 Particularizing, generalizing and partially overlapping translation

Assignment

(i) Starting at line 5 ('Aber moralische...') of the ST printed on p. 87, make a detailed analysis of particularizing, generalizing and overlapping translation in the TT printed below the ST.

(ii) Where possible, give an edited TT that is a more exact translation, and explain your decisions.

Contextual information

The passage is taken from the same Thomas Mann Novelle, *Der Tod in Venedig* (1912), used in Practicals 4 and 5. The present extract comes from the 'literary-biographical' section of the Novelle mentioned in Practical 5; it contains a continuation of the literary biography of the Novelle's fictional main protagonist, the writer Gustav von Aschenbach.

NB Here is an example of how to lay out your material for this exercise:

ST 1–5: 'War es eine... verlieh?'

1. 'perhaps' is a particularization that not only adds unnecessarily to the TT, but actually alters the illocutionary impact of the sentence.
2. 'intellectual' is a particularization of 'geistig' (intellectual/spiritual/mental/psychological) which, in this context, comes close to mistranslation: of the available choices, 'mental' and 'psychological' are defensible in context, but 'intellectual' seems to be the worst alternative.
3. 'Würde' remains untranslated in the TT; thus generalization results from the omission of a detail.
4. 'austerity' is a particularization of 'Strenge' (whose meaning covers both 'austerity' and 'discipline').
5. 'his style showed' is an overlapping rendering of 'man beobachtete' (explicit reference to an observer is omitted and explicit reference to the observed is added); however, this is an appropriate solution in the TT.

6 'exaggerated' is an overlapping translation of 'übermäßiges Erstarken'; the notion of 'strengthening' is lost, while the element of 'wilfully overdoing' is added to the TT (note that 'exaggerated' translates German 'übertrieben').
7 'a[n]... sense of beauty' is a generalizing translation of 'sein Schönheitssinn', and it is one that, in context, could be misleading: the TT might suggest that beauty is a quality noted in Aschenbach's style, whereas in the ST what is at issue is the author's aesthetic sensibility (see *seines*).
8 In so far as 'symmetry' generally includes a notion of 'harmony' in form, 'symmetry' is a particularizing translation of 'Ebenmäßigkeit': this is a gratuitous choice in the TT, as there are many ways other than symmetry in which an object can display a quality of being evenly proportioned.
9 The omission of an explicit rendering of 'Formgebung' (admittedly difficult to translate), and its replacement by 'style', is an unfortunate case of partially overlapping translation, since the concept of 'Form' is of great significance to the subject matter of the ST.
10 The rendering of 'so' has been omitted from the TT, resulting in generalization; this could be easily remedied by adding 'such' to the TT.
11 'conscious' is a mistranslation of 'sinnfälliges'.
12 'gave' is an unnecessary generalizing translation of 'verlieh': 'lent' is both a closer literal equivalent, and can be worked into an idiomatic English TT.

Ed TT: Was it a psychological consequence of this 'rebirth', of this new dignity and discipline, that at around the same time observers noted an almost excessive strengthening of his aesthetic sensibility, of that lofty purity, simplicity and proportion of formal structure, which was thenceforth to lend his work such an unmistakable, indeed deliberate, stamp of the masterly, the classical?

Source text

War es eine geistige Folge dieser 'Wiedergeburt', dieser neuen Würde und Strenge, daß man um dieselbe Zeit ein fast übermäßiges Erstarken seines Schönheitssinnes beobachtete, jene adelige Reinheit, Einfachheit und Ebenmäßigkeit der Formgebung, welche seinen Produkten fortan ein so sinnfälliges, ja gewolltes Gepräge der Meisterlichkeit und Klassizität verlieh? Aber moralische Entschlossenheit jenseits des Wissens, der auflösenden und hemmenden Erkenntnis, – bedeutet sie nicht wiederum eine Vereinfachung, eine sittliche Vereinfältigung der Welt und der Seele und also auch ein Erstarken zum Bösen, Verbotenen, zum sittlich Unmöglichen? Und hat Form nicht zweierlei Gesicht? Ist sie nicht sittlich und unsittlich zugleich, – sittlich als Ergebnis und Ausdruck der Zucht, unsittlich aber und selbst widersittlich, sofern sie von Natur eine moralische Gleichgültigkeit in sich schließt, ja wesentlich bestrebt ist, das Moralische unter ihr stolzes und unumschränktes Szepter zu beugen?

Reprinted from Thomas Mann, *Der Tod in Venedig* (Fischer-Bücherei, Frankfurt: Lizenzausgabe des S. Fischer Verlages, 1954, pp. 17–18), by permission of S. Fischer Verlag GmbH, Frankfurt am Main.

Target text

Was it perhaps an intellectual consequence of this rebirth, this new austerity, that from now on his style showed an almost exaggerated sense of beauty, a lofty purity, symmetry, and simplicity, which gave his productions a stamp of the classic, of conscious and deliberate mastery? And yet: this moral fibre, surviving the hampering and disintegrating effect of knowledge, does it not result in its turn in a dangerous simplification, in a tendency to equate the world and the human soul, and thus to strengthen the hold of the evil, the forbidden, and the ethically impossible? And has not form two aspects? Is it not moral and immoral at once; moral in so far as it is the expression and result of discipline, immoral – yes, actually hostile to morality – in that of its very essence it is indifferent to good and evil, and deliberately concerned to make the moral world stoop beneath its proud and undivided sceptre?

Reprinted by kind permission from Thomas Mann, *Death in Venice*, translated by H. T. Lowe-Porter (Harmondsworth: Penguin 1956, pp. 17–18), copyright © Martin Secker & Warburg Ltd and Alfred A. Knopf Inc.

7.2 Speed translation

Assignment

Your tutor will give you a text to be translated in class within a certain time limit. You should try to apply the lessons learned so far, while meeting the demands of speed and accuracy.

8

Connotative meaning and translation problems

As was pointed out in Chapter 7, literal meaning is only one aspect of verbal meaning. To deal with meaning in terms of the literal reference conventionally attached to verbal signs is a necessary part of unravelling a complex message, but it is not, in itself, enough. In actual fact, the meaning of a text comprises a number of different layers: referential content, emotional colouring, cultural associations, social and personal connotations, and so on. The many-layered nature of meaning is something translators must never forget.

Even within a single language, so-called referential synonyms are as a rule different in their overall semantic effects. For instance, 'the police' and 'the fuzz' must be rated as synonyms in terms of referential content, but they may be said to have different overall meanings. This is because, while 'the police' is a relatively neutral expression, the 'fuzz' is usually understood to carry pejorative overtones. These overtones are not part of the literal meaning of the expression, but it is clear that a reference to 'the fuzz' could be taken as disrespectful or hostile in a way that reference to 'the police' could not. It is impossible to ignore such overtones in responding to messages in one's own language, and one certainly cannot afford to overlook them when it comes to translating. For example, a speaker who refers to 'die Bullen' does not merely designate members of a particular organization, but also conveys a certain attitude to them. Consequently, while translating 'die Bullen' as 'the police' would accurately render the literal meaning of the ST, it would fail to render the disrespectful attitude connoted by 'die Bullen' (better translated as 'the cops' or 'the fuzz').

We shall call such overtones **connotative meanings** – that is, associations which, over and above the literal meaning of an expression, form part of its overall meaning. In fact, of course, connotative meanings are many and varied, and it is common for a single piece of text to combine several kinds into a single overall effect. Nevertheless, there are six major types of commonly recognized connotative meaning, which we will review in turn. We should perhaps add that, by definition, we are only concerned with socially widespread connotations, not private ones – as long as private connotations are recognized for what they are, and not allowed to influence the production of a TT that does justice to the ST, they are the translator's own affair.

ATTITUDINAL MEANING

Attitudinal meaning is that part of the overall meaning of an expression which consists of some widespread *attitude to the referent*. That is, the expression does not merely denote the referent in a neutral way, but, in addition, hints at some attitude to it on the part of the speaker.

Our examples of 'die Bullen' and 'the fuzz' versus 'die Polizei' and 'the police' are clear cases of attitudinal connotations. As these examples show, attitudinal meanings can be hard to pin down. (For instance, just how hostile is the expression 'the fuzz'? Is it simply familiar, or perhaps even affectionately derogatory? This will vary from context to context.) There are two main reasons why attitudinal meanings are sometimes hard to define. First, being connotations, they are by definition meant to be suggestive – the moment they cease to be suggestive, and become fixed by convention, they cease to be connotations and become part of literal meaning. Second, being controlled by the vagaries of usage, they can change very rapidly. Both these factors are illustrated by the evolution of the word 'Tory', originally a term of abuse imported from Irish ('tóriadhe', meaning 'outlaw'), but later proudly adopted by the parties so labelled.

ASSOCIATIVE MEANING

Associative meaning is that part of the overall meaning of an expression which consists of stereotypical *expectations* rightly or wrongly *associated with the referent* of the expression.

The word 'nurse' is a good example. Most people automatically associate 'nurse' with the idea of female gender, as if the word were synonymous with 'female who looks after the sick'. This unconscious association is so stereotypical and automatic that the term 'male nurse' has had to be coined in order to counteract its effect. Even so, the female connotations of 'nurse' continue to persist: witness the fact that 'he is a nurse' still feels semantically odd.

Any area of reference where prejudices and stereotypes, however innocuous, operate is likely to give examples of associative meaning. Even something as banal as a date may trigger an associative meaning, for example July 14 or November 5. Similarly, in Germany and England – though not in Scotland – 'golf' will automatically trigger associations of an 'upper- or middle-class' milieu.

The appreciation of associative meanings requires cultural knowledge, and the translator must constantly be on the lookout for them. Take, for instance, Spoerl's earlier mentioned essay *Mädchen ohne Singular* (Spoerl, 1961, p. 112). Associatively, the term 'Renaissance' evokes the name of a well-known vaudeville theatre – the Renaissance Theatre in Berlin – and through this, by further association, the image of a chorus-line of dancing girls. This enables Spoerl to create a word-play in the expression 'Renaissancebeine' ('legs with Renaissance proportions' / 'legs like those of a chorus-girl at the Renaissance Theatre'). In English, 'Renaissance' would evoke images associated with the art of the historical period designated, but the association with the chorus-line at the Renaissance Theatre could not be recreated, which makes Spoerl's joke about 'Renaissancebeine' virtually impossible to translate effectively into English. This difficulty is a direct consequence of associative meaning. (Depending on the context, a possible solution might be 'theatrical legs', which does at least reproduce a play on two different senses of 'theatrical'; but the translation loss in this TT is admittedly considerable.)

AFFECTIVE MEANING

Affective meaning is that part of the overall meaning of an expression which consists in an *emotive effect worked on the addressee* by the choice of that expression. The expression does not merely denote its referent, but also hints at some attitude of the speaker/writer to the addressee.

Features of linguistic politeness, flattery, rudeness, or insult are typical examples of expressions carrying affective meanings. Compare, for instance, 'Bitte, nehmen Sie doch Platz' with 'Hinsetzen!'. These expressions share the same literal meaning as English 'sit down', but their overall impact in terms of affective meaning is quite different: polite and deferential in the first case, brusque and peremptory in the second. That is, the speaker's tacit or implied attitude to the listener produces a different emotive effect in each case.

Not only imperative forms, but also statements and questions, can have alternative forms identical in basic literal meaning yet totally different in affective meaning, as in 'Excuse me, Madam, I think that's my seat' versus 'Oy, Ducky, that's my seat'; or 'Where are the toilets, please?' versus 'Where's the bog?'.

Clearly, translators must be able to recognize affective meanings in the ST. But they must also be sure not to introduce unwanted affective meanings into the TT. Take, for example, someone making a date to be picked up by an acquaintance and saying 'Sie holen mich also morgen ab'. This would sound rude and peremptory if translated literally as 'You'll pick me up tomorrow, then'. A better TT would cushion what sounds to English ears as brutally assertive: '(So) you'll fetch me tomorrow, then?'.

REFLECTED MEANING

Reflected meaning is the meaning given to an expression over and above its literal meaning by the fact that its form is reminiscent of the completely different meaning of a homonymic or near-homonymic expression (that is, one that sounds or is spelled the same, or nearly the same).

An often-cited example of reflected meaning compares the connotative difference between the two synonyms 'Holy Spirit' and 'Holy Ghost' (see Leech, 1974, p. 19). Through homonymic association, the 'Ghost' part of 'Holy Ghost' is reminiscent of the reflected meaning of 'ghost' ('spook' or 'spectre'). Although such an association is not part of the literal meaning of 'Holy Ghost', it has a tendency to form part of the overall meaning of the expression, and therefore may actually interfere with its literal meaning. By another, near-homonymic, association, the 'Spirit' part of 'Holy Spirit' may call to mind the reflected meaning of 'spirits' ('alcoholic drinks'); here again, the association tends to interfere with the literal meaning. Clearly, then, while 'Holy Spirit' and 'Holy Ghost' are referential synonyms, their total semantic effects cannot be called identical, in so far as they evoke different images through different reflected meanings.

When a term is taken in isolation, its reflected meaning is usually merely latent – it is the *context* that triggers or reinforces latent reflected meanings. In the case of 'Holy Ghost' and 'Holy Spirit', if there is anything in the context that predisposes the hearer to think about 'spooks' or 'alcoholic drinks', reflected meaning may come across as a *double entendre*. If one were translating 'Heiliger Geist' (which does not have the reflected meanings of its English synonyms), one would have to take care that the TT context did not trigger the latent reflected meaning of whichever English expression was selected for the TT. Otherwise the TT could be marred by infelicitous innuendo, as for example if one wrote 'Holy Spirit' just after a reference to Communion wine.

Conversely, a ST may deliberately trade on innuendo, using an expression primarily for its literal meaning, yet implicitly expecting the addressee to perceive a connotation echoing the meaning of some similar expression. A good example is the *double entendre* in Spoerl's use of 'Renaissancebeine', which we have already discussed as an example of associative meaning. (It is very common for an expression to combine more than one type of connotative meaning, as in this example.) In such cases, a fully successful TT would be one which deliberately traded on innuendo similar to that in the ST; but such a TT may be extremely difficult to construct.

COLLOCATIVE MEANING

Collocative meaning is given to an expression over and above its literal meaning by *the meaning of some other expression with which it collocates to form a commonly used phrase*. Thus, in the clichéd expression 'a resounding crash', the word 'resounding' collocates regularly with the word 'crash', forming such a strong stereotyped association that 'resounding' is capable of evoking the meaning of its collocative partner. This no doubt is why a collocation like 'resounding tinkle' feels incongruous – there is nothing in the literal meaning of 'resounding' to prevent its qualifying 'tinkle', but the connotation it has through collocative association with 'crash' is carried over and clashes with the literal meaning of 'tinkle'. Similarly, the gender-specific connotations of 'pretty' and 'handsome' can be said to be collocative meanings, deriving from the tendency of 'pretty' to collocate with words denoting females ('girl', 'woman', and so on) and the tendency of 'handsome' to collocate with words denoting males ('boy', 'man', and so on).

Some collocative meanings are so strong that they need very little triggering by context. For example, the word 'intercourse' (literally 'mutual dealings') can hardly be used at all without evoking its collocative partner 'sexual', and is well on the way to becoming a synonym of 'sexual intercourse'. Other collocative meanings need to be activated by the context, as with the humorous innuendo in 'I rode shotgun on the way to the wedding', based on activating the collocative echo of 'shotgun wedding'.

Collocative meanings are important for the translator, not only because they can contribute significantly to the overall meaning of a ST, but also because of the need to avoid unwanted collocative clashes in a TT. For example, translating 'die Heidelberger Landstraße ist gesperrt' as 'the Heidelberg road is shut' produces a collocative clash or infelicity – doors or windows are shut, but roads are *closed*. An analogous collocative clash is produced by translating 'er hat die Rechnung abgeschlossen' as 'he shut the account'.

Collocative clashes are always a threat to idiomaticity when the TL offers an expression closely resembling the ST one. Compare, for instance, 'shut your mouth' with 'hold your mouth' as translations of 'halt den Mund'; or 'the engine is too noisy' and 'the engine is too loud' as translations of 'der Motor ist zu laut'. In fact, collocative clashes are often produced by failure to spot the need for a communicative translation, as in rendering 'stocknüchtern' by 'sober as a stick' instead of 'sober as a judge'. Worse still, translating 'er ist ein hübscher Kerl' as 'he is a pretty fellow' produces a collocative clash which totally distorts the meaning of the ST (better rendered as 'he's a good-looking chap').

ALLUSIVE MEANING

Allusive meaning is present when an expression evokes, beyond its literal meaning, the meaning of some associated saying or quotation, in such a way that the meaning of that saying or quotation becomes part of the overall meaning of the expression.

Allusive meaning hinges on indirectly evoking sayings or quotations that an informed hearer can recognize, even though they are not fully spelled out. The evoked meaning of the quotation alluded to creates an added innuendo that modifies the literal meaning of what has explicitly been said. For example, saying that 'there are rather a lot of cooks involved' in organizing an event evokes the proverb 'too many cooks spoil the broth', and by this allusive meaning creates the innuendo that the event risks being spoilt by over-organization.

In the case of allusive meaning in STs, the translator's first problem is to recognize that the ST does contain an allusive innuendo. The second problem is to understand the allusive meaning by reference to the meaning of the saying or quotation evoked. The third problem is to convey the force of the innuendo in the TT, ideally by using some appropriate allusive meaning based on a saying or quotation in the TL.

There is a simple example in an advertisement for a German electrical firm, where the text contains the slogan 'SEIN WISSEN IST IHR SANFTES RUHEKISSEN', evidently based on an allusion to the proverbial saying 'Ein gut Gewissen ist ein sanftes Ruhekissen'. In the advertising text, the meaning of this proverb blends by allusion with the literal meaning of the slogan used, producing the innuendo that the firm advertised is conscientious, trustworthy and fully reliable. To translate this advertising slogan would present considerable difficulties, since there seems to be no well-known proverbial equivalent to 'Ein gut Gewissen ist ein sanftes Ruhekissen' in English; but even if there were one, weaving an allusion to it into the TT would still tax the translator's ingenuity. (At best the translator would need to resort to some form of compensation in devising an appropriate TT slogan, say: 'SAFE HANDS MAKE LIGHT WORK', or 'RELAX! HE'S GOT A GOOD HEAD FOR LIGHTS'.)

Even this relatively simple example, then, is potentially problematic, but really drastic difficulties can arise if an apparent allusive meaning in the ST is obscure. Considerable research may be necessary to track down the allusion; and even after it has been identified and understood, the translator faces another challenge if there is no parallel to it in the TL culture. The solution, as in the example above, is usually to compensate by some other means for the absence of a suitable allusion.

Take the following example: 'Denn laß dir sagen, und damit sprech' ich ein großes Wort gelassen aus: die Kommerzienrätin will *nicht*' (Fontane, 1966, p. 70). Fontane's dialogue contains here a mischievous allusion to the famous lines (lines 306–7) spoken at a highly dramatic moment in Goethe's *Iphigenie* (1787):

IPHIGENIE:	[...] Vernimm! Ich bin aus Tantalus' Geschlecht.
THOAS:	Du sprichst ein großes Wort gelassen aus.

In Goethe's text, the Taurian king has been pressing the mysteriously arrived priestess Iphigenie to marry him, as he needs an heir. Under great pressure she at last reveals that she is descended from the race of Tantalus, that is, her ancestry is full of horrors.

The Fontane allusion, also occurring in the context of a marriage, is a mother-in-law joke: the speaker is sure that the marriage in prospect will not take place because the prospective bridegroom's mother (the formidable *Kommerzienrätin* Frau Jenny Treibel) will veto it, and will prevail. The translation of this allusion cannot afford to be too ponderous, as the tone of this particular Fontane novel is light and satirical throughout. The joke here takes its spice from the incongruity between the immediate issue and the weighty and tragic context of the allusion; and yet, the weightiness of the allusion is a back-handed tribute to Jenny's power. It might be necessary to turn to some classical source in English literature for adequate compensation in translating this allusion. (Fontane's novels are exceptionally rich in such allusions, to the extent that no serious translator can afford to be without a considered strategy on how to handle them.)

A different sort of example of the same problem of allusive meaning is afforded by the title of Ulrich Plenzdorf's *Die neuen Leiden des jungen W*. Here the allusion is, of course, to Goethe's classic *Die Leiden des jungen Werther* which forms the intertextual background to Plenzdorf's text (Plenzdorf, 1973). In order to retain the allusion in the title of an English TT of *Die neuen Leiden des jungen W*, the important consideration must be to allude to the English title under which Goethe's original work is known to English readers. This raises interesting problems in its own turn: should the allusion be to the British title *The Sufferings of Young Werther* (translated by Bayard Quincy Morgan, 1957), or to the American title *The Sorrows of Young Werther* (translated by Catherine Hutter, 1962)? In the first instance, the translation of Plenzdorf's title might be *The New Sufferings of Young W*; in the second, *The Modern Sorrows of Young W*. (For making a choice between these two versions, one will need to consider whether the translation is intended mainly for a British, or an American, readership.)

PRACTICAL 8

8.1 Connotative meaning

Assignment

(i) Discuss the strategic problems confronting the translator of the following text, paying particular attention to connotation. Outline your strategy for translating the text.
(ii) Translate the text into English.
(iii) Explain the main decisions of detail you made in producing your TT.

Contextual information

This short satirical piece by Kafka is a self-contained text, that is to say, not an extract from a longer work.

Source text

WIR HABEN EINEN NEUEN Advokaten, den Dr. Bucephalus. In seinem Äußern erinnert wenig an die Zeit, da er noch Streitroß Alexanders von Mazedonien war. Wer allerdings mit den Umständen vertraut ist, bemerkt einiges. Doch sah ich letzthin auf der Freitreppe selbst einen ganz einfältigen Gerichtsdiener mit dem Fachblick des kleinen Stammgastes der Wettrennen den Advokaten bestaunen, als dieser, hoch die Schenkel hebend, mit auf dem Marmor aufklingendem Schritt von Stufe zu Stufe stieg.

Im allgemeinen billigt das Barreau die Aufnahme des Bucephalus. Mit erstaunlicher Einsicht sagt man sich, daß Bucephalus bei der heutigen Gesellschaftsordnung in einer schwierigen Lage ist und daß er deshalb, sowie auch wegen seiner weltgeschichtlichen Bedeutung, jedenfalls Entgegenkommen verdient. Heute – das kann niemand leugnen – gibt es keinen großen Alexander. Zu morden verstehen zwar manche; auch an der Geschicklichkeit, mit der Lanze über den Bankettisch hinweg den Freund zu treffen, fehlt es nicht; und vielen ist Mazedonien zu eng, so daß sie Philipp, den Vater, verfluchen – aber niemand, niemand kann nach Indien führen. Schon damals waren Indiens Tore unerreichbar, aber ihre Richtung war durch das Königsschwert bezeichnet. Heute sind die Tore ganz anderswohin und weiter und höher vertragen; niemand zeigt die Richtung; viele halten Schwerter; aber nur, um mit ihnen zu fuchteln, und der Blick, der ihnen folgen will, verwirrt sich.

Vielleicht ist es deshalb wirklich das beste, sich, wie es Bucephalus getan hat, in die Gesetzbücher zu versenken. Frei, unbedrückt die Seiten von den Lenden des Reiters, bei stiller Lampe, fern dem Getöse der Alexanderschlacht, liest und wendet er die Blätter unserer alten Bücher.

8.2 Connotative meaning

Assignment

(i) Taking the expressions printed in bold type in the ST on pp. 96–8, comment on the types of connotative meaning these expressions exemplify.
(ii) Working in groups, attempt an effective rendering of a stanza of the ST.

Contextual information

This is the full text of an early poem by Brecht. It appeared in the appendix to the *Hauspostille* in 1927. At the point when it was written, Brecht had not been to America.

Source text

Vom armen B.B.

1

Ich, Bertolt Brecht, bin aus den **schwarzen Wäldern**.
Meine Mutter trug mich in die Städte hinein
Als ich in ihrem Leibe lag. Und die Kälte der Wälder
Wird in mir bis zu meinem **Absterben** sein.

2

In der **Asphaltstadt** bin ich daheim. Von allem Anfang
Versehen mit jedem **Sterbsakrament**:
Mit Zeitungen. Und Tabak. Und Branntwein.
Mißtrauisch und faul und zufrieden am End.

3

Ich bin zu den Leuten freundlich. Ich setze
Einen steifen Hut auf nach ihrem Brauch.
Ich sage: Es sind ganz **besonders riechende Tiere**
Und ich sage: Es macht nichts, ich bin es auch.

4

In meine leeren **Schaukelstühle** vormittags
Setze ich mir mitunter ein paar Frauen
Und ich betrachte sie sorglos und sage ihnen:
In mir habt ihr einen, **auf den könnt ihr nicht bauen**.

5

Gegen Abend versammle ich um mich Männer
Wir reden uns da mit **'Gentlemen'** an.
Sie haben ihre Füße auf meinen Tischen
Und sagen: Es wird besser mit uns. Und ich frage nicht: Wann?

6

Gegen Morgen in der grauen Frühe **pissen die Tannen**
Und ihr **Ungeziefer,** die Vögel, fängt an zu schrein.
Um die Stunde trink ich mein Glas in der Stadt aus und schmeiße
Den Tabakstummel weg und **schlafe beunruhigt ein**.

7

Wir sind gesessen, **ein leichtes Geschlechte**
In Häusern, die für unzerstörbare galten
(So haben wir gebaut **die langen Gehäuse** des Eilands Manhattan
Und **die dünnen Antennen**, die das Atlantische Meer unterhalten).

8

Von diesen Städten wird bleiben: der durch sie hindurchging, der Wind!
Fröhlich machet das Haus den Esser: er leert es.
Wir wissen, daß wir **Vorläufige** sind
Und nach uns wird kommen : nichts Nennenswertes.

9

Bei den Erdbeben, die kommen werden, werde ich hoffentlich
Meine **Virginia** nicht ausgehen lassen durch Bitterkeit
Ich, Bertolt Brecht, in die Asphaltstädte **verschlagen**
Aus den schwarzen Wäldern in meiner Mutter in früher Zeit.

9

Language variety in texts: dialect, sociolect, code-switching

In this chapter and Chapter 10, we discuss the question of language variety and translation. By way of introduction to the notion of language variety, here is a text from *Steiler Zahn und Zickendraht. Das Wörterbuch der Teenager- und Twensprache.* It consists in a pastiche of a dialogue between two 1960s German teenagers and its interlingual translation into rather formal standard German. This text can be used as a point of reference for both Practicals 9 and 10, and would repay some discussion in class.

Hallo Zahn!	Guten Tag, mein Fräulein!
Hallo Typ!	Guten Tag, mein Herr!
Ist meine Schlägerpfanne nicht das Allergrößte?	Ist mein Sturzhelm nicht schön?
Ich finde sie ein bißchen krank. Aber für dein vergammeltes Pennerkissen ist sie vielleicht nicht so undufte.	Ich finde ihn ein bißchen blöd. Aber für Ihren unordentlichen langen Haarschnitt ist er vielleicht nicht so unpassend.
Willste was auf meinem Feuerstuhl gefahren werden?	Darf ich Sie zu einer Fahrt auf meinem Motorrad einladen?
Steh ich nicht drauf. Außerdem habe ich die kanischen Röhren nicht dabei.	Das bereitet mir keine Freude. Außerdem habe ich meine amerikanischen langen Hosen nicht angezogen.
Wollen wir ne Menage nehmen?	Wollen wir etwas essen?
Ne, lieber ein Rohr brechen.	Nein, lieber eine Flasche trinken.
Willste nicht mit in die Scheune gehen? Es gibt da den letzten Heuler mit Gary Cooper. Die Kohlen kommen von mir. Ich	Wollen Sie nicht mit mir ins Kino gehen? Es gibt dort eine großartige Sache mit Gary Cooper. Ich werde auch bezahlen. Ich bin zwar schon

bin zwar noch die Miete für den Stall scharf, aber ich werde wegen der Mäuse sowieso noch mit meiner Regierung sprechen.	im Rückstand mit der Wohnungsmiete, aber ich werde wegen des Geldes sowieso noch mit meinen Eltern sprechen.

Reprinted from *Arbeitstexte für den Unterricht. Fach- und Sondersprachen* (Stuttgart: Philipp Reclam jun., 1974, pp. 85–6).

Discussing this text and how to translate the version in the left-hand column will immediately highlight certain features: the markers of sociolect, the colloquialisms, the grammar and vocabulary, and the slangy tone. It is, in fact, an excellent example of one of the most difficult aspects of textual 'meaning', namely the appreciation not of referential content, but of characteristics *in the way the message is expressed* that voluntarily or involuntarily reveal information about the speaker or writer. These stylistically conveyed meanings are connotations: they share with the types of connotation discussed in Chapter 8 the character of meanings 'read between the lines' on the basis of associations that are widespread, although not enshrined in the dictionary.

Sorting out significant information carried by such stylistic features can be a daunting practical problem – details have to be separated out as one comes to them. However, this is no reason for not trying to discuss the problem in general terms. There are two essential questions that arise. The first is: what are the objective textual characteristics from which stylistic information about the speaker or writer can be inferred? The simple answer must be: the way the message is expressed as compared with other possible ways it might have been expressed; the parallel between the two columns in the text above offers an immediate way of making such comparisons. From comparing the two columns it is evident that, in each case, the *manner in which the message is formulated* is the basic carrier of information about the speaker/writer.

The second question that arises is: what *kind of information* can be carried through the particular manner in which the message is formulated? The answer is twofold: first, the manner, or style, reveals things about speakers/writers that they do not necessarily intend to reveal, notably social and/or regional affiliations, and the social stereotype they appear to belong to; second, it reveals things that they do intend to reveal, notably the calculated effect they want their utterances to have on the listener/reader. Naturally, any or all of these features can and do occur together in overlap with one another. Social stereotype and effect on a listener/reader, in particular, are sometimes so closely associated that they cannot easily be distinguished; we shall discuss them, as different aspects of 'register', in the next chapter. In the present chapter, we look at translation issues raised by dialect, sociolect and code-switching.

DIALECT

To speak a particular **dialect**, with all its phonological, lexical, syntactic and sentential features, is to give away information about one's association with a particular region. A simple phonological example, drawn from Carl Zuckmayer's play *Des Teufels General* (an extract from which is used in Practical 10) is 'Da ha ick 'n mächtgen Drang nach': an utterance heavily marked by phonic features characteristic of extreme Berlin dialect speech. The same text offers a lexical example in the choice of the dialectal variant 'Köppche' as opposed to Hochdeutsch 'Kopf '. It is sometimes also possible to infer the degree of speakers' regional affiliations from the proportion of dialectal features in their speech; for instance, whether they are natives of the region and have little experience of other regions, or whether they are originally from the region, but retain only traces of that origin overlaid by speech habits acquired elsewhere; or whether they are incomers who have merely acquired a veneer of local speech habits. Furthermore, some speakers are notable for having a repertoire including several dialects between which they can alternate (that is, they are capable of 'code-switching'), or on which they can draw to produce a mixture of dialects. All these aspects of dialectal usage are stylistic carriers of information about a speaker, and no sensitive translator can afford to ignore them. Four main problems arise from taking account of them.

The first problem is easily defined: it is that of recognizing the peculiarities from which dialectal affiliation can be inferred in a ST. Clearly, the more familiar the translator is with SL dialects, the better.

The second is that of deciding how important the dialectal features in a ST, and the information they convey, are to its overall effect. The translator always has the option of rendering the ST into a bland, standard version of the TL, with no notable dialectal traces. This may be appropriate if the dialectal style of the ST can be regarded as incidental, at least for the specific purposes of the TT. For example, in translating an eyewitness account of a murder for Interpol, one might be well advised to ignore all dialectal features and concentrate on getting the facts clear. However, if the dialectal nature of the ST cannot be regarded as incidental – for example, in a novel where plot or characterization actually depend to some extent on dialect – the translator has to find means for indicating that the ST contains dialectal features. This creates some difficult practical problems.

For instance, suppose that the ST is so full of broad dialectal features as to be virtually incomprehensible to a SL speaker from another region. The translator's first strategic decision is whether to produce a TT that is only mildly dialectal, and totally comprehensible to any TL speaker. Arguments against this solution might be similar to those against 'improving' a ST that is badly written. However, there can be circumstances where this is the best alternative, since, in making any strategic decision, the translator has to consider such factors as the nature and purpose of the ST, the purpose of the TT, its intended audience, the requirements of the person or organization paying for the translation, and so on. One may decide to inject a mere handful of TL dialectal features into the TT, just to show the audience that it is based on a ST in dialect. On the other hand, the very obscurity of a piece of ST dialect may serve important textual purposes which would be vitiated in the TT if the piece were not rendered in an equally obscure TL dialect. In such a case – and probably *only* in such a case – it may be necessary for the translator to go all the way in the use of a TL dialect.

The third problem arises if the translator does opt for a broad TL dialect: just what dialect should the TT be in? Supposing that the ST is in Berlin dialect, is there any dialect of English that in some way corresponds to Berlin dialect, having similar status and cultural associations among English dialects to those held by Berlin dialect among German dialects? There is no obvious objective answer to this question – after all, what *is* the exact position of Berlin dialect among German dialects?

Of course, there may be certain stereotypical assumptions associated with given ST dialects which might be helpful in choosing a TT dialect (for instance, 'people from Berlin have a "große Schnauze"', or 'Cockneys are cheeky and cheerful'). When a dialect is used in the ST specifically in order to tap into such stereotypes, it could conceivably be appropriate to select a TL dialect with similar popular connotations. In other cases, the choice of TL dialect may be influenced by geographical considerations. For instance, a south-western dialect of German, in a ST containing references to 'southerners', might be plausibly rendered in a southern dialect of English. Even more plausibly, a German ST with a plot situated in an industrial setting, say, in Gelsenkirchen, might be rendered in a TL dialect from an industrial city in the Midlands, perhaps Birmingham or Sheffield.

A final difficulty, if one decides to adopt a specific TL dialect, is of course the problem of familiarity with the characteristics of this dialect. If the translator does not have an accurate knowledge of the salient features of the TL dialect chosen, the TT will become as ludicrous as all the texts which, through ignorance, have Scots running around saying 'hoots mon' and 'och aye the noo'.

It will be clear by now that rendering ST dialect with TL dialect is a form of cultural transplantation. Like all cultural transplantation, it runs the risk of incongruity in the TT. For instance, having broad Norfolk on the lips of country folk from Bavaria could have disastrous effects on the plausibility of the whole TT. The safest way of avoiding this would be to transplant the entire work – setting, plot, characters and all – into Norfolk; but, of course, this might be quite inappropriate in the light of the contents of the ST. Short of this extreme solution, the safest decision may after all be to make relatively sparing use of TL features that are recognizably dialectal without being clearly recognizable as belonging to a specific dialect. Fortunately, there are many features of non-standard accent, vocabulary and grammar that are widespread in a number of British dialects. Nevertheless it would be even safer, with a ST containing direct speech, to translate dialogue into fairly neutral English, and, if necessary, to add after an appropriate piece of direct speech some such phrase as 'she said, in a broad Gelsenkirchen accent', rather than have a woman from Gelsenkirchen speaking Scouse or Glaswegian.

SOCIOLECT

In modern sociolinguistics, a distinction is made between regional dialects (dialects proper) and language varieties that are, as it were, 'class dialects'. The latter are referred to by the term **sociolect.** Sociolects are language varieties typical of the broad groupings that together constitute the 'class structure' of a given society. Examples of the major sociolects in British culture are those designated as 'lower class', 'urban working class', 'white collar', 'public school', and so on. It is noticeable, and typical, that these designations are relatively vague in reference. This vagueness is due partly to the fact that sociolects are intended as broad, sociologically convenient labels, and partly to the lack of rigid class structure in British society. In more rigidly stratified societies, where there is a strict division into formally recognized 'castes', the concept of sociolect is more rigorously applicable.

A further possible reservation as to the usefulness of purely sociolectal labels is that, very often, a social classification is virtually meaningless without mention of regional affiliations. For example, the term 'urban working-class sociolect' cannot designate a particular language variety of English unless it is qualified by geographical reference. While 'upper class' and 'public school' sociolects are characteristically neutral to regional variations, the further 'down' one goes on the social scale, the more necessary it is to take social and regional considerations together, thus creating concepts of mixed regional and sociolectal language varieties such as 'Norwich urban working class', 'Edinburgh "Morningside" urban middle class', and so on. Such mixed socio-dialectal designations are generally more meaningful labels for recognizable language variants than purely sociological ones. (The situation in a German context is similar to the situation in Britain: regional variations are increasingly marked as one moves 'down' in the social scale, while regional variations within the range of 'upper class' and 'upper middle class' variants of Hochdeutsch are limited.)

Whatever one's reservations about the notion of sociolect, it remains true that sociolectal features can convey important information about a speaker or writer. If they are obtrusive in the ST (in the form of non-standard features of accent, grammar, vocabulary or sentential marking), the translator cannot afford to ignore them. Characteristic features of 'lower class' sociolect in German include 'willste' (instead of 'willst du'), double negative 'keine...nicht' (instead of 'keine'), 'melde ich mir' (instead of 'melde ich mich') and 'nich' (instead of 'nicht'); even here, the question arises of regional differences between various 'lower class' non-standard versions of 'nicht', such as 'nich' and 'net'.

There are, clearly, literary texts in which sociolect is a central feature and requires attention from the translator. However, the mere fact that the ST contains marked sociolectal features does not necessarily mean that the TT should be just as heavily sociolectally marked. As with translating dialects, there may be considerations militating against this, such as whether the sociolect has a definite textual role in the ST, or the purposes for which the ST is being translated. In many cases it is sufficient for the translator to include just enough devices in the TT to remind the audience of the sociolectal character of the ST. Alternatively, there may be good reasons for producing a TT that is in a bland 'educated middle-class' sociolect of the TL – this also is a sociolect, but, for texts intended for general consumption, it is the least obtrusive one.

Once the translator has decided on a TT containing marked sociolectal features, the problems that arise parallel those created by dialect. The class structures of different societies, countries and nations never replicate one another. Consequently, there can be no exact matching between sociolectal varieties of one language and those of another. At best, something of the prestige or the stigma attached to the ST sociolect can be conveyed in the TT by a judicious choice of TL sociolect. The translator may therefore decide that a valid strategy would be to render, say, an 'urban working-class' SL sociolect by an 'urban working-class' TL sociolect. But this does not solve the question of *which* 'urban working-class' sociolect. The decision remains difficult, especially as the wrong choice of TL sociolect could make the TT narrative implausible for sociological reasons. This question of the socio-cultural plausibility of the TT is one of the translator's major considerations (assuming, of course, that the ST is not itself deliberately implausible). Finally, as with dialect, it goes without saying that the translator must actually be familiar enough with features of the chosen TL sociolect(s) to be able to use them accurately and convincingly (in general, it is also safest to use them sparingly).

CODE-SWITCHING

Passing mention was made above of **code-switching**. This well-known phenomenon occurs in the language-use of speakers whose active repertoire includes several language varieties – dialects, sociolects, even distinct languages. It consists of a rapid alternation from one moment to another between different language varieties. Code-switching is used, by ordinary speakers and writers, for two main strategic reasons: first, to fit style of speech to the changing social circumstances of the speech situation; and second, to impose a certain definition on the speech situation by the choice of a style of speech. Examples of both are to be found in Practical 10.

Since code-switching is a definite strategic device, and since its social-interactional function in a text cannot be denied, the translator of a ST containing code-switching should convey in the TT the effects it has in the ST. For written dialogue, the possibility of explaining the code-switch without reproducing it in the TT does exist, as in 'he said, suddenly relapsing into the local vernacular'. There is, of course, no such option for the text of a play or a film, except as an instruction in a stage direction. At all events, it would be more effective, if possible, to reproduce ST code-switching by code-switching in the TT. Such cases place even greater demands on the translator's mastery of the TL, two or more noticeably different varieties of the TL needing to be used in the TT.

The parallel texts at the beginning of this chapter do not directly illustrate code-switching, but rather the difference between two markedly distinct codes (registers) displayed side-by-side. Such differences constitute the basis for code-switching; as an example of code-switching, one may usefully consider the effects that could be created, if, in a 'dramatized' text, the protagonists alternated between these distinct codes:

Hallo Zahn!
Guten Tag!
Ist meine Schlägerpfanne nicht das Allergrößte?
Ich finde sie ein bißchen blöd. Aber für Ihr unordentliches Pennerkissen ist sie vielleicht nicht so unpassend.
Willste was auf meinem Feuerstuhl gefahren werden?
Das bereitet mir keine Freude... Außerdem habe ich meine kanischen langen Hosen nicht angezogen.

PRACTICAL 9

9.1 Language variety: dialect and sociolect

Assignment
You will be played a sound recording of an extract from the sound-track of a television interview. The interviewee is giving his views of environmental issues. After brief discussion of the salient features of the text, you will be given a transcript of it. Working in groups:

(i) Identify and discuss the dialectal and sociolectal features in the text.
(ii) Reconstruct a standard German (Hochdeutsch) version of the text.
(iii) Discuss the strategic problems involved in translating the text (a) for voice-over in a television documentary and (b) for a speech in a play.
(iv) Produce a translation for voice-over for discussion in class.

9.2 Language variety: code-switching

Assignment
Working in groups on the text below:

(i) Discuss the strategic problems it poses for the translator. Outline your strategy for translating it, particularly with reference to code-switching, bearing in mind that it is a dialogue in a novel.
(ii) Translate the text into English.
(iii) Explain the main decisions of detail you made in producing your TT.

Contextual information

The extract is taken from Theodor Fontane's novel *Mathilde Möhring*. Mathilde, aged twenty-three and plain, living with her timid widowed mother on a low income in a Berlin apartment, bettered herself by accepting the lodger's proposal of marriage and using her own brains, personality and determination to get him to take and pass his law examinations, then secure and successfully assert himself in the position of a small-town mayor. Mathilde ensures that her husband, Hugo, gets the limelight and the credit, but also does everything expected of her in her own public role, thereby earning the liking and respect of the local gentry, including an elderly Polish aristocrat. When Hugo falls ill and dies after only a year or so, Mathilde returns to her mother in Berlin. She has decided to study in order to become a teacher.

Text

'Thilde, schläfst du schon?'

'Nein, Mutter, aber beinah.... Willst du noch was?'

'Nein, Thilde, wollen will ich nichts. Mir is bloß so furchtbar angst wegen deiner Lernerei. Du siehst so spack aus und hast solchen Glanz in den Augen. Er hat ja doch die Schwindsucht gehabt, und am Ende....'

'Nun?'

'Am Ende wär' es doch möglich... und wenn es so is, is doch frische Luft immer das beste und nicht soviel sitzen.'

'Gewiß, frische Luft ist immer gut, aber wo soll ich sie hernehmen? Hier ist sie nicht gut, und wenn es nicht wegen deines Rheumatismus wäre....'

'Nein, Thilde, daß das Fenster offensteht, das geht nich, aber du könntest doch die frische Luft haben.'

'Ich? Woher denn?'

'Ja, Thilde, du hast mir doch gleich in deinem ersten Brief geschrieben, ich meine in deinem ersten, als er tot war, da hast du mir geschrieben von wegen "Hausdame" und mit Gehalt. Und wenig kann es doch nich gewesen sein, weil er ja so reich is, wie du mir geschrieben hast. Und alt is er auch, und da hättest du nu die schöne frische Luft gehabt und die gute Verpflegung. Ich will ja nichts sagen, aber was wir heute hatten, hatte doch keine Kraft mehr. Und wenn du ihn ordentlich gepflegt hättest, und das hättest du gewiß, denn du hast ja Mitleid mit jedem und mit mir auch, denn du bist gut, Thilde, ja, Thilde, denn hätten wir jetzt vielleicht was. Einer, der so reich is, kann doch nich so mir nichts, dir nichts sterben, ohne was zu hinterlassen. Und vielleicht, daß er noch ganz zuletzt.... War er denn katholisch?'

'Natürlich war er katholisch.'

'Na, denn ging es nich.'

10

Language variety in texts: social register and tonal register

From dialect and sociolect, we move on to conclude our survey of language variety by looking at two other sorts of information about speakers/writers that can often be inferred from the way the message is formulated. Both are often referred to as 'register', and they do often occur together, but they are different in kind. We shall distinguish them as 'social register' and 'tonal register'.

SOCIAL REGISTER

A **social register** is a particular style from which the listener reasonably confidently infers what kind of person the speaker is, in the sense of what social stereotype the speaker belongs to. To explain this concept, we can start by taking two extremes between which social register falls.

It is possible to imagine, at one extreme, a way of formulating messages that is so individual that it instantly identifies the author, narrowing down the possibilities to just one particular speaker and writer. Writers with very clearly recognizable individual styles, such as Kafka, Thomas Mann or James Joyce, and singer-song-writers for whom a characteristic voice quality acts as an additional identifying mark, such as Wolf Biermann (see Practical 3, pp. 34–5), Frank Sinatra, or Queen, come to mind as obvious examples. At the other extreme, a message can be formulated in such a bland, neutral and ordinary way as to give away virtually no personal information about its author: the speaker/writer could be almost any member of the SL speech community.

Usually, however, a style will be recognized as characteristic of a certain *kind* of person, seen as representing some previously encountered social stereotype. This information is, obviously, distinct from information carried specifically by dialectal features. Perhaps less obviously, it is also distinct from information carried specifically by sociolect: though dialect and sociolect may be ingredients of a given social register, dialect only conveys regional affiliations, and sociolect corresponds to very broad conceptions of social grouping (limited to sociological notions of 'class structure'), whereas social register designates fairly narrow stereotypes of the sorts of people one expects to meet in a given society. (For example, the grammatical, orthographical and lexical features of the left-hand text in the extract from *Steiler Zahn und Zickendraht* on pp. 99–100 indicate a social register more immediately than they do a sociolect.) Since, in general, we organize our interactions with other people (especially those we do not know intimately) on the basis of social stereotypes to which we attach particular expectations, likes and dislikes, it is easy to give examples of social register.

For instance, encountering a man given to using four-letter expletives, one may perhaps infer that he is the vulgar, macho type. (Terms like 'vulgar' and 'macho' are typical stereotyping terms.) Difficulties of precisely pinpointing the appropriate stereotype are similar to those of precisely pinpointing attitudinal meaning (see p. 90). Nevertheless, what is significant is that a whole section of the population is eliminated from conforming to this type – one's genteel maiden aunt is unlikely to speak like this – while other types (such as the young, unskilled urban manual worker) remain likely candidates. Similarly, a style full of 'thank you' and 'please' is not indicative of just any speaker. A middle-class, well-bred, well-mannered person (note again the typical stereotyping terms) may be implied by such a style.

As these examples suggest, whatever information is conveyed by linguistic style about the kind of person the speaker/writer is will often be tentative, and will require support from circumstantial and contextual evidence before it adds up to anything like the 'characterization' of an individual. For example, in the *Steiler Zahn und Zickendraht* text, while the slang elements of grammar and lexis suggest that the speakers are stereotypical city teenagers, it is circumstantial details like references to motorbikes, motor-cycle gear, films and financial dependence on parents that allow one to be reasonably confident in this inference. (In any case, that example also shows that, as we have suggested, sociolect is subordinate to social register as an indication of what 'kind of person' is speaking.)

Despite reservations, the fact remains that the mere observing of linguistic style invites unconscious social stereotyping, both of people and of situations in which they find themselves. Linguistic style is understood as an unconscious reflex of a speaker's perception of 'self', of situations and of other people present. All the time that one is unconsciously stereotyping oneself and others, and situations, into various social categories, one is also unconsciously correlating the various stereotypes with appropriate styles of language-use. Inferences from social stereotype to linguistic stereotype and vice versa are virtually inevitable.

As soon as a particular stylistic indication places a speaker and/or a social situation into one of the relatively narrowly circumscribed social categories used in stereotyping personalities and social interactions in a given society, the amount of stylistic information is seen to be relatively rich. In such cases, that information is likely to include fairly clear pointers to a combination of specific characteristics of speaker and/or situation. Among these characteristics may figure the speaker's educational background and upbringing; the social experience of the speaker (for example, social roles the speaker is used to fulfilling); the speaker's occupation and professional standing; the speaker's peer-group status, and so on – the list is in principle inexhaustible.

This, then, is the sort of information carried by what we are calling 'social register'. In other words, when speakers provide linguistic clues about their social personae and specific social milieux (as distinct from broad class affiliations), we say that they are using particular social registers, each one held in common with other speakers answering a similar stereotypical description. Equally, if the style reveals details of the way participants perceive the social implications of the situation they are speaking in, we refer to this style as the social register appropriate both to a type of person and to a type of situation.

When authors' social credentials are of some importance (perhaps because of the need to establish authority for speaking on a particular subject), they will select and maintain the appropriate social register for projecting a suitable social persona. This use of social register accounts for much of the use of jargon, not only the jargon in technical texts (which is at least partly used to maintain the author's self-stereotyping as a technical expert), but also jargon consisting of clichés, catch-phrases and in-words that build up other social stereotypes.

Use of jargon frequently springs from expectations, and the fulfilling of expectations, with respect to social register. In moderation, this does work as a successful means of signalling social stereotype. However, when taken to excess, jargon may become ridiculous, putting its users into stereotypes they do not welcome. The ridiculing of social stereotypes by pastiche that uses jargon to excess is illustrated in an anonymous parody, *Definition des 'Reichsgerichts'*, which appeared in W. Gast's 1975 Reclam anthology. It is worth analysing this extract in Practical 10, to identify the social register the pastiche is caricaturing, to determine how the caricature is done and how successful it is, and to attempt a TT:

14a. Anonym: Definition des 'Reichsgerichts'

> Ein Reichsgericht ist eine Einrichtung, welche eine dem allgemeinen Verständnis entgegenkommen sollende, aber bisweilen durch sich nicht ganz vermeiden lassende, nicht ganz unbedeutende bzw. verhältnismäßig gewaltige Fehler im Satzbau auf der schiefen Ebene des durch verschnörkelte und ineinandergeschachtelte Perioden ungenießbar gemachten Kanzleistils herabgerollte Definition, welche eine das menschliche Sprachgefühl verletzende Wirkung zu erzeugen fähig ist, liefert.
>
> (Gast, W. (ed.), 1975, p. 37)

This example clearly shows the potential of exaggeration in social register as a comic device, and also the attendant problem of finding an appropriate social register, as well as getting the degree of exaggeration right, when translating a ST parodying some SL social register. The example also shows a different, but related, problem in translating *serious* STs: while it may be important to choose an appropriate social register, it is just as important not to over-mark it, otherwise the TT may become unintentionally comic.

In a narrative or play, an essential part of making sure the characters stay plausibly true to type is to ensure that they express themselves consistently in an appropriate social register. (The 'dramatized' text on p. 105 shows this need for consistency with respect to social register.) It would indeed be very odd for a street-corner hooligan suddenly to assume the social register of a contemplative intellectual or an aristocrat, unless, of course, there were special textual/narrative reasons for doing this deliberately. (Still more interesting in the text on p. 105 is the mixing of slang with standard German by both speaking characters – to what extent do they share a common repertoire consisting of both 'Teenagersprache' and an educated Hochdeutsch?) Good characterization demands two things: insight into the way in which people belonging to identifiable social stereotypes tend to express themselves, and the ability to use consistently the stylistic quirks and constraints of these social registers. (By *quirks* we mean the kind of thing representatives of a given stereotype would say; by *constraints,* the kind of thing they would never say.)

It is important to remember that, in literature and real life, social register can be marked on any or every level of textual variable, including accent and delivery. Practical 10 may include discussion of two taped extracts, both from recordings of interviews, given here in transcript:

Text 1

Ich habe gelebt bis neunz'nhundertachtzehn in einer Monarchie, die praktisch für mich eine gemäßigte Diktatur war. Dann bin (sic!) ich ungefähr vierzehn Jahre in einer Demokratie gelebt, indem die Deutschen von Demokratie noch nichts verstanden. Dann kam das tausendjährige Reich Hitlers, eine reine Diktatur, abgelöst durch die Diktatur der Besatzungsmächte. Deutschland ist seit achtundvierzig ein sogenannter demokratischer Staat, in dem man nicht... von dem ma...man nicht verlangen kann, daß die Masse etwas von Demokratie versteht.

Adapted from Frank Carter, *Quer durch Deutschland* (Oxford: OUP, 1975, p. 65), by permission of Oxford University Press.

Text 2

Auframma sagn mir zon Ausweissln. Dös ischt an Arwat, de grod de Weiberleit bleib. Waar oan scho gnua, bal ma an ganzn Winta de Fluigngschiss oschaugn müassat. Und si'scht – da Haustenna, da Stall, Kammer und Kammerlen, es braucht an Arwat, bis ma überall durch ischt. Freili, es trickert it so leicht mehr, aber mi muass es halt toan bal ma Derweil hat. Da Putzaus und da Kehraus bringen koa Geld is Haus.

Hochdeutsch version

Aufräumen sagen wir zum Ausweißen. Das ist eine Arbeit, die den Weiberleuten bleibt. Wäre schlimm, wenn man den ganzen Winter die Fliegenschisse anschauen müßte. Und sonst – die Tenne, der Stall, Kammer und die Kämmerlein – es braucht viel Arbeit, bis man überall durch ist. Freilich, es trocknet jetzt nicht mehr so leicht, aber man muß es dann tun, wenn man Zeit hat, mit dem Putzen und Kehren ist nämlich kein Geld verdient.

Reprinted from Kultureller Tonbanddienst, *Deutsche Dialekte* (Bonn: Inter Nationes, p. 245).

It will be clear by now that in translating a ST that has speaking characters in it, or whose author uses a social register for self-projection, the construction of social register in the TT is a major concern. Equally clearly, in translating, say, P.G. Wodehouse into German, one would have to do something about the fact that Jeeves speaks in the social register of the 'gentleman's gentleman', and Bertie Wooster in that of the aristocratic nitwit. The fundamental problem is this: how can essentially English stereotypes like Jeeves and Bertie be transplanted into a German-speaking context, produce plausible dialogue in German, and still remain linguistically stereotyped so as to hint at the caricatures of gentleman's gentleman and inane aristocrat? There are no obvious global answers to such questions.

A choice of appropriate TL registers can, however, sometimes seem relatively easy when the translator is operating between similar cultures, where certain social stereotypes (such as the street-corner hooligan) and stereotype situations (such as an Embassy ball) do show some degree of cross-cultural similarity. It may well be that some social stereotypes can be fairly successfully matched from one culture to another. The translator is then left with a two-stage task. First, a ST stereotype must be converted into an appropriate target-culture stereotype; and second, a plausible social register must be selected and consistently applied for each of the target-culture stereotypes chosen.

However, 'parallels' in social stereotyping are in fact far from exact. There are obvious discrepancies between, for example, the stereotypes of British aristocrat and German aristocrat, or British hooligan and German hooligan. In any case, is it desirable for Bertie Wooster to become every inch the German aristocrat in a German TT? Does the translator not need to remind the German reader of Wooster's essential Britishness (or even Englishness)?

Even greater difficulties arise when it comes to matching stereotypes that have no likely parallels in the target culture. For instance, are there close target-culture parallels for the British *gentleman farmer* or for the German *Spießbürger?* Given either of these types in a ST, what social register would be appropriate for the corresponding character in the TT? Or should their speech be rendered in a fairly neutral style, with very few marked features of social register? For that matter, should these characters be rendered as culturally 'exotic'? After all, for Sternheim's Spießbürger to lose all trace of Germanity in an English translation of *Die Hose* (1911) might be as disappointing as for Bertie Wooster to come across as completely German. Even once the strategic decisions have been taken, there remains the eternal double challenge to the translator's linguistic skill: to be familiar with the quirks and constraints of TL varieties, and to be able to produce a consistently plausible TL social register.

TONAL REGISTER

A fourth type of speaker-related information that can be inferred from the way a message is formulated is what we shall call **tonal register**. Tonal register is what is often called 'register' in dictionaries and textbooks on style. It often combines with any or all of dialect, sociolect and social register in an overall stylistic effect, but it is qualitatively different from them. Tonal register is *the tone that the speaker/writer takes* – perhaps vulgar, or familiar, or polite, or formal, or pompous, and so on. That is, the effect of tonal register on listeners is something for which speakers can be held responsible, in so far as they *are being* familiar, pompous, and so on. Dialect, sociolect and social register are different from tonal register in that they are not matters of an attitude that speakers intentionally adopt, but the symptomatic result of regional, class and social-stereotype characteristics that they cannot help. So a listener might reasonably respond to tonal register by saying 'don't take that tone with me', but this would not be a reasonable response to dialect, sociolect or social register. If, in a given situation, Bertie Wooster *is being* polite, that is a matter of tonal register; but it would be odd to suggest that he *is being* an upper-class nitwit – he *is* an upper-class nitwit, as one infers from his sociolect, social register and general behaviour. (Of course, it is a different matter when someone *puts on* an accent, sociolect or social register as a form of mimicry or play-acting at 'being', say, Glaswegian or Sloane; in 'playing the Sloane' the speaker is not taking a tone with the listener, but is consciously or unconsciously projecting herself as having a particular social persona.)

Many of the labels dictionaries attach to certain expressions, such as 'familiar', 'colloquial', 'formal', and so on, are, in fact, reflections of the tone a speaker using these expressions can be said to be taking towards the listener or listeners. It is, therefore, helpful to assess levels of tonal register on a 'politeness scale', a scale of stylistic options for being more or less polite, more or less formal, more or less offensive, and so on.

Looked at in this way, tonal register is relatively easy to distinguish from social register. As we have suggested, being polite on a particular occasion is different from being stereotyped as a well-brought-up kind of person. Nevertheless, tonal register often overlaps with social register, in two ways.

First, there are ambiguous cases where it is not clear whether a style of expression is a reflection of social stereotyping or of the speaker's intentions towards the listener. For example, it may be impossible to tell whether a speaker 'is being' deliberately pompous in order to convey a patronizing attitude (tonal register), or whether the pomposity is just a symptom of the fact that the speaker fits the stereotype of, for example, the self-important academic (social register).

Thus, the difference in register between 'this essay isn't bad' and 'this essay is not without merit' might equally well be classified as social or as tonal.

Second, the characteristics of particular social registers are very often built up out of features of tonal register – and of dialect and sociolect, for that matter. This is especially true of social stereotypes characterized by 'downward social mobility'. For instance, a middle-class, educated person who is adept at the jargon of criminals and down-and-outs will have an active repertoire of vulgarisms and slang expressions. As we have seen, 'vulgarism' and 'slang' mark points on the politeness scale of tonal register; but, at the same time, they go towards building up the complex of features that define a particular social register. Similarly, the girl pretending to be a Sloane is thereby also using the amalgam of tonal registers that helps to constitute the Sloane social register.

The notions of 'social register', 'tonal register', 'dialect' and 'sociolect' do therefore overlap to some extent, and all four are likely to occur intermingled in a text. Their separation is consequently something of a methodological abstraction, but, practically speaking, it is still very useful to keep them as clearly distinct as possible in analysing style, because this helps the translator to recognize what is going on in the ST, and therefore to make correspondingly important strategic decisions. Where it does remain unclear whether a particular case is an instance of tonal or of social register, it is legitimate to use the cover-term 'register'. (Similarly, where dialect, sociolect and social register overlap indistinguishably, the cover-term 'language variety' can be used.)

The implications of tonal register for the translator are essentially no different from those of dialect, sociolect and social register. Since tonal register is linked to intended effects on the listener/hearer, interpreting the impact of a ST depends very greatly on identifying its tonal register. Once this has been done, care must be taken to match the tonal register of the TT to intended audience effect. Inappropriateness or inconsistency in register can all too easily spoil a translation. For example, there would be unacceptable translation loss in rendering 'als Negschdes, muß ich mer mol werrer de Grobb leermache' by 'if I may continue, I just 'ave to get the following off me chest', or 'äs is noch mäih wie e Schann – äs is en Frewel' by ''taint just a disgrace – it is a bloody liberty'. As with the other language varieties, looking for suitable renderings of tonal register puts translators on their mettle, giving ample scope for displaying knowledge of the SL and its culture, knowledge of the target culture, and, above all, flair and resourcefulness in the TL.

PRACTICAL 10

10.1 Language variety: social register and tonal register

Assignment

(i) Identify and discuss the salient features of language variety in the following text. Pay special attention to social register and tonal register, but do not ignore important instances of dialect and sociolect. In the case of features of social register, say what sort of social stereotype they signal.

(ii) Using appropriate English social and tonal registers, translate the ST expressions that you have identified as indicators of register. Explain your decisions in each case.

Contextual information

Carl Zuckmayer's drama *Des Teufels General* was written in exile in the USA between 1942 and 1944 and first performed in 1946. The play is set in autumn 1941, in Berlin. The central figure, Harras (the *General* referred to in the title), holds a key responsibility for military aircraft production and has the rank of General in the Luftwaffe. He has not concealed his contempt for Nazism. The extract below comes from early in the third act. Harras has been given ten days to clear up a series of crashes which look like the result of sabotage and which he believes may have been instigated by the Gestapo. His situation at this moment in the play is one of extreme stress. (His 'Schnauze!' is a stock response already established in the play as a feature of his relationship with Korrianke.)

Text

HARRAS: [...] Du bist noch nicht übers Alter, sie werden versuchen, dich an die Front zu stecken – vielleicht könntest du Druckpunkt beziehen, bei einem meiner Freunde in den besetzten Ländern. Du kennst dich ja aus. Aber Vorsicht, Alter – scharf aufpassen, Maul halten und so weiter! Die vergessen nicht. Gib ihnen keine Chance!

KORRIANKE: Kommt nicht in Frage, Herr General. Im Falle eines Falles, da melde ick mir freiwillig zur Infanterie. Mitm nächsten Schub nach Osten.

HARRAS: Nach Osten? Du hast wohl'n Furz im Kopp?

KORRIANKE: Wetten, daß nein, Herr General? Det Köppche vakoof ick nich – nicht für ne Kaffeebohne. Nach Osten – immer nach Osten! Da ha ick 'n mächtgen Drang nach. Im Osten, auf Posten, in finstrer Mitternacht – *Hebt die Hände.* 'Towarischtschi-Towarischtschi!' Kann ick schon.

HARRAS: Ich glaube – um dich muß ich mir keine Sorgen machen.

KORRIANKE: Nein, Herr General. *Das Telephon schnarrt wieder.*

HARRAS *drückt eine Klappe nieder*: Im übrigen – bleibt alles wie vereinbart. Klar? Du hältst dich bereit und wartest – für alle Fälle – bis es dunkel wird.

KORRIANKE: Bis zum Jüngsten Tag, Herr General.

HARRAS: Solang kann es auch dauern – bis wir uns wiedersehn. Und was werden wir dann sagen, Korrianke?

KORRIANKE: 'Prost!' werden wir sagen. Ohne mit der Wim – ohne mit der Wimper – *Starrt ihn an, ganz erschrocken.*

HARRAS *am Telephon*: Na? Was ist?

KORRIANKE: Sie haben 'Schnauze' vergessen.

HARRAS: Verzeihung. Ich bin ein bißchen zerstreut. *Brüllt ihn an.* Schnauze!

KORRIANKE *in militärischer Haltung – schluckend:* Danke, Herr General! *Rasch ab.*

HARRAS: *am Arbeitstisch, knüllt den Briefbogen zusammen, wirft ihn in den Papierkorb. Knipst die Lampe aus. Nimmt das Telephon auf, drückt auf den Summer:* Chefingenieur, bitte. – Oderbruch? Ausgeschlafen? – Na, sosolala. – Nein, nichts Wesentliches. Immer das gleiche Bild. – Ja, die Vernehmung der beiden Arbeiter. Schicken Sie mir den Kommissar herein! Oder nein, kommen Sie mit, bitte, und bleiben Sie dabei! *Er knöpft seinen Rock zu, schaut zur Tür. Herein treten Oderbruch und ein Kommissar in Zivil.*

KOMMISSAR: Mor'n, Herr General! Ich hab Ihnen wunschgemäß die beiden Vögel hergebracht. Aber aus denen kriegen Sie nichts heraus, das sind Verstockte. Kreuzfragen, Scheinwerferverhör, Vertraulichkeit – zieht nich bei denen. Für die Sorte reicht unsere altmodische Polizeimethode nicht aus. Und für die neue sind wir nicht geeicht.

HARRAS: Oder aber, die Vögel sind unschuldig und wissen wirklich nichts.

KOMMISSAR: Dann gnade ihnen Gott. – Sind Sie im Bilde?

HARRAS: Ich habe die Akten eingesehen. *Zu Oderbruch.* Sie sind doch von der verdächtigten Belegschaft?

ODERBRUCH: Soweit man von verdächtig reden kann. Sie haben in einer Schicht gearbeitet, durch deren Hände nachweislich einige der Unglücksmaschinen gegangen sind. Mehr wissen wir nicht.

HARRAS: Und warum hat man diese beiden herausgefischt?

KOMMISSAR: Der eine ist alter SPD-Mann, unbeliebt in der Arbeitsfront, als Nörgler verschrien. Hat mehrmals Bemerkungen gemacht, zum Beispiel: Dr. Ley könne ihn und so weiter. Der andere steht im Verdacht, mit einer geheimen kommunistischen Jugendorganisation zu sympathisieren.

HARRAS: Das ist nicht grade ein Beweis, daß sie in diese Affäre verwickelt sind.

KOMMISSAR: Nein – nicht grade ein Beweis. Sie leugnen alles ab, natürlich. Und wenn man scharf wird, verlegen sie sich auf totale Verdunkelung.

HARRAS: Wollen Sie mir einen Gefallen tun, Herr Kommissar? Lassen Sie uns mit ihnen allein sprechen. Ich halte es für möglich, daß es erfolgreicher wäre.

KOMMISSAR *zuckt die Achseln:* Ich bezweifle es. Aber, bitte, wie Sie wünschen, Herr General. *Wendet sich zur Tür, gibt ein Kommando.*

Eine Wache bringt die beiden Arbeiter herein, entfernt sich mit dem Kommissar. Die Verhafteten sind ungefesselt und tragen ihre eigenen Kleider, ohne Kragen und Krawatten, aber keine Sträflingstracht. Der Ältere, um die Fünfzig, hat ein knochiges, verwittertes Gesicht und angegraute Haare, der Jüngere ist mager und sehr bleich. Beide scheinen ruhig, schauen unter sich.

HARRAS *beobachtet sie einen Augenblick*: Wollen Sie sich setzen?

DER ÄLTERE *ohne aufzuschauen*: Danke! Wir stehen lieber.

HARRAS: Sie sind schon sitzmüde, kann ich mir denken. Gehen Sie ruhig auf und ab, wenn Sie Lust haben. Ich biete Ihnen mit Absicht jetzt keine Zigarette an, das macht jeder Bulle, wenn er Sie ausquetschen will. Aber ich könnte leichter mit Ihnen reden, wenn Sie sich entschließen würden, mich mal anzuschauen.

DER ÄLTERE *mit einem Anflug von Lächeln*: Das läßt sich machen.

HARRAS: Na also! Ich will Sie nämlich nicht ausquetschen. Ich bin nicht Ihr Feind. Ich halte Sie in der Sache nicht für schuldig, solange man Ihnen nichts bewiesen hat. Ich will Sie auch nicht verleiten, Kameraden zu verpfeifen und so weiter. Ich möchte Ihnen nur einen Rat geben – solang wir allein sind.

DIE ARBEITER *schauen ihn an – unbewegt.*

HARRAS: Ich will vorausschicken, daß mir persönlich Ihre politische Gesinnung und Ihr Vorleben gänzlich piepe sind. Ich stehe hier nicht als Polizeimann und nicht als Regierungsvertreter. Für mich ist diese Untersuchung kein Spaß und erst recht keine Schikane. Ich habe die Verantwortung für unsere Flugzeuge und für die Sicherheit unserer Flieger, das ist alles. Es ist Sabotage vorgekommen, und ich will erreichen, daß sie aufhört, sonst nichts. Früher oder später wird sie doch entdeckt – und dann unter erschwerenden Umständen, für alle Beteiligten. Wenn Sie Vertrauen zu mir hätten – könnten wir gegenseitig unsere Lage verbessern. Ich meine das so, wie ich es sage.

DIE ARBEITER *schauen ihn an – schweigen.*

HARRAS: Es ist Ihnen doch klar, daß Sie in der Scheißgasse sind. Ob mit Recht oder Unrecht, steht hier nicht zur Frage. Aber Sie wissen ja Bescheid. Wenn man jemanden verdächtigen will, findet man immer was Verdächtiges, und je weniger dabei herauskommt, desto schärfer geht man vor. Solange Sie in regulärer Untersuchungshaft sind, passiert Ihnen nichts, und wenn Sie in ein Gefängnis kämen oder sogar in ein Zuchthaus, wären Sie fein heraus. Ich will Ihnen hier nicht einreden, sich was aus den Fingern zu saugen.

Reprinted from Carl Zuckmayer, *Des Teufels General* (Frankfurt: S. Fischer Verlag, 1954, pp. 133–6), by permission of S. Fischer Verlag GmbH, Frankfurt am Main.

10.2 Language variety: dialect, social register and tonal register

Assignment

(i) Listen to the recording played to you by your tutor and identify the salient features of language variety in the text. (Your tutor may give you a transcript of the spoken text.) Discuss the strategic problems of translating the text as (a) part of a dramatised text and (b) a voice-over spoken by an actor in a television documentary on environmental issues.

(ii) Working in groups, translate 'Die Duwaksblanze...' into English, paying appropriate attention to language variety. The TT should be suitable as a text for voice-over. (Your tutor may give you an intralingual translation of the transcript into Standard German.)

(iii) Explain the decisions of detail you made in producing your TT.

11

Textual genre as a factor in translation: oral and written genres

At various times in this course we have spoken of the ST both as a starting-point for translation and as a point of reference in evaluating TTs. However, before it is ever thought of as a ST requiring translation, any text is already an object in its own right, something that belongs to a particular genre of the source culture. Because any ST shares some of its properties with other texts of the same genre, and is perceived by a SL audience as being what it is on account of such genre-typical properties, the translator must, in order to appreciate the nature of the ST, be familiar with the broad characteristics of the appropriate source-culture genre. Furthermore, since any source culture presents a whole array of different textual genres, the translator must have some sort of overview of genre-types in that culture. This does not imply an exhaustive theory of genres – even if such a theory were available, it would be too elaborate for a methodology of translation. All that is needed is a rough framework of genre-types to help a translator to concentrate on characteristics that make the ST a representative specimen of a particular source-culture genre.

The most elementary subdivision in textual genres is into *oral* text types and *written* ones. Both these major categories, of course, break down into a number of more narrowly circumscribed minor categories, and ultimately into specific genres.

ORAL GENRES

In the case of oral genres, we suggest the following breakdown into sub-genres:

conversation
oral narrative

dramatization
oral address
oral reading
lyrics

Conversation

As a sub-genre, conversation is characterized by its genuinely unscripted nature, and by the fact that its guiding structural principle is 'turn-taking' (the rule-governed alternation between participant speakers).

Oral narrative

The sub-genre of oral narrative includes the continuous (though not necessarily uninterrupted) telling, by one speaker, of tales, stories, anecdotes, jokes and the like, and the recounting of events (whether true or apocryphal). Characteristic of such texts is the fact that they are organized by a narrative structure, which may be idiosyncratic to specific genres (e.g. 'There was an Englishman, a Scotsman and an Irishman....').

Dramatization

By this category we mean the entire gamut of plays, sketches, dramatized readings, films and the like, manifested in actual spoken performance (whether on stage, screen, radio, or television). Such texts are characterized by the necessary role of an actor or actors in their performance, and by the fact that their effectiveness depends on a dramatic illusion entered into by both actors and audience.

Oral address

In this subcategory are placed all forms of public speaking (lectures, talks, seminars, political speeches, verbal pleadings in a court of law, and so on). The defining feature of this genre-type is that, nominally at least, a single speaker holds the floor, and elaborates on an essentially non-narrative theme. There is a clearly felt intuitive distinction between oral narratives and oral addresses: while stories are 'told', addresses are said to be 'delivered'. (Though an address may be interspersed with items of oral narrative, for instance anecdotes or jokes, its structural guiding principle is clearly not a narrative structure, being geared to information, instruction or persuasion rather than to entertainment.)

Oral reading

Oral reading is introduced as a separate genre-type in order to distinguish, not only 'reading aloud' from 'silent reading', but also the 'flat' reading-out of written texts from 'dramatized reading'. In other words, what is typical of oral reading is that readers do not attempt to act out the script by assuming the characters of imaginary unscripted speakers. (This, incidentally, is distinct from the habitual manner of poetry recitation, where the reader normally assumes and interprets the part of the poet.) Where dramatized reading tries to give the impression of unscripted oral performance, oral reading is simply the vocalized delivery of a written text. Oral reading is also distinct from oral address: witness the clear intuitive difference between a lively lecturing style (oral address) and the technique of 'reading a paper' at a seminar or conference.

Lyrics

The subcategory of lyrics includes all oral texts set to music, whether figuring as songs performed in isolation, or as part of a performed libretto. It is important to remember that, even where these may be written down, it is not the printed text of a song or libretto itself that is denoted by the term 'lyrics', but the verbal content of actual oral renderings of songs, musicals, operas, operettas and the like. Consequently, lyrics should not be considered in the abstract, but as objects forming part of a live musical performance.

This list, while it does not claim to be exhaustive, gives a good general coverage of oral genres in Western cultures. Each genre-type can, of course, be further subdivided (for example, oral narrative into folk tales, ghost stories, anecdotes, autobiographical accounts, jokes, and so forth). However, even as it stands, the list enables us to pick out the basic features that concern translators of oral texts.

The defining property all these genres have in common is the fact that they are realized in a vocal medium. This truism has important implications. First, an oral text is in essence a fleeting and unrepeatable event that strikes the ear and 'then is heard no more'. Second, vocal utterance may be accompanied by visual cues (such as gestures or facial expressions) that are secondary to it, and equally transitory, but which do form a part of the overall text and play a role in colouring its meaning. This all means that, on every level of textual variable, oral texts must obey the 'rules' of a spoken language first and foremost. It also means that an effective oral text avoids problems of comprehension arising from informational overloading, elaborate cross-reference, excessive speed, and so forth. Of course, in all these respects, what is true for oral STs is also true for oral TTs – an obvious fact, but one that is all too often overlooked.

Another important implication is the appearance of spontaneity that characterizes the majority of oral genres (with the exception of oral reading). This goes not only for impromptu conversation or unrehearsed narrative, but for prepared texts as well: stories told and retold in a carefully formulated version; memorized lines in a play or film; even such texts as speeches or lectures, where the speaker may stick closely to a script but the delivery is imitative of unscripted oral texts.

Though to a lesser degree, dramatized reading, recited verse, song lyrics and libretti, if well performed, all give the audience a chance to enter into the illusion of spontaneous vocal utterance.

As these remarks suggest, an oral text is always quite different in nature and impact from even its most closely representative written version. For instance, a recited poem is quite distinct from its printed counterpart, and so is a performed song from the bare text set down on paper. Even the most blatant oral reading has nuances of oral delivery, such as intonation and stress, that make its reception quite different from the experience of silent reading.

An awareness of these properties of oral texts and genres is a necessary starting-point for discussing the particular types of problem that confront anyone wanting to translate an oral ST into an oral TT. The most specialized branch of oral-to-oral translating is on-the-spot interpreting. (In fact, terminologically, interpreting is usually distinguished from other kinds of translating.) There are three major types of interpreting.

The first is *bilateral interpreting* of conversation, where the interpreter acts as a two-way intermediary in unrehearsed dialogue. Bilateral interpreting can be the most relaxed of the three types; as part of the multi-lingual social situation, the interpreter can even clarify obscure points with the speakers. What this kind of interpreting involves mainly is a broad facility in understanding and speaking the languages involved, familiarity with the relevant cultures, and sensitivity to the conversational nuances of both languages (including awareness of tonal registers and of visual cues of gesture and facial expression).

The second type is *consecutive interpreting*. This requires all the same skills as bilateral interpreting, and more besides. The interpreter listens to an oral text, makes detailed shorthand notes and, from these, ad libs an oral TT that relays the content and some of the nuances of the ST. The training for consecutive interpreting is intensive, and takes several months at least.

The third type is *simultaneous interpreting*. Here, the interpreter relays an oral TT at the same time as listening to the oral ST. This is the most specialized form of interpreting, and requires the longest training. Grasping the content and nuances of a continuous oral ST, while at the same time producing a fluent oral TT that does justice to the content and nuances of the ST, can be very taxing. Trainees do not usually start learning simultaneous interpreting until they have acquired considerable skill in consecutive interpreting.

Since it is a specialized skill, interpreting is not part of this course, and we shall not dwell on it. It is very useful, however, to try a session of bilateral interpreting and one of consecutive interpreting, partly as an exercise in gist translation (as defined on p. 9), but mostly because it sharpens awareness of specifically oral textual variables, which may require special attention in translating any kind of text, spoken or written.

An exercise in interpreting will also confirm that spoken communication has stylistic quirks and constraints that are very much language-specific. The eternal problem of translating jokes is a good example of this. It is not merely that some jokes are hard to translate because they depend on word-play, but that both humour itself and techniques of joke- and story-telling are to a great extent culture-specific. Translating oral jokes is an especially clear illustration of the fact that oral translation is not simply a matter of verbal transposition from one spoken language to another: the genre-related norms and expectations of the target culture must be respected as well, including gestures, facial expressions, mimicry, and so on. Texts in most oral genres are not only utterances, but also dramatic performances. This will have been vividly seen by anyone who tried putting 'Die Duwaksblanze...' (Practical 10.2, p. 117) into colloquial English. To do so, one is almost bound to produce a written TT, but this will only be an interim approximation to the combination of phonic and prosodic features essential to a successful, performed, oral TT.

Another oral genre dealt with in Practical 11, the genre of the song lyric, highlights a second set of difficulties peculiar to oral translation. Assuming that the TT is to be sung to the same tune as the ST, overriding strategic priority will have to be given to the prosodic and phonic levels of textual variables. It is therefore hardly surprising that translators of songs, and even libretti, sometimes take considerable liberties with the literal meanings of STs. Popular songs may, of course, have completely new TL lyrics made up for them; and if they are translated, it is very freely. Libretti cannot enjoy the same degree of freedom, since the TT still has to make sense within the framework of a plot that does not depart significantly from that of the original ST. Libretto translators have an extremely demanding task, because they have to do three things: respect the dramatic needs of the ST (with its linguistic and stylistic implications); produce a dramatic TT matching the expectations that a TL audience has of the genre; and work under the very strict prosodic constraints imposed by the music. As we have seen (pp. 46–8), different languages have differently organized prosodic properties. Consequently, when translating from German to English, one needs to understand the prosodic features not only of the SL, but also of the TL, so that the TT can actually be sung without sounding ridiculous.

In addition, the translator of lyrics must be alert on the phonic level, and pay attention to the quality of syllabic vowels as they correspond with notes in the score. For example, in German lyrics it is feasible to sing a long note on a syllabic [ə], as in Lotte Lenya's rendering of 'Seg**e**ln'; but an [ə] on a long musical note in English is incongrous if it falls on a syllable that is unstressed in ordinary speech – compare 'ret**ur**n', which is acceptable, and 'etern**a**lly', which is not. Consonant clusters must also be attended to, so that the performer is not given a tongue-twister to sing.

In Chapter 12, where we look at the issues that arise in translating written STs for oral delivery and oral STs into written TTs, this brief survey of the main requirements of oral-to-oral translation will need to be borne in mind. First, however, we need to survey – equally briefly – the field of written genres.

WRITTEN GENRES

There are, in Western cultures, so many different varieties of written text that any typology of practical use for translation is bound to be even more approximate than the one suggested for oral genres. We shall approach the categorization of written genres by looking back to a time immediately predating the literary explosion that has continued to escalate since the sixteenth and seventeenth centuries. The approach implies that innovation in written textual genres, for at least the past four centuries, has been limited to the invention of new subdivisions of five already existing genres, the seeds of which were probably sown in classical antiquity. On this assumption, the fundamental and most general categories of written genres are:

literary/fictional
religious/devotional
theoretical/philosophical
empirical/descriptive
persuasive/prescriptive

This classification is primarily based on a global view of textual subject matter, or, more precisely, on *the author's implicit attitude to the treatment of subject matter.*

Literary/fictional genres

The essence of texts in this category is that they are about a 'fictive', imaginary world of events and characters created autonomously in and through the texts themselves, and not controlled by the physical world outside. However close a text of this type may be to autobiography, it still approaches its subject matter by re-creating experience in terms of a subjective, internal world, which is fundamentally perceived as fictive, for all its similarities to real life. In texts in this category, the author is understood to be ultimately in control of events and characters.

Literary genres have, of course, subdivided and diversified very greatly. Even poetry, which is just one genre in this category, has split up over the past two centuries into innumerable sub-genres, each with different characteristic styles. (One need only compare the poems used in this course to begin to appreciate this proliferation.) As for prose fiction, there are not just the genres of novel and short story, but a wide variety of minor genres such as detective stories, thrillers, historical romances and science fiction.

Religious/devotional genres

The subject matter of devotional and religious works implies belief in the existence of a 'spiritual world'. Seen from the outside (that is, by an atheist or agnostic), there may seem to be little difference between this and the fictive and imaginary subject matter of literary/fictional genres. However, and this is the point, seen in terms of the author's attitude to the treatment of the subject matter, there is nothing fictive about the spiritual world dealt with in religious/devotional texts: it has its own extratextual realities and unshakeable truths. That is, this category has more in common with 'empirical/descriptive' than with 'literary/fictional' genres. The author is understood not to be free to create the world that animates the subject matter, but to be merely instrumental in exploring it.

Of all five categories of genre, this one seems to have changed and diversified least of all. Even the Good News Bible represents only a minor diversion from the Authorized Version, and Thomas Aquinas or Julian of Norwich have only to be brought modestly up to date to feel remarkably modern.

Theoretical/philosophical genres

These genres have as their subject matter a 'world' of *ideas*, which are understood to exist independently of the individual minds that think them. So-called pure mathematics is the best example of the kind of subject matter and approach to subject matter that define theoretical/philosophical genres. The vehicle used by authors is not fictional imagination or spiritual faith, but reasoning. (In Western cultures, the primary form of abstract, rational thinking is deductive logic.) The author of a theoretical/philosophical text, however original it may be, is understood not to be free to develop theoretical structures at will, but to be constrained by standards of rationality.

The proliferation of genres in this category has been less spectacular than that of literary genres, but it is strikingly diverse nonetheless – compare, for instance, Leibniz's *Theodizee,* Wittgenstein's *Tractatus* and Kant's *Kritik der reinen Vernunft*.

Empirical/descriptive genres

Genres in this category purport to treat of the real objective world as it is experienced by specialist observers. An empirical/descriptive text is one with a necessarily 'factual' reference (though, again, sceptics may refuse to accept that factuality); a text that sets out to give an objective account of phenomena.

This category has diversified in direct proportion to the creation and diversification of specialized scientific and technical disciplines. Each discipline and each school of thought tends to develop its own technical vocabulary and its own style. In this way, a virtually endless list of minor genres is being constantly generated.

Persuasive/prescriptive genres

The essence of these genres is that they aim at influencing readers to act and think in textually prescribed ways. This aim can be pursued through various means: explicit and helpful instructions; statutory orders, rules and regulations; oblique suggestions. Thus, we are uniting in a single category the entire gamut of texts from instruction manuals, through documents stating laws, rules and regulations, to propaganda leaflets, advertisements, and so forth. Like the other four genre-categories, this one can be broken down into an indefinite number of sub-categories. Nevertheless, it is held together by a common purpose, the purpose of getting readers to take a certain course of action, and perhaps explaining how to take it.

The category of persuasive/prescriptive genres has also undergone immense proliferation, thanks not only to the growth of bureaucracy, technology and education, but also to the modern escalation in advertising.

The reason why this classification is useful for translation methodology is that *differences in approach to subject matter* entail fundamental *differences in the way a text is formally constructed.* In other words, differences in genre tend to correspond to characteristic differences in the use of textual variables. So – to take a simple example – sound-symbolism and the deliberate use of connotative meanings are inappropriate in English empirical/descriptive texts. Apart from the interesting case of 'hybrid' texts that cut across categories, linguistic and stylistic expectations are in general distinct from one genre-category to another.

The importance of genre-distinctions for the practice of translation is actually very clearly illustrated by the phenomenon of 'hybrid genres'. There are three main ways in which a particular text can cut across basic genre-distinctions. Either it can belong by subject matter to one category, but borrow the stylistic form of another (as in Norman Mailer's *The Armies of the Night,* or Goethe's scientific treatises in verse): hybrids of this type have a double purpose, such as providing literary enjoyment along with empirical description. Or a text may be compounded of sections allocated to subject matters falling into different genres (as in *Time* magazine, *The Listener*, or *Der Spiegel*): the Bible itself is a good example of such a 'hybrid' text in which different books represent different genre-categories (for instance, the Song of Songs represents a literary genre, Paul's Epistle to the Romans a religious/devotional genre, the Acts of the Apostles a historical/descriptive genre, and Leviticus a prescriptive one). Alternatively, a text can use genre-imitative subsections as a conscious stylistic device. A good example is this descriptive passage from Th. Mann's *Felix Krull* parodying the persuasive style of a certain type of travel guide:

> Der Rheingau hat mich hervorgebracht, jener begünstigte Landstrich, welcher, gelinde und ohne Schroffheit sowohl in Hinsicht auf die Witterungsverhältnisse wie auf die Bodenbeschaffenheit, reich mit Städten und Ortschaften besetzt und fröhlich bevölkert, wohl zu den lieblichsten der bewohnten Erde gehört. Hier blühen, vom Rheingaugebirge vor rauhen Winden bewahrt und der Mittagssonne glücklich hingebreitet, jene berühmten Siedlungen, bei deren Namensklange dem Zecher das Herz lacht, hier Rauenthal, Johannisberg, Rüdesheim, und hier auch das ehrwürdige Städtchen, in dem ich, wenige Jahre nur nach der glorreichen Gründung des Deutschen Reiches, das Licht der Welt erblickte. Ein wenig westlich des Knies gelegen, welches der Rhein bei Mainz

beschreibt, und berühmt durch seine Schaumweinfabrikation, ist es Hauptanlegeplatz der den Strom hinauf und hinab eilenden Dampfer und zählt gegen viertausend Einwohner. Das lustige Mainz war also sehr nahe und ebenso die vornehmen Taunusbäder, als: Wiesbaden, Homburg, Langenschwalbach und Schlangenbad, welch letzteres man in halbstündiger Fahrt auf einer Schmalspurbahn erreichte.

Reprinted from Thomas Mann, *Bekenntnisse des Hochstaplers Felix Krull* (Fischer TaschenbuchVerlag, Frankfurt: Lizenzausgabe des S. Fischer Verlages, 1981, p. 6), by permission of S. Fischer Verlag GmbH, Frankfurt am Main 1954.

This passage repays discussion in class. It is also very instructive to compare it with real tourist guides such as the *HB Bildatlas Südlicher Schwarzwald* cited in Chapter 3 (p. 31).

'Hybrid' texts, especially literary ones, show why translators need to have a clear view of available genres and of their linguistic and stylistic characteristics. For instance, the point of the text from *Felix Krull* would be lost if the typical style of TL tourist guides were not used (with appropriate adaptation) in the TT. A sense of genre characteristics enables translators to set themselves clearly formulated targets before they start producing TTs. It also forewarns them about any special needs in translating a particular text, such as finding the necessary dictionaries and source materials, doing the necessary background reading, and so on. No translation can be undertaken without due preparation, and identifying the genre of the ST is the first step towards adequate preparation.

As the example from *Felix Krull* shows, awareness of genre is vital in that translators have to be familiar with the styles of presentation and language-use expected from particular genres in particular cultures. It is often genre that makes a communicative rendering preferable to literal translation. For instance, if, as the criminal draws a pistol, a policeman shouts 'Paß auf! er hat 'nen Revolver' in a cops-and-robbers film, genre demands that this be rendered by 'Look out! he's got a gun', the familiar cry from countless English-language cops-and-robbers films. This generalizing translation could easily be avoided by translating literally – 'Look out! he's got a revolver' – but, as very often happens, the demands of the genre outweigh those of literal accuracy. These considerations are as valid for written as for oral genres, and will be of central importance in Practicals 11–14.

Between textbook and poetry

There is another parameter on which genres can be compared in a way relevant to translation. This parameter can be visualized as a scale or continuum defined by the relative textual importance of explicit literal meaning at one extreme, and of implicitly conveyed connotative and/or stylistic meaning at the other. At one end of the scale are texts like scientific or legal documents, or textbooks, that require maximum attention to precision in literal meaning and minimum attention to 'aesthetic' effects. What connotative nuances or overtones do exist in these texts can be virtually ignored by the translator – indeed, care must be taken not to let such effects creep into the TT inadvertently, as they could be a distraction from the literal meaning.

At the opposite end of the scale are texts that depend maximally on subtle nuances of non-literal meaning and aesthetic effect, and minimally on the explicit, literal meaning. Poetry clusters towards this extreme. In poetry, understanding the literal content of sentences is often no more than perceiving the vehicles of a more subtle textual meaning. A lyric poem may have relatively slight content in literal meaning, and yet be both a serious poem and a very rich one (Goethe is the supreme case in point). It is inherent in poetry that a given poem's precise combination of literal meaning, connotative (or 'emotive') meanings, syntactic articulation, prosody and phonic patterning produces a text which works largely through *suggestion*. Experienced commentators will usually agree broadly – but never in all details – on the 'import' of the poem. Poetry may, simply because it has words, tempt the inexperienced translator to identify its meaning with its literal content – whereas, in fact, to reproduce the total import of a poem in a TT would require re-creating the whole unique bundle of meanings and sounds presented in the ST. That is the prime reason why poetry is often said to be untranslatable. In our view, however, if one accepts that translation loss is *inevitable*, and that the translator's role is to reduce it as much as possible, then it is feasible to envisage at least highly honourable failure in translating poetry – witness the many excellent translations of modern German poetry by Michael Hamburger and Christopher Middleton (Hamburger and Middleton, 1962).

Translators can usefully gauge the genre of a ST, and also of their own TT, by rating its position on this scale between textbook and poetry. Obviously, this cannot be done objectively or precisely, but it is possible roughly to assess the *proportions* in which literal meanings and connotative 'resonances' contribute to the overall meaning of a given text. So, for example, poetry is to be taken as increasingly 'poetic' the less important literal meaning is in proportion to connotative resonances; and it will be taken as increasingly 'prosaic' the more important literal meaning is relative to connotative resonances. Certain examples of verse disguised as prose (such as the Thomas Mann passage studied in Practical 4) would seem to occupy the middle ground in the continuum; but, in principle, connotative meaning has a slight edge over literal meaning in even the most prosaic forms of poetry. (It is, incidentally, important not to be misled by textual layout: verse is not necessarily poetry, and prose may well be.) Conversely, even the most poetic prose will not be classified as poetry if literal meaning has overall precedence over connotative meaning.

At the other end of the scale, scientific texts represent the extreme point of meaning in directly expressed and logically structured form. But the translator must be on the alert for the pseudo-scientific text, in which apparent 'objectivity' is a consciously adopted register, and therefore constitutes a stylistic device requiring attention in translating.

In conclusion, then, we can say that even a rough-and-ready typology of oral and written genres pays dividends by concentrating the translator's mind on four vital strategic questions.

First, what genre is represented by the ST? What problems are expected in connection with this genre? Second, given the genre of the ST, what ST features should be given priority in translation? Does the ST have recognizable, perhaps clichéd, genre-specific characteristics that require special attention? Third, what genre(s) in the TL provide a match for the ST genre? What can a scrutiny of available specimens of these TL genres suggest about the manner in which the TT should be formulated? Finally, what genre should the TT be ultimately couched in, and what genre-specific linguistic and stylistic features should it have?

PRACTICAL 11

11.1 Genre

Assignment
Working in four groups:

(i) Listen to the song, without following the printed text. *Treating it as an oral text*, discuss its genre, content and impact.
(ii) Examine the script of the song (on pp. 129–31) and discuss its salient features *as a written text*.
(iii) Listen to the song again, following it on the text, and discuss the relation between the words and the music. (Note the points where there are discrepancies between the sung lyrics and the written text.)
(iv) Discuss the strategic problems of translating the song into a TT as part of the libretto of an English production of the Brecht/Weill musical.
(v) Each group taking one stanza, produce a TT suitable for musical performance on stage.

Contextual information
'Die Seeräuber-Jenny' comes from B. Brecht's opera *Die Dreigroschenoper*, first produced in Berlin in 1928. The music is by Kurt Weill. Ronald Taylor writes:

> *Die Dreigroschenoper*, a ballad opera adapted from John Gay's *Beggar's Opera* of 1728 and set in the Soho of the Victorian age, enjoyed a huge popular success from the moment of its first performance in the Theater am Schiffbauerdamm. [...] As a satire on modern capitalist society, portrayed as a world in which success equals villainy and corruption, it had the standard-bearers of that society squealing with delight. And there is no more sardonic representation of the slick, sordid, light-headed, don't-want-to-know world of the tottering Weimar Republic than the spiky yet sentimental, bitter-sweet music of Kurt Weill, which is an inseparable part of the work.

The song forms part of Scene 2 of *Die Dreigroschenoper*, set in a disused stable, and entitled:

TIEF IM HERZEN SOHOS FEIERT DER BANDIT MACKIE MESSER SEINE HOCHZEIT MIT POLLY PEACHUM, DER TOCHTER DES BETTLER-KÖNIGS

The song is offered by the bride as a contribution to the wedding breakfast entertainment. Brecht elaborately 'alienates' the presentation; the dialogue leading directly to the song accordingly belongs to the contextual information:

POLLY:	Meine Herren, wenn keiner etwas vortragen will, dann will ich selber eine Kleinigkeit zum besten geben, und zwar werde ich ein Mädchen nachmachen, das ich einmal in einer dieser kleinen Vier-Penny-Kneipen in Soho gesehen habe. Es war das Abwaschmädchen, und Sie müssen wissen, daß alles über sie lachte und daß sie dann die Gäste ansprach und zu ihnen solche Dinge sagte, wie ich sie Ihnen gleich vorsingen werde. So, das ist die kleine Theke, Sie müssen sie sich verdammt schmutzig vorstellen, hinter der sie stand morgens und abends. Das ist der Spüleimer und das ist der Lappen, mit dem sie die Gläser abwusch. Wo Sie sitzen, saßen die Herren, die über sie lachten. Sie können auch lachen, daß es genau so ist; aber wenn Sie nicht können, dann brauchen Sie es nicht. *Sie fängt an, scheinbar die Gläser abzuwaschen und vor sich hin zu brabbeln.* Jetzt sagt zum Beispiel einer von Ihnen – *auf Walter deutend* –, Sie: Na, wann kommt denn dein Schiff, Jenny?
WALTER:	Na, wann kommt denn dein Schiff, Jenny?
POLLY:	Und ein anderer sagt, zum Beispiel Sie: Wäschst du immer noch die Gläser auf, du Jenny, die Seeräuberbraut?
MATTHIAS:	Wäschst du immer noch die Gläser auf, du Jenny, die Seeräuberbraut?
POLLY:	So, und jetzt fange ich an.

Songbeleuchtung: goldenes Licht. Die Orgel wird illuminiert. An einer Stange kommen von oben drei Lampen herunter, und auf den Tafeln steht:

DIE SEERÄUBER-JENNY

Text

1

Meine Herren, heute sehen Sie mich Gläser abwaschen
Und ich mache das Bett für jeden.

Und Sie geben mir einen Penny und ich bedanke mich schnell
Und Sie sehen meine Lumpen und dies lumpige Hotel
Und Sie wissen nicht, mit wem Sie reden.
Aber eines Abends wird ein Geschrei sein am Hafen
Und man fragt: Was ist das für ein Geschrei?
Und man wird mich lächeln sehn bei meinen Gläsern
Und man sagt: Was lächelt die dabei?
  Und ein Schiff mit acht Segeln
  Und mit fünfzig Kanonen
  Wird liegen am Kai.

2

Man sagt: Geh, wisch deine Gläser, mein Kind
Und man reicht mir den Penny hin.
Und der Penny wird genommen, und das Bett wird gemacht!
(Es wird keiner mehr drin schlafen in dieser Nacht.)
Und Sie wissen immer noch nicht, wer ich bin.
Aber eines Abends wird ein Getös sein am Hafen
Und man fragt: Was ist das für ein Getös?
Und man wird mich stehen sehen hinterm Fenster
Und man sagt: Was lächelt die so bös?
  Und das Schiff mit acht Segeln
  Und mit fünfzig Kanonen
  Wird beschießen die Stadt.

3

Meine Herren, da wird wohl Ihr Lachen aufhörn
Denn die Mauern werden fallen hin
Und die Stadt wird gemacht dem Erdboden gleich
Nur ein lumpiges Hotel wird verschont von jedem Streich
Und man fragt: Wer wohnt Besonderer darin?
Und in dieser Nacht wird ein Geschrei um das Hotel sein
Und man fragt: Warum wird das Hotel verschont?
Und man wird mich sehen treten aus der Tür gen Morgen
Und man sagt: Die hat darin gewohnt?
  Und das Schiff mit acht Segeln
  Und mit fünfzig Kanonen
  Wird beflaggen den Mast.

4

Und es werden kommen hundert gen Mittag an Land
Und werden in den Schatten treten
Und fangen einen jeglichen aus jeglicher Tür
Und legen ihn in Ketten und bringen vor mir
Und fragen: Welchen sollen wir töten?

Und an diesem Mittag wird es still sein am Hafen
Wenn man fragt, wer wohl sterben muß.
Und dann werden sie mich sagen hören: Alle!
Und wenn dann der Kopf fällt, sag ich: Hoppla!
  Und das Schiff mit acht Segeln
  Und mit fünfzig Kanonen
  Wird entschwinden mit mir.

Reprinted by kind permission from Bertolt Brecht, *Gesammelte Werke Band 2*, (Frankfurt: Suhrkamp Verlag, 1967, pp. 414–17),

11.2 Genre

Assignment
Working in groups:

(i) Discuss the strategic problems confronting the translator of the following text, paying careful attention to considerations of genre.
(ii) Translate a section of the text allocated to your group. (For the purposes of the exercise, assume that the TT will be published in a Christian magazine.)
(iii) Explain the main decisions of detail you made in producing your TT.

Contextual information
The text was first published in the *Amtsblatt des Erzbistums Köln*, 15.9.1980. It was subsequently reprinted in newspapers as a statement of the official position of the Roman Catholic episcopate.

Text

Wort der Bischöfe zur Bundestagswahl

Liebe Brüder! Liebe Schwestern!

Am 5. Oktober wird der 9. Deutsche Bundestag gewählt. Jede Wahl ist nicht nur ein politischer Vorgang, sondern zugleich eine sittliche Entscheidung darüber, welche Werte und Ziele die Politik in den kommenden Jahren bestimmen und tragen. Dazu wollen wir Bischöfe heute ein Wort sagen.

Der Christ wird bei seiner Wahlentscheidung bedenken, was die Gebote Gottes in der Politik fordern. Sie betreffen ja nicht nur das Leben des einzelnen Menschen, sie sind zugleich Richtschnur für das öffentliche Leben. Die Gebote Gottes sind das Fundament jeder wahren Humanität. Sie begründen die unbedingte Achtung vor dem Menschen als Person und als Träger unantastbarer Rechte und Pflichten. Die Gebote Gottes fordern Gerechtigkeit und Liebe im gesellschaftlichen und politischen Zusammenleben und verpflichten zum Dienst am Frieden.

Vier Gesichtspunkte seien eigens hervorgehoben:

Erstens: Eine Politik, die nicht einer Ideologie, einem Prestige- oder Machtdenken dient, sondern Gottes Gebot folgen will, muß die Würde jedes Menschen und seine Rechte achten und fördern. Unser Grundgesetz bekennt sich zu diesem Maßstab. Wir dürfen dankbar anerkennen, daß in den zurückliegenden dreißig Jahren vieles geschaffen wurde, was soziale Notstände beseitigte, Ungerechtigkeiten abbaute und die Entfaltungsmöglichkeiten der Bürger erweiterte. Um so schmerzlicher ist es, feststellen zu müssen, daß Menschen in unserer Gesellschaft vielen ungeborenen Kindern das Recht auf Leben verweigern und daß unsere Rechtsordnung dieses Grundrecht nicht mehr umfassend schützt. Wir dürfen uns über die Folgen einer solchen Entwicklung nicht hinwegtäuschen: Die Aushöhlung des Grundrechts auf Leben untergräbt auch die Grundwerte der Gerechtigkeit und der Solidarität. Sie zerstört die Liebe und gefährdet den Frieden.

Zweitens: Ein Volk verliert die Hoffnung auf Zukunft, wenn die Werte von Ehe und Familie nicht mehr erkannt, geschützt und auch nicht mehr vorgelebt werden. Gesetze, die die Ehescheidung begünstigen und den auf Lebenszeit geschlossenen Bund aushöhlen, zerstören die Ehe. Gesetze, die von der falschen Annahme ausgehen, die Mehrzahl unserer Familien sei zerrüttet und deshalb müsse immer mehr der Staat die Familie ersetzen oder in sie hineinregieren, solche Gesetze tragen nicht dazu bei, personale Freiheit und Verantwortung zu stärken. Sie schwächen die Familie. Familienpolitik darf kein Lippenbekenntnis bleiben. So sehr die Erhöhung des Kindergeldes zu begrüßen ist, so wenig kann sie eine Politik ersetzen, die der Familie den ihr gebührenden hohen Rang zuerkennt. Darum aber geht es, daß die wichtige Rolle der Familie für die Gesellschaft geistig, rechtlich und materiell gestärkt wird.

Drittens: Notwendig ist auch eine Politik, die das Gemeinwohl gegen ausufernde Privat- und Gruppeninteressen durchsetzt und zugleich die Grenzen der Zuständigkeit des Staates achtet. Seit Jahren stehen wir in der Bundesrepublik Deutschland in der Gefahr, über unsere Verhältnisse zu leben und damit die Lebenschancen unserer Kinder zu belasten. Die Ausweitung der Staatstätigkeit, die damit verbundene Bürokratisierung und die gefährlich hohe Staatsverschuldung müssen jetzt korrigiert werden. Es ist ein Trugschluß zu meinen, der Staat könne alles, und insbesondere, er könne alles besser machen. Der Staat ist dem Gemeinwohl, also der Sicherung und der Förderung des friedlichen Zusammenlebens der Bürger verpflichtet. Dieser Verpflichtung wird er am besten gerecht, wenn er die Initiative, die Anstrengung und die persönliche Verantwortung der einzelnen und der Gruppen herausfordert und stärkt.

Viertens: Die vornehmste Aufgabe der Politik ist die Sicherung des Friedens. Die schweren Konflikte und kriegerischen Auseinandersetzungen, die in nicht wenigen Teilen der Welt ausgebrochen sind und so vielen Menschen schreckliches Leid zufügen, gefährden den Frieden. Sie gehen auch uns an. Wahrer Friede ist Friede in Freiheit. Wie der Friede in Freiheit erhalten, gesichert, beziehungsweise wiedergewonnen werden kann, darüber gehen die Auffassungen auseinander. Darum muß in der Politik gerungen werden. Den Weg zum dauerhaften Frieden geht nur, wer – innerhalb des Staates und der Völkergemeinschaft – sich an der Menschenwürde, an der Freiheit und an der Gerechtigkeit für alle ausrichtet.

Die demokratischen Parteien in unserem Land wissen sich seit der Gründung der Bundesrepublik Deutschland dem Frieden als dem obersten Ziel der Politik verpflichtet. Dieses gemeinsame Fundament unserer Demokratie darf nicht verspielt werden. Keine demokratische Partei sollte der anderen den Willen zum Frieden oder die Fähigkeit, ihm in Politik und Diplomatie zu dienen, absprechen.

Alle Bürger stehen bei der Wahl vor einer Gewissensentscheidung. Nichtwählen ist in der Regel eher ein Zeichen der Flucht vor der Verantwortung, entweder, weil man sich nicht festlegen möchte, oder, weil man eine ideale Alternative ohne Fehler und Tadel sucht, die es auf dieser Welt nicht gibt. Der Frage, wie wir unserer Verantwortung gerecht werden für eine Lebensordnung, die nach Gottes Willen dem Menschen dient, müssen wir uns stellen.

Es segne Euch der allmächtige Gott, der Vater, der Sohn und der Heilige Geist.

Die Deutschen Bischöfe
Für das Erzbistum Köln
+ **Joseph Card. Höffner**

Reprinted by kind permission of the Sekretariat der Deutschen Bischofskonferenz.

12

Genre marking and the crossover between oral and written genres

In Chapter 11 we concentrated mainly on the ST as an object belonging to a given genre. We outlined certain major categories of oral and of written genres, and suggested that translators should be familiar with the characteristics of SL and TL genres and have the ability to couch a TT in a form appropriate to the chosen TL genre. We also suggested that demands of genre often outweigh those of literal accuracy in a TT. In this chapter, we shall explore two related themes, one of which follows on from the other. The first of these themes concerns the use of features that mark a TT as being a plausible text in a particular TL genre. The second concerns the problems attendant on the fact that, in the course of translation, there is very frequently a 'crossover' between oral and written texts and their corresponding genres. As we shall see below, a careful view of such a crossover is of vital importance for minimizing translation loss. At the same time, such a view invites direct comparison between oral and written texts, providing the clearest and most economical way of bringing out features specific to each. The theme of 'crossover' also builds on lessons drawn from Practical 11, linking these to Practical 12.

GENRE MARKING

A TT must stand, independently of any support from the ST, as a plausible text in terms of the expectations of a TL audience. While this holds for any genre, it is probably most immediately obvious in the case of certain oral genres, since the audience can publicly applaud, or boo, or walk out.

Making a TT 'fit' a particular genre means not only tailoring it to the standard 'grammar' of the TL genre, but also giving it features that conform to typical stylistic properties of that genre. Some of these features may be simply formulaic;

certainly, formulaic features give the most tangible examples of what we mean. For instance, in translating a traditional fairy story told by a German story-teller, it would be reasonable to open the TT with the phrase 'Once upon a time there was...'. This is a genuine choice, since one could translate the formulaic German beginning 'Es war einmal' as 'There was once'. Choosing 'Once upon a time' is an autonomous TL-biased decision motivated by the fact that English fairy tales typically begin with this standard formula. This formulaic expression is a simple genre-marking feature of fairy tales, and is a good example of genre marking as a significant option for the translator. Similarly, TL linguistic etiquette suggests that the German expression 'Meine Damen und Herren' should, in the genre of an oral address, be rendered by the English formula 'Ladies and Gentlemen'. Even ordinary conversation has its share of genre-marking formulae, such as 'ritualized' greetings, to which interpreters need to be sensitive and where the choice of a given formula is a matter of TL etiquette. So, for example, whether to render 'Guten Tag' by 'How do you do', 'Good morning' or 'Hello' has to be an autonomous decision made in the light of target-culture etiquette, with ST tonal register acting as a guideline.

As these simple examples show, genre-marking a TT influences the process of translation in the direction of TL-orientation. This may affect small details or general translation strategy; both types of effect are illustrated in the following extract from Friedrich Dürrenmatt's play *Romulus der Große*. (*Contextual information*. The play is set in 476 AD with the Roman Empire in the very last stages of decadence and bankruptcy and under immediate threat from invading hosts of *Germanen* under Odoaker. Cäsar Rupf, wealthy trouser manufacturer, has just obtained an audience with the Emperor Romulus and is offering to buy off the impending invasion at the price of a marriage alliance with the Imperial family and a law making trouser-wearing compulsory.)

CÄSAR RUPF: Sie sehen, Majestät, ich bin eiskalt. Sie müssen mir ohne mit der Wimper zu zucken zugeben, daß das römische Imperium nur noch durch eine solide Verbindung mit einer erfahrenen Firma gerettet werden kann, sonst kommen die Germanen, die schon vor Rom lauern, mit krachenden Riesenschritten heran. Sie werden mir heute nachmittag Ihre Antwort geben. Wenn nein, heirate ich die Tochter Odoakers. Die Firma Rupf muß an einen Erben denken. Ich bin in den besten Jahren und die Stürme des Geschäftslebens, gegen die eure Schlachten nur Zimperlichkeiten sind, machten es mir bis jetzt unmöglich, das Glück in den Armen einer trauten Gemahlin zu suchen.

(Dürrenmatt, 1957, pp. 32–3)

This text is clearly intended for oral delivery in the social register of the stereotypical 'captain of industry' and in a high-handed, blustering tonal register. Dürrenmatt's text is not, of course, a **transcript** – that is, it does not represent and record a pre-existing oral text. It may (perhaps deliberately) be inconsistent in register in some details – compare the moderately formal 'Sie sehen, Majestät' with the more casual, even contemptuous, 'eure Schlachten' and the peremptory 'Sie werden mir heute nachmittag Ihre Antwort geben'. Nevertheless, Dürrenmatt has included enough features drawn from an appropriate genre of oral address to act as genre-marking cues. Whatever other components there are in the genre to which this monologue belongs (theatre; anachronistic setting; social and political satire), an essential feature is use of a genre of oral address. In the following literal TT, there is no allowance made for these genre-marking features of the ST; this translation strategy yields a poor text for stage performance:

CAESAR RUPF: You see, Majesty, I am as cold as ice. You must admit without batting an eyelid that the Roman Empire can now only be saved by a solid alliance with an experienced firm, otherwise the German tribes, who are already lurking outside Rome, will come crashing in with giant steps. You will give me your answer this afternoon. If not, then I shall marry Odoaker's daughter. The firm of Rupf must think about an heir. I am in my best years, and the storms of business life, compared to which your battles are mere prissiness, have made it impossible for me, until now, to seek happiness in the arms of a faithful spouse.

Compare this TT with one that, in strategic approach, resembles the ST in being a **script** – that is, a written text designed for oral performance. In detail, this TT makes plausible use of communicative translation, clichés, illocutionary particles, contracted forms and pause marks, all as genre-marking features:

CAESAR RUPF: I must make it clear to you, Your Majesty, that I am adamant about this. Look me in the eye and tell me I'm wrong when I say that you've only one option left for saving the Roman Empire at this juncture: and that's by securing a solid alliance with a well-established business firm... otherwise you'll have the Teutons – remember they are lurking outside Rome at this very moment – come crashing in on you like a pack of wolves. I'll expect your answer by this afternoon. If it's 'no', then I'll just have to marry Odoaker's daughter. The Rupf Company must consider the need for an heir. I'm in the prime of life, and the commercial wars I have fought, which, I may say, would make your piffling battles look like storms in a teacup, have so far prevented me from seeking conjugal bliss in the arms of a loving spouse.

As we saw in Chapter 3, communicative translation is a form of cultural transposition. It is usually a crucial factor in genre-marking a TT. In the case of the

Dürrenmatt extract, the translator might decide to go still further by introducing an element of cultural transplant, in order to increase the TL bias of the TT: 'Caesar Rupf' might then give way, say, to 'Caesar Warp', 'the Rupf Company' to 'Warp Incorporated', and 'Teutons' to 'Huns'. (Whether to go this far would, of course, depend on an initial strategic decision about whether to keep Germany as the target of political satire, or to substitute Britain, or the United States.)

TL genre-marking characteristics can be over-used, of course. Compare, for example, these four lines from Brecht's 'Surabaya-Johnny' with the TT that follows:

[...]
Ich hatte es nicht beachtet
Warum du den Namen hast
Aber an der ganzen langen Küste
Warst du ein bekannter Gast.

(Brecht, 1993, pp. 345–6)

[...]
I ne'er did stop to wonder
Why it was that this name you bore
But so well-known a guest you must have been
All along that whole distant shore.

Unlike the ST, the TT is heavily marked for some kind of archaic or folksy 'poetic' genre. This is done through lexical items ('ne'er', 'wonder', 'bore', 'distant'); archaic syntax ('ne'er did stop'); and a combination of rhymes and a dominant anapestic metre bought at the cost of inversion in line 2, padding ('distant') in line 4, and both inversion and padding ('so') in line 3.

The lesson to be learnt from these examples is simple but important: there is a middle course to be steered between under-marking genre-features, as in the literal translation of the Dürrenmatt extract, and over-marking them, as in the Brecht TT.

A particular genre-marking translation problem occurs in the case of STs heavily marked by slang. Sociolect and register are crucial here, but so is the fact that languages differ from one another in respect of the referential domains covered by slang, and in the kinds of slang available. The example given below comes from U. Plenzdorf's *Die neuen Leiden des jungen W.*; we suggest devoting some time in Practical 12 to the translation problems it raises. (*Contextual information.* The teenage first-person protagonist has just been reading Goethe's *Die Leiden des jungen Werther* and is voicing his reactions to the story.)

Nach zwei Seiten schoß ich den Vogel in die Ecke. Leute, das konnte wirklich kein Schwein lesen. Beim besten Willen nicht. Fünf Minuten später hatte ich den Vogel wieder in der Hand. Entweder ich wollte bis früh lesen oder nicht. Das war meine Art. Drei Stunden später hatte ich es hinter mir.

Ich war fast gar nicht sauer! Der Kerl in dem Buch, dieser Werther, wie er hieß, macht am Schluß Selbstmord. Gibt einfach den Löffel ab. Schießt sich ein

Loch in seine olle Birne, weil er die Frau nicht kriegen kann, die er haben will, und tut sich ungeheuer leid dabei. Wenn er nicht völlig verblödet war, mußte er doch sehen, daß sie nur darauf wartete, daß er was *machte*, diese Charlotte. Ich meine, wenn ich mit einer Frau allein im Zimmer bin und wenn ich weiß, vor einer halben Stunde oder so kommt keiner da rein, Leute, dann versuch ich doch *alles*. Kann sein, ich handle mir ein paar Schellen ein, na und? Immer noch besser als eine verpaßte Gelegenheit. Außerdem gibt es höchstens in zwei von zehn Fällen Schellen. Das ist Tatsache. Und dieser Werther war...zigmal mit ihr allein. Schon in diesem Park. Und was macht er? Er sieht ruhig zu, wie sie heiratet. Und dann murkst er sich ab. Dem war nicht zu helfen.

(Plenzdorf, 1973, p. 36)

CROSSOVER BETWEEN ORAL AND WRITTEN GENRES

Except in some forms of (bilateral or simultaneous) interpreting, translators actually do a great deal of their work in a written medium. This means that when their ST is in an oral medium, or in a written medium whose basis lies in an oral genre, or when the eventual TT is meant for oral performance, the translation process crosses over the important boundary between oral and written texts. This is easily overlooked, but merits serious attention by translators. Given that both ST and TT are, ideally, carefully genre-marked, one should not lose sight of the inevitable metamorphoses resulting from the conversion of an oral text into a written one, and conversely, of a written text into an oral one. These metamorphoses are due partly to the lack of precise correspondence between speech and writing (see Chapter 6, pp. 63–5), which makes writing a pale copy of speech in terms of expressive force, and partly to the different genre-marking expectations associated with oral and written genres. The point is that in crossing over from oral to written versions of a ST important genre-marking features may be lost in transcription (for example, the oral register features of the Dürrenmatt extract on p. 135); while, in producing a written TT that is ultimately to be converted into an orally performed one, the translator may fail to indicate, or even allow for, the inclusion of suitable oral genre-marking features in the TT script (as in the first version of the Dürrenmatt TT on p. 136). There is also the analogous problem of transposing or implanting into written texts genre-marking features with oral origins, like the slang in the extract from *Die neuen Leiden des jungen W.* given above.

Crossover in the process of translation may take a number of forms. Four in particular deserve mention here. In the first, the translator starts with a live or recorded ST in an oral medium, transfers to the use of a written transcript, and then composes a TT which is a script suitable for oral performance: *song lyrics* are typically translated in this way. In the second form of crossover, the translator starts with a written script, transfers to considerations of how the ST might be orally performed and then composes a TT which is a script suitable for eventual oral performance: this is the usual process by which *plays* are translated. In a third type of case, the translator starts with an oral ST and its transcript, but produces a TT suitable for silent reading (though perhaps with some suggestion of the oral origins of the ST): *film subtitles* are typically produced in this way. In the fourth type, the translator starts with a written script, has recourse to oral performance of the ST, but produces a TT suitable for silent reading (though, again, perhaps with a hint of the oral properties of the ST): poetry will usually be translated in this way.

In discussing crossover between oral and written genres, drama texts deserve special mention. Dramatic traditions in different cultures are usually markedly different, despite various degrees of cross-fertilization. This implies that the translation of stage-plays will often involve an element of genre-transposition, in deference to the different expectations and tastes of TL audiences. (In any case, as the Dürrenmatt example shows, the appearance of spontaneity essential to a stage performance often implies that a faithful ST-oriented translation is inappropriate, since it would not sound plausible.) On the other hand, complete transposition of the TT into some traditional TL genre may mean that the point is lost, and with it the merits of the ST. Thus, a translation of the later Schiller plays as an imitation of the genre of Shakespearean tragedy would fail on at least two counts: the TT would convey none of the merits of the genre of the Schiller works, and retain little or nothing of the merits of the genre of Shakespearean tragedy. The translations of stage drama that are most successful from the performing point of view are usually based on compromises between reflecting some of the features that confer merit on the ST and adopting or adapting features of an existing TL dramatic genre.

(Care must be taken, of course, in translating plays that deliberately trade on incongruity for the creation of absurd effects resulting from the clash between the improbability of the plot or dialogue and the apparent spontaneity of performance. Our earlier example of Dürrenmatt's *Romulus der Große* is a case in point. In such cases, one of the translator's main tasks is to preserve the absurdity of this clash, otherwise the TT could lose its satirical impact.)

Related to theatre is film, but film dialogue presents special problems for translators. Putting aside the alternatives of subtitling and voice-over (which is normally only used in certain kinds of documentary), actual oral translation of film dialogue requires *dubbing* – that is, creating the impression that the TT heard by the audience is actually the text spoken by the characters on screen. This impression depends largely on the skill of the dubbing specialist in synchronizing the oral TT with the movements, facial expressions and lip movements of the screen actors.

Dubbing is difficult to do successfully, and a more feasible alternative is subtitling. A subtitle is not an oral TT, but an excellent example of crossover between an oral ST and a written TT. It has special requirements, however. First, it is essentially a form of gist translation. Second, while working in a written medium, under very tight constraints of time and space, the translator will usually want to produce a TT that, within reason, hints at some of the characteristics of the oral style of the ST. These may include features of social register, tonal register, dialect, sociolect, and so on. While it would be difficult, unnecessary and undesirable to pay attention to every little quirk of the oral delivery of the ST, it could also be unfortunate to produce an over-polished TT suggesting that the ST speaker 'talks like a book'. Here, as ever, compromise seems to be indicated, between making the subtitles easily digestible as a written text and injecting into them features reminiscent of an appropriate oral style.

The special requirements of subtitling make it into a very useful exercise for students, because it forces them to focus especially clearly on many of the issues raised in this chapter and the previous one. Even without the equipment for subtitling film or videotape, a useful practical can still be done simply using an audiocassette. An exercise of this types figures in Practical 12. To assist in preparation for it, we end this chapter with some general notes on subtitling as practised by professionals (for which we are indebted to John Minchinton), followed by a sample of the amateur version using an audiocassette.

NOTES ON SUBTITLING

The subtitler-translator usually has a dialogue list, that is, a transcript of all the verbal contents of the film. The dialogue list does not include details of cuts. The subtitler runs the film on a viewing/editing table, measuring the time of each phrase, sentence and shot to determine when titles should start and stop. This process is called 'spotting'. The technicalities of spotting vary, depending on whether one is working with 35mm film or videotape, but the essential rules are the same:

- A single-line subtitle requires at least two seconds' viewing time.
- A double-line subtitle requires at least four seconds.
- Never show a title for less than two seconds or more than six seconds.
- Avoid carrying a title over a cut (except, for example, in newsreel with many cuts).
- Voices off, such as telephone voices or narrations, are in italics (unless the speaker is present but simply not in camera view).
- Observe the basic rules of punctuation, but, where the end of a subtitle coincides with the end of a sentence, omit the full stop.
- In double-line titles, try to make the second line shorter than the first, but do not be inflexible: it is most important that the first line should read well and not end clumsily.
- Make every title a clear statement. Avoid ambiguity (unless the ST is deliberately or significantly ambiguous): viewers have only a limited time to take in the message, and cannot turn back as they can with a book or a newspaper.
- When a sentence is split over more than one title, end the first one with three suspension points, and begin the next one with three suspension points.
- Do not use telegraphese, because viewers do not have the time to work it out.

When timings are short, it is sometimes helpful to have two speakers' dialogue as a double-line subtitle (ideally for question and answer). In such cases, use a dash to introduce each line, and justify left, so that the titles are not centred on the screen. For example:

– Where have they gone today?
– To the country

Here is an example of how to split a sentence over two or more titles. The text itself conveys the point we are making: 'In such cases, it is especially important to make each title sensible in itself, unless the speaker is rambling, delirious, or similar, so that viewers maintain a steady understanding of the dialogue'. This sentence might be effectively subtitled as follows:

Title 1	In such cases...
Title 2	...it is especially important to make each title sensible in itself...
Title 3	...unless the speaker is rambling, delirious, or similar...
Title 4	...so that viewers maintain a steady understanding of the dialogue

Here is an example of how *not* to do it:

Title 1	In such cases, it is especially...
Title 2	...important to make each title sensible...
Title 3	...in itself, unless the speaker is rambling, delirious, or similar, so that...
Title 4	...viewers maintain a steady understanding of the dialogue

Apart from other errors, the weakness of this version is that breaks between titles correspond to neither the structure nor the oral phrasing of the sentence. Despite the suspension points, Title 2 looks like the end of a sentence or clause, and Title 3 like the start of one. The result is that the 'unless...' clause looks like a clause parenthetically inserted in mid-sentence: the text might seem to be saying 'In itself, unless the speaker is rambling in such a way that viewers maintain a steady understanding [...]'. But the anticipated resolution of this apparent sentence does not materialize, so that the viewer is (at best) momentarily puzzled.

NB The maximum number of spaces allowed for a line of title varies, depending on the equipment used. We shall take as an example a maximum of 36, which is not untypical. This includes letters, spaces between words, and punctuation marks. So, for instance, the following line of title is exactly 36 spaces long:

...so that viewers maintain a steady

Sample subtitling exercise using audiocassette

Dialogue list (from the television interview in Practical 9)

> Als Negschdes, muß ich-mer mol werrer de Grobb leermache, – dann weller Häpprumer is net voll Rouches – weil-se uns die Schiller-Lind an de Poscht umgemoacht häwe!! Äs letschde griene Pläckel im Härze där Stadt! Äs is noch mäih wie-e Schann – äs is-en Frewel. Do is uff alle 'Planerei' gepeffe, wann niks woas ahm lieb wa, erhalde wärrn konn. Un a-noch Bensemer solles gewäst soi – häb ich-mer-soa-losse – die wu-se umgeläigt heen.

Spotting
Following the taped text on the dialogue list, mark off convenient sections coinciding, if possible, with pauses and intonational cues in the spoken delivery. Each of these sections will subsequently form the basis of a subtitle. At the end of spotting, the dialogue list should look something like this:

> Als Negschdes, muß ich-mer mol werrer de Grobb leermache,/ – dann weller Häpprumer is net voll Rouches/ – weil-se uns die Schiller-Lind an de Poscht umgemoacht häwe!!/ Äs letschde griene Pläckel im Härze där Stadt!/ Äs is noch mäih wie-e Schann – äs is-en Frewel./ Do is uff alle 'Planerei' gepeffe,/ wann niks woas ahm lieb wa, erhalde wärrn konn./ Un a-noch Bensemer solles gewäst soi – häb ich-mer-soa-losse – die wu-se umgeläigt heen./

Timing
The sections marked off in spotting are numbered, and the time between the start of one section and the start of the next is measured (with a stopwatch if possible, but the second-hand of a watch will do very well for our purposes). The timing of the subtitles is based on these measurements. (*Remember that any pauses in and between sentences are part of the overall time the text lasts.* They are invaluable allies for the subtitler, because they give extra time for viewers to read and digest the titles.) The timed list should look like this:

Title 1	4.0 sec	Als...leermache,
Title 2	3.5	– dann weller...Rouches
Title 3	4.0	– weil-se...umgemoacht häwe!!
Title 4	3.5	Äs letschde...där Stadt!
Title 5	4.0	Äs is...en Frewel.
Title 6	7.0	Do is...wärrn konn.
Title 7	6.5	Un a-noch...umgeläigt heen.

Creating subtitles
Each of the spottings into which the dialogue list has been divided is translated into English, observing the following constraints:

(i) *Not more than two lines* can be shown on the screen at once.
(ii) *Lines cannot be longer than 36 spaces*, as explained on p. 141.
(iii) The maximum time available for displaying each subtitle is given by the

timing measurements above; allow at least *two seconds for a single-line title*, and at least *four seconds for a double-line title* (but not more than six seconds for any title).

Here is a possible TT:

Title 1	4.0 sec	And now, I've just *got* to get another thing off my chest
Title 2	3.5	'Cos everyone in Heppenheim...
Title 3	4.0	...is up in arms about how they've cut down our Schiller-tree
Title 4	3.5	The last patch of green in the town!
Title 5	4.0	And it was people from Bensheim that did it, let me tell you
Title 6	6.0 (+1)	It's not just a shame – it's a bloomin' liberty!
Title 7	6.0 (+0.5)	So much for planning, if you can't keep something everybody loves

(NB The times given in brackets are moments during which no title is shown.) Note that the order of the speaker's sentences has been changed, for the express purpose of subtitling. The TT follows a more 'logical' order of the speaker's grievances, not the order in which she mentions them. To see why this was done, compare our TT with the following one, which keeps the ST order:

Title 1	4.0 sec	And now, I've just *got* to get another thing off my chest
Title 2	3.5	'Cos everyone in Heppenheim...
Title 3	4.0	...is up in arms about how they've cut down our Schiller-tree
Title 4	3.5	The last patch of green in the town!
Title 5	4.0	It's not just a shame – it's a bloomin' liberty!
Title 6	6.0 (+1)	So much for planning, if you can't keep something everybody loves
Title 7	6.0 (+0.5)	And it was people from Bensheim that did it, let me tell you

As with any subtitled text, the message is given in a series of short bursts, each of which disappears for good after a few seconds. Therefore, as we have seen, viewers need to concentrate harder than readers (who can see the whole text on a page and go at their own pace) or even listeners (who have phonic and prosodic cues to help them assimilate important information). These factors create a particular problem in the last sentence of our second TT where information is fed in 'out of turn'. That is, although the speaker is complaining that the people who actually cut down the tree came from neighbouring Bensheim (one suspects a history of ill-feeling between the two localities), the TT reads as if the Bensheimers were responsible for the 'planning'. For the reader to realize that the antecedent of 'that did *it*' is not in the immediately preceding title, but in the earlier 'cut down our Schiller-tree', requires a certain mental agility of anyone, but most of all of film viewers. Keeping the ST order in the subtitles may well put viewers on the wrong track, or puzzle them momentarily by making them ask 'What did the Bensheimers do? Were they the town planners?'. While they are sorting this out, they will not register the next subtitle properly, and could end up losing the thread altogether. (Students should be on the lookout for similar problems in Practical 12.)

This, then, is why we changed the ST order in our first TT. Normally, 'improving' a ST in this or any other way is not necessary or desirable, but, for reasons of 'user-friendliness', it is sometimes a serious option in oral-to-oral translating (especially interpreting), in cases of crossover between oral and written texts (in either direction, but especially in subtitling), and, as we shall see in Chapter 13 and Practical 13, in empirical/descriptive or persuasive/prescriptive texts where the paramount concern is maximal clarity.

PRACTICAL 12

12.1 Subtitling

Assignment
Working in groups:

(i) Listen to the recording of the following ST, and discuss the strategic decisions that have to be made before translating it into film subtitles; outline your own strategy for doing so.
(ii) Treating the text as a dialogue list, use a stopwatch or wristwatch to convert it into a list with timed spottings.
(iii) Translate the text into English subtitles; lay your TT out as already shown. (Remember to indicate 'gaps' during which no title is shown.)
(iv) Explain the main decisions of detail you made in producing your TT.

Contextual information
The ST is a narrative told in Westfälisch dialect by a man reminiscing about the old days of his childhood. The names he mentions are 'Professor Dr Franz Hitze' and 'Pfarrer Sievering'. The place-name 'Haanentse' corresponds to Hochdeutsch 'Hanemicke'. For the purposes of subtitling, imagine that the soundtrack is taken from a documentary film about pre-war Germany, to be shown on Channel 4. A true dialogue list does not contain details of cuts, but, since this is an audiocassette, you are here given details of the cuts; these are marked by asterisks in the text.

Text

*Un wo ik da graad fon den Missedaine schreake, då möcht ik doch ens, iäbm doch dat Stückelsin fertällen, wat mir sainertsait passeerte unger dem allen Proofesser Frants Doktor Frants Hitse, der Raichstagsabjeordnete. Dä kam hiir in siinen Feeriien in siine Heïmat hiin, nå Haanentse, **un kaam dann Sunndachmarjens met siinem Kutchwaagen jefooert un deï dann in die Ruua so'n Schnappmissken, dat duurte so'n Veertelstunt oder twintich Minuuten. ***Un wai immer de Misse dainte, dai kreech dåfiir twintich odder fiiwentwintich Penninge. Då wåren wii jewant bii unserm Paschtooor, då hockte wii uns in de Sakrischtai, wen we 'n Altåår affjerüümet haant un kreïgent dann den Siägen. ****Un ... ik haat nuu de Misse gedaint, un dachte de ganße Misse an deï fiiwentwintich Pennige, un da ho' ik mii natüürlik as ik et jewann un jelaart haa, fom 'me Siiverink, hock ik mik in dä Schtuuf in de Sakrischtai un da schtallte sik de groute Mann für mik un sachte: 'Na, Junge, wat is dii nuu laiwer, de Siägen odder fiiwentwintich Penninge?' Ik dachte, wann die jäts sächs: 'De Siägen', dann geïst de widder liäch heïme; ik sachte gants äärlik: 'Fiiwentwintich Pennige!' 'Hast rächt jemaaket', sacht' he, 'dann kriss de auk noch dain Siägen dabii.'

* cut to interviewee
** cut to view of village, with church
*** cut to inside of church, with view of altar
**** cut to interviewee

Reprinted from Kultureller Tonbanddienst,
Deutsche Dialekte (Bonn: Inter Nationes, pp. 88–9).

12.2 Speed translation

Assignment

You will be asked to translate a text given to you in class by your tutor, who will tell you how long you have for the exercise.

13

Technical translation

In so far as all texts can be categorized in terms of genre, there is no reason why one particular genre should be singled out for special attention rather than any other. However, since most language students lack training in science or technology, and are often in awe of 'technical' texts, we feel the need to devote a separate chapter to problems confronting the translator of texts in this genre-category. By 'technical' translation we mean translation of empirical/descriptive texts written in the context of scientific or technological disciplines. As a matter of fact, any specialist field, from anthropology to zymurgy via banking, history, numismatics and yachting, has its own 'technical' register, its own jargon, its own genre-marking characteristics, with which translators should be familiar if they are to produce convincing TTs in the appropriate field. In any case, the problems met in translating technical texts are to a great extent no different from those met in translating in any genre, specialized or not. Textual variables are textual variables, particularizations are particularizations, whatever the genre and whatever the subject matter; and the relative merits of literal and communicative translation need to be considered in translating any text. Nevertheless, the very fact that technical texts are at the far extreme of unfamiliarity for most language students makes them especially valuable illustrations of all these points. There are two reasons, then, for devoting a chapter to technical translation: first, because it is often so unnerving for language students; and second, because it is so exemplary of issues crucial to translation methodology.

A notable generic property of technical texts is that they are seldom aimed at complete non-specialists. Thus, in subject matter and comprehension, the typical technical ST is not easily accessible to most native SL speakers, let alone to those who have learnt the SL as a foreign language. There are three main reasons for this relative inaccessibility. One is lexical and the other two are conceptual. All three can be illustrated from the following text, to which we shall refer in our discussion:

Hinweise auf Funktionstrennung bei *Parus*-Arten ergeben sich wie folgt:

1) Bei Territorialgesang: Bestimmte Strophentypen wurden besonders bei Auseinandersetzungen (bei Anlockung mit Klangattrappen), jedoch nicht

so oft spontan gesungen (z.B. SMITH 1972, MARTENS 1975, FICKEN et al. 1978). Hier liegt also eine Funktionstrennung im Sinne von Revierverteidigung im Gegensatz zu Revierproklamation vor.

2) ♀-bezogene Strophentypen: Eine Trennung des Repertoires in ♀-bezogene und revierverteidigungsbezogene Strophentypen ist nachzuweisen (vgl. z.B. ROMANOWSKI 1978, SCHROEDER & WILEY 1983b, GADDIS 1983).

(F. Goller, 1987, p. 306)

LEXICAL PROBLEMS IN TECHNICAL TRANSLATION

There are three sorts of problem arising from the specialized use of technical terms. First, there is the obvious problem of terms not used in everyday, ordinary language, and which are, therefore, unfamiliar to the lay translator. The text given above contains an example of this problem. A term such as ‘Klangattrappen’ is instantly recognizable as belonging only to a specialized scientific context. Without specialist knowledge, therefore, translators can neither guess the exact meaning of the term nor make a reliable guess at its correct TL rendering.

The second problem is that of terms whose ordinary uses are familiar to the translator, but which are manifestly used in some other, technically specialized, way in the ST. That is, the familiar senses of the terms do not help the translator to find a rendering of their technical senses. Almost any technology has such lexical pitfalls. Mining technology, for example, appropriately enough, is rich in these. No one who has lived in the Ruhr will fail to gloss ‘über Tage’ as ‘surface’, but the UK-based translator may find this puzzling. Similarly puzzling is ‘Raubaktion’ (in a 1980s EC publication) used in the sense of ‘recovery operation’. (Another source of such pitfalls in German lies in the fact that compound words may occasionally cleave in an unexpected way: ‘die Strebenden’ in mining is probably not (romantically) ‘the toilers’ but (prosaically) ‘the face ends’.)

Third, a term may have an ordinary, everyday sense that is not obviously wrong in the context. This is the most dangerous sort of case, because the translator may not even recognize the term as a technical term, and carelessly render it in its ordinary sense. For example, ‘Auseinandersetzung’, in the ornithology text above, is glossed in a standard 1980 dictionary as ‘discussion, debate; argument; clash; examination; analysis’. A standard 1990 dictionary offers much the same range, but additionally ‘dispute’ – with a field-name linking it to industrial relations. The right technical translation in animal behaviour certainly lies well within the range of meanings implied by the dictionary glosses; but the translator needs experience or advice in order to select ‘dispute’, and in the present context no other term will do. Likewise, a translator in a hurry might (especially if Arts-trained) translate ‘Anlockung mit Klangattrappen’ (in the same text) as ‘enticement with sound-lures’, where the ornithologist expects ‘attracting with playbacks’.

As these examples show, access to technical dictionaries and up-to-date data-banks is indispensable for translators of technical texts. However, not even these source materials can be guaranteed to keep the translator out of difficulties. For one thing, technical texts are liable to be innovative – why publish them unless they make some new contribution? This means that dictionaries and data-banks must always lag slightly behind the most up-to-date use of technical terms. Second, even the best source materials do not necessarily give a single, unambiguous synonym for a particular technical term, so that the translator may still have to make an informed choice between alternatives. Finally, even established technical terms are sometimes used loosely or informally in technical texts, in which case it may be misleading to render them by their technical TL synonyms. All of this suggests that the normal limitations on the use of dictionaries apply also to technical translation, but in a particularly acute form. That is, translators can only select the appropriate TL terminology from a range of alternatives offered by the dictionary if they have a firm grasp of the immediate textual context and of the wider technical context. The problem is not lessened, of course, by the awkward fact that some of the context may remain obscure until the correct sense of the ST terms has been identified. This brings us to the two conceptual reasons why technical texts may be difficult to translate.

CONCEPTUAL PROBLEMS IN TECHNICAL TRANSLATION

The first type of conceptual problem is caused by failure to understand the background assumptions and knowledge taken for granted by experts in a science, but not shared by non-specialists and not explicit in the ST. This is another point that can be illustrated from the above text. In the sentence '♀-bezogene Strophentypen: Eine Trennung des Repertoires in ♀-bezogene und revierverteidigungsbezogene Strophentypen ist nachzuweisen', the phrase 'ist nachzuweisen' is potentially ambiguous. Purely syntactically, it may be construed either as meaning 'is/needs to be demonstrated' or 'is demonstrable'. This ambiguity is almost certainly not present for the author or for the expert SL reader who is up to date with current research and knows whether the distinction in question has been proved or not. But the translator effectively has to choose between 'remains to be demonstrated' and 'is demonstrable'; the wrong choice will seriously mislead the less expert TL reader, and will damage the translator's reputation (and possibly the author's too) with those who do know the score. In this case, it took a bird-song specialist to resolve the issue in favour of 'remains to be demonstrated'. Translation problems like this are generally easily resolved by any TL speaker with a basic grasp of the technical discipline in question. Non-specialist translators, however, may reach a conceptual impasse from which no amount of attention to syntax or vocabulary can rescue them. In that case they have only two options: study the technical field in which they are translating, or work in close consultation with experts.

The most intractable problems in technical translation arise in translating the development of new ideas. In such an instance, even basic background knowledge may be insufficient to save the translator from a conceptual impasse. This is the second conceptual reason for inaccessibility in technical texts. What one might call the 'logic' of a discipline – methods of argumentation, the development of relations between concepts – is normally specific to that discipline. There may therefore be translation problems that hinge crucially on that logic. It may transpire that the translator is quite unable to solve a conceptual problem of this nature, and that the only alternative is to consult either an expert or, if necessary (and if possible), the author of the ST.

Even in less advanced texts, the translator may face serious conceptual difficulties in grasping the 'logic' of a discipline, in particular the relationship between concepts. This is illustrated in the following sentence from the biochemistry text used in Practical 13 (p. 153):

> Die Isolierung von Enzymfragmenten oder defekten Enzymen aus Mutanten erlaubt jedoch die kinetische Analyse einzelner Aminosäurebindungsstellen.

Without a grasp of enzyme chemistry in general, and of the particular problems and research techniques discussed in the text, one cannot be absolutely sure whether, in the above sentence, 'kinetische Analyse' is the *object* or the *subject* of the verb 'erlaubt'. Judging by its internal syntax and morphology, the sentence may potentially be construed in either of two diametrically opposed ways: 'But the isolation... makes kinetic analysis... possible', or 'But kinetic analysis... makes the isolation... possible'.

Experience in German will tell the non-biochemist translator two things: first, there is an excellent chance that the correct order here is object-verb-subject; second, the essential evidence (when not available from word-endings or word-order internally) must be sought in the context, more precisely, in terms of the development of the argument. (The only real internal evidence, 'jedoch', underlines the relevance of context.) But the surrounding argument throughout the abstract is so technical that even the closest and most sensitive linguistic analysis is bound to be less reliable (and less cost-effective) than a brief consultation with a biochemist. Trying to 'crack' a technical text on linguistic experience alone is valuable for honing one's translation skills, and fun as a challenge; but to deliver a *useful* TT (in this case the subject-verb-object version) may well require consultation.

To summarize thus far: the non-specialist is not sufficiently equipped for producing reliable technical TTs guaranteed to be useful to technical experts in the target culture. Prospective technical translators must acquire as soon as possible some degree of technical competence in the field in which they intend to work. Training technical translators usually has this as its main target. Such training cannot be general, however: technical translators can only train by specializing in particular fields. Naturally, a combination of an academic degree in a science and a qualification in a foreign language is an ideal background for a technical translator. However, not even people with this kind of qualification can expect to keep abreast of research while at the same time earning a living as translators, and they will sooner or later come up against problems that can only be solved by consulting technical experts.

These remarks about the need for consultation are not to be taken lightly. They raise the important question of the responsibility – and perhaps the legal liability – of the translator. There is a difference here between literary translation and technical translation. It is not that literary translators are not held responsible for their published TTs, but that the practical implications of mistranslation are seldom as serious for them as for technical translators, whose one mistake could cause financial damage or loss of life and limb. This is another respect in which technical translation is exemplary, bringing out extremely clearly a golden rule which is in fact essential to all translation: *never be too proud or embarrassed to ask for help or advice.*

The spectre of legal liability is a reminder that even the minutest error of detail on any level of textual variables is typically magnified in a technical text. This is not surprising, given that matters of factual correctness rank maximally high in empirical/descriptive genres. Some such errors are in the category of *faux amis* – banal, but no less potentially embarrassing. For example, in a medical text, translating 'Ambulanz' as 'ambulance' where it should be 'Outpatients Department' could at the very least cause confusion.

Much more dangerous (and more likely, if the translator is not a specialist) is confusion between closely similar technical names. Consider, for example, the profusion of possible permutations between minutely differentiated prefixes and suffixes that can be attached to the root 'sulph':

per-		
bi-		-ate
di-	sulph	-ite
hypo-		-ide
hydro-		-onate

Obviously, the slightest error in affixation here will constitute a major factual error, whereas, in non-technical language, slight differences in affixation may often be unimportant. For example, in German, there is a fine but clear distinction of meaning between the adverbs 'rechtens' and 'rechtlich'. 'Rechtens' might well be used by a lawyer in court to mean 'legally', but it has its natural place in the field of private judgement and can have moral connotations. At the personal/moral end of its range, it approximates to 'by rights'. 'Rechtlich' means 'legally' in the sense of 'in law', 'in the eyes of the law', 'as defined by law'. In technical texts, the difference between the two terms must be scrupulously observed. In non-technical texts, the translator *may* choose to render either term as (among other options) 'by rights', prompted more by considerations of genre and register than by those of literal accuracy. Similarly, there is only a relatively subtle difference in English between 'disbelieving' and 'unbelieving', or between 'continuous' and 'continual'. In literary texts one can, to some extent, base such choices on questions of euphony or style. But that temptation must be resisted absolutely in translating technical terms.

Again, in a literary text, choosing the wrong synonym is, at worst, a stylistic error; but in a technical text it might create a serious misnomer showing ignorance, thus undermining the reader's confidence in the text. For example, it is not immaterial, in a given chemical context, whether vanilla is referred to by its trivial name 'vanilla', its technical name 'vanillin', its old systematic name '4-hydroxy-3-methoxybenzaldehyde', or its empirical formula $C_8H_8O_3$.

Some parts of technical texts may be expressed with mathematical precision. (Indeed they may actually be formulated in mathematical symbols, in which case they only need a modicum of effort in translation. Mathematical formulae cannot always be literally transcribed, however; one of the elementary things to note in this respect is the mathematical use of the comma on the Continent, where British conventions require the use of a decimal point.) In these cases, the most important thing is for the TT to achieve the same standard of mathematical precision as the ST.

However, even the driest technical text is bound to have more informal passages – perhaps introductory, parenthetical or concluding remarks in ordinary, or even colloquial, prose. Such passages pose another kind of problem for the technical translator, for it is here that the technical author may let personality intrude, or even deliberately cultivate a persona. Thus, although technical translators are chiefly accountable for the literal and factual content of the ST, they cannot always remain insensitive to such stylistic ploys as register, connotation, humour, polemic, and so on. The TT should at least not spoil, cancel or contradict what is to be read between the lines in the ST. The overall register of the text – if only the question of pompous versus casual style – is also a matter of concern. To this extent at least, no text can avoid being the result of stylistic choices. In short, as we suggested at the beginning of this chapter, technical translators should not see themselves as having nothing in common with, for example, literary translators. On the contrary, because problems of style affect all texts, all translators have problems and methods in common. To this we must add that, while 'factuality' may on the face of it appear antithetical to 'style', textual factuality can itself be a kind of style, or even a pose.

Returning finally to the question of error and accuracy, there is – as with any text – the problem of what to do if the ST is badly written, or ungrammatical, or even factually deficient. Should the deficiencies of the ST be reflected in the TT, or should they be ironed out? This is a general and controversial issue. In our view, translators are not in principle responsible for 'improving' defective STs. However, we saw in the last chapter that this may sometimes be advisable in dealing with oral texts. It is more strongly advisable, perhaps even necessary, in the case of technical texts – or indeed any empirical/descriptive or prescriptive text – because the paramount concern is factual accuracy. If there is any ambiguity, obscurity or error in the ST, and it is potentially misleading or dangerous, there is every reason to keep it out of the TT – if necessary (as ever) after consultation with the author or an expert. Failing that, the translator may feel the need to append a translator's note to the TT calling attention to the deficiency in the ST.

Many of our examples in this chapter were drawn from the text on pp. 146–7. As part of Practical 13, the problems in this text should be analysed, and a translation attempted. The work on Practical 13 will show that, apart from the lexical and conceptual problems outlined above, technical translation is not essentially different from most other sorts of prose translation: as long as specialist help can be called on (and students should be strongly encouraged to enlist the aid of their own technical advisers), there is no reason why technical translation in most fields should be more daunting than translation in any other genre.

PRACTICAL 13

13.1 Technical translation

Assignment

(i) Discuss the strategic problems confronting the translator of the text given on pp. 146–7, and outline your own strategy for translating it.
(ii) Translate the text into English.
(iii) Explain the main decisions of detail you made in producing your TT.

NB We give no contextual information for this text (apart from the points made in Chapter 13). This is so that you can distinguish clearly between the problems requiring specialist knowledge and those raised by the usual characteristic differences between German and English.

13.2 Technical translation

Assignment
Working in groups:

(i) Discuss the strategic problems confronting the translator of the following text, and outline your own strategy for translating it.
(ii) Translate the text into English.
(iii) Explain the main decisions of detail you made in producing your TT.

Contextual information
The passage is the final section of an abstract of about 200 words, published in a German scientific journal. (One footnoted reference has been omitted.)

Text

Problematisch ist die Untersuchung der Bindung von Substratanaloga von Valin und Leucin. So wird in Abwesenheit von Valin die Synthese von 3,3′-Leucin-GS katalysiert. Isoleucin und Norleucin werden ebenfalls an beiden Bindungsstellen aktiviert. Die Isolierung von Enzymfragmenten oder defekten Enzymen aus Mutanten erlaubt jedoch die kinetische Analyse einzelner Aminosäurebindungsstellen. Aus der Kurahashi-Mutante *hh* von *Bacillus brevis* konnte ein GS 2-Fragment von 2.6 x 10^5 Dalton isoliert werden, das Leucin nicht aktiviert, jedoch eine unveränderte Valin-Bindungsstelle besitzt. Limitierte Proteolyse mit Chymotrypsin führt zur Inaktivierung der Valin-Bindungsstelle auf GS 2.

Adapted from Altmann, M. und Kittelberger, R., 'Gramicidin-S-Synthetase: Kinetik der Aktivierungsreaktionen', *Hoppe-Seyler's Zeitschrift für physiologische Chemie*, Vol. 360, 1, 1979, pp. 224–5.

13.3 Technical translation

Assignment
Working in groups:

(i) Discuss the strategic problems confronting the translator of the following text, and outline your own strategy for translating it.
(ii) Translate the text into English.
(iii) Explain the main decisions of detail you made in producing your TT.
(iv) Discuss the published TT, which will be given to you by your tutor.

Contextual information
The passage is the German abstract at the beginning of an article, 'Superoxiddismutasenaktivität von Ginkgo-biloba-Extrakt', by Matthias Diwok, Bodo Kuklinski and Bruno Ernst, published in a German medical journal. (Footnoted references have been omitted.)

Text

Superoxiddismutasenaktivität von Ginkgo-biloba-Extrakt
Matthias Diwok, Bodo Kuklinski, Bruno Ernst
3 Abbildungen und 3 Tabellen

Zusammenfassung

Das Ginkgo-biloba-Extrakt wird aus grünen Blättern des Ginkgo-biloba-Baumes gewonnen. Präparate mit diesem Wirkstoff werden u.a. zur Behandlung von Hirnleistungsstörungen und arteriosklerotischen Erkrankungen genutzt. In In-vitro- und In-vivo-Studien wurden Radical Scavenger- und PAF (platelet activating factor)-antagonistische Wirkungen beschrieben. In dieser Arbeit konnte eine konzentrationsabhängige Superoxiddismutasenaktivität des Ginkgo-biloba-Extraktes rökan-flüssig nachgewiesen werden.

Code: Ginkgo-biloba – Superoxiddismutasenaktivität – freie Sauerstoff-radikale

Adapted from Diwok, M., Kuklinski, B. and Ernst, B., 'Superoxiddismutasenaktivität von Ginkgo-biloba-Extrakt', in *Zeitschrift gesamte Inn. Med.*, 47, 1992, pp. 308–11, copyright © Georg Thieme Verlag, Stuttgart – New York.

14

Translation of consumer-oriented texts

A real translation, as distinct from a translation done as an academic exercise, is always produced in response to the specific demands of an audience, a publisher or some other paymaster. This puts a particular kind of pressure on the translator. We have tried to simulate such demands and pressures in some of the practicals in this course, for example by asking for a TT that can be sung to a particular tune, or a TT suitable for subtitles. These exercises are necessarily artificial, but they do make it clear that TTs are purpose-made texts, their manner of formulation heavily influenced, both strategically and in detail, by who and what they are intended for. It is to emphasize this vital point that we are giving an entire chapter to consumer-oriented texts, for the decisive influence of 'translation-for-a-purpose' is nowhere more strongly felt than in translating such texts.

Of course, all texts are in a certain sense consumer-oriented. One may assume that every type of text appeals to the tastes of a particular audience. In that sense, short stories are consumer-oriented to satisfy readers who enjoy short stories, television soap operas are consumer-oriented to satisfy viewers who like watching soap, and so forth. The first thing a publisher asks when offered a manuscript is what potential readership there is for the text. The whole question of saleability turns primarily on this kind of consumer orientation.

However, consumer orientation has a much more acute form in texts that do not merely 'sell' themselves, but have other things to 'sell'. These are texts that fall into the persuasive/prescriptive genre, texts whose main purpose is to recommend commodities, attitudes, or courses of action.

The most transparently consumer-oriented sub-category of this genre is advertising. Indeed, one may initially think of this genre as epitomized by advertising copy. The self-evident consumer-oriented purpose of advertising is to boost sales of particular commodities. However, many advertising campaigns show that sales promotion techniques shade into the promotion of opinions, beliefs, attitudes and courses of action. Examples are government health warnings about smoking, drug-abuse and AIDS. Along with party-political election campaigns, these examples point to a flourishing genre of texts directly aimed at instructing and persuading audiences to do or not to do (as well as to think or not to think) a wide gamut of things. Consumer-oriented texts consequently share common imperatives: they must capture attention and hold it, they must in some sense speak directly to their public, and they must convey their message with neatly calculated effect.

That much is clear. What is perhaps less immediately clear is that the range of texts suitably grouped under 'publicity' is wider than one would think at first sight. It includes, for instance, things like tourist brochures and information leaflets, public notices, posters, and even instructions for the use of appliances, recipe books, and so on.

It is therefore necessary to bear in mind that the title or explicit description of a text (for example, 'Instructions for Use') does not always clearly indicate that the text belongs to the same persuasive genre as those that are explicitly labelled as advertisements. It could be argued, in fact, that some of the most successful advertisements are those that appear to belong to some other genre, masking their consumer-oriented purposes under the guise of being informative or educational, or even literary. The upshot of this is that translators may sometimes have to look carefully at STs in order to recognize and identify their covert consumer-oriented persuasive/prescriptive features.

Take the average recipe book, for instance. On the face of things, it may seem to belong to the category of empirical/descriptive genres, for it appears to classify different cooking techniques in a descriptively systematic manner, to offer factual and objective accounts of the contents and appearance of dishes, as well as of their preparation. In itself, this almost makes recipe books sound like scientific texts. But it does not account for a number of manifest textual features of recipe books: the fact that even the most 'objective' recipe books are rarely written in a technical and scientifically neutral style; their use of tonal register is often calculated to draw the reader into a comfortable, possibly flattering, relationship; they have a transparently helpful organization, beyond what could be expected of the most indulgent scientific textbook; and they are often lavishly furnished with glossy pictures. (Some of these features are illustrated in the three extracts from recipe books on pp. 161–2.) Such features indicate a consumer-oriented purpose in recipe books that contain them, and are well worth looking out for when translating certain kinds of 'commercial' ST. Even if not directly consumer-oriented to the sale of particular foodstuffs or the promotion of fashionable cuisine, most recipe books are, at the very least, specimens of a hybrid genre characterized by the dual purpose of description and persuasion.

One must, then, be alert to covertly persuasive STs, in order to be able to translate them into appropriately persuasive TTs. But this is only the tip of the iceberg. The more methodologically interesting aspects of consumer orientation in STs and TTs are revealed when it is realized that literal translation of persuasive STs is likely to produce TTs that are far from persuasive for TL audiences.

This point, too, shows up most transparently of all in the case of advertising copy. To find examples hinging on cultural differences one need only observe differences of style and impact in different English-speaking cultures. For instance, hectoring and hard-sell styles appear in general to be more acceptable in American than in British advertising, where overpraising a product is seen as unpleasantly boastful, and any kind of overkill can only be used for humorous purposes. Much of British television advertising is based on comic effects of some kind or another, whereas American-style advertisements may strike British customers as bombastic and unsubtle. For the rest, the tendency in British advertising is to stereotype the customer as a discerning equal, not someone to be browbeaten or condescended to; consequently, the tonal register of some American advertisements might be considered 'insulting' to British customers. In cultures where they are in favour, hard-sell techniques may spread over the entire range of persuasive genres – not just commercial, but also ethical and political publicity, as well as many of the less obviously consumer-oriented textual types. To the extent that this is so, importing, for example, an American-style consumer-oriented text without modification from an American to a British context runs the risk of producing adverse effects on British consumers.

This intercultural comparison holds a lesson for translators. The fact that different cultures (even those nominally speaking the same language) have different expectations with regard to style in consumer-oriented genres explains why literal translations of persuasive STs are likely to turn out less than persuasive in the TL. In other words, persuasiveness in consumer-oriented texts is culture-specific.

The advice to the translator of persuasive/prescriptive texts is therefore the same as for translating any other genre of text. Look not only at the style of the ST, but also at the style(s) of other SL texts in the same or similar genres. Look not only at the surface literal meaning of the ST, but also at the details of the stylistic choices made in the ST. From detailed observation of stylistic choices in a number of texts in a given genre it is possible to build up a general picture of the stylistic tendencies or expectations associated with particular types of text in a given culture. Naturally, only a specialist will have the requisite time and experience to develop a clear and detailed sense of stylistic appropriateness in a given genre. (Practical 14 may be seen as a first step towards becoming a specialist translator of recipe books, by considering some general tendencies in the style of German recipes as compared with English ones.)

Further recommendations to the translator of consumer-oriented texts concern the nature of TTs. Here, again, the same principles apply as to any other text: do not be afraid to break away from literal translation where the needs of persuasive effect indicate such a break; do not produce TTs without having first built up a knowledge of the style of specimen TL texts in the appropriate genre. First-hand analysis of such TL specimens means building up, through careful observation, a kind of 'genre grammar' consisting of generalizations concerning the stylistic norms, tendencies and expectations typical of the genre of the eventual TT. This does not mean that the TL specimens are models for slavish copying; but comparing the stylistic tendencies of the ST genre with those of the TT genre is the best starting-point for tackling decisions about departures from literal translation.

Conducting the kind of investigation we are talking about may typically involve contrasting texts relating to the same product in the SL and TL. An example is given here from the English and German versions of the blurb packaged with Kodachrome 40 Movie Film cartridges. This should be prepared for discussion in Practical 14. Corresponding passages are given in the order in which they appear in the original texts, and are, as far as possible, arranged opposite one another.

KODACHROME 40 Movie Film (Type A) *In super 8 cartridge* This film can be used only in super 8 cameras and projected only in projectors that accept super 8 film.	*KODACHROME 40 (Type A) Farbfilm* *in der super 8 Filmkassette* Dieser Film kann nur in Cameras und Projektoren für super 8 Film verwendet werden. Der Film ist vollständig durchgelaufen, wenn auf dem Filmende das Wort EXPOSED (belichtet) erscheint.
Do not move film in slot on cartridge front, or turn core by hand.	
DAYLIGHT MOVIES: Use daylight filter. With *automatic cameras*, simply expose whenever the camera indicates there is enough light. With *non-automatic cameras*, set your exposure meter at *ASA 25* (*15 DIN*) and use the lens opening nearest 1/40-second shutter speed, or follow the exposure table on your camera.	*TAGESLICHTAUFNAHMEN*: Verwenden Sie ein Tageslichtfilter. Filmen Sie, wenn die *automatische Camera* ausreichende Lichtverhältnisse anzeigt. Bei *einstellbaren Cameras* richten Sie sich nach der Belichtungstabelle der Camera. Wenn Sie einen Belichtungsmesser verwenden, so stellen Sie diesen auf *15 DIN* (*ASA 25*) ein und lesen die Blende für ca. 1/40 Sekunde ab.
INDOOR MOVIES: Use movie lights (3400 K) and remove the daylight filter. With *automatic cameras* expose whenever the camera indicates there is enough light.	*INNENAUFNAHMEN*: Verwenden Sie Filmlampen (3400 K) und schwenken Sie das Tageslichtfilter aus. Mit einer *automatischen Camera* können Sie filmen, solange die Camera ausreichende Lichtverhältnisse anzeigt.
With *non-automatic cameras*, set your exposure meter at *ASA 40* (*17 DIN*) and use the lens opening nearest 1/40-second shutter speed, or use the settings indicated on the movie light or lamp package.	Bei *einstellbaren Cameras* stellen Sie den Belichtungsmesser auf *17 DIN* (*ASA 40*), und wählen die Blende, die ca. 1/40 Sekunde entspricht, oder Sie stellen die Blende nach der Tabelle der Filmlampe ein.

PROCESSING: Film price includes processing by Kodak. The film itself is so identified. To mail film for processing, put the cartridge in the mailing envelope and address it to one of the processing labs listed.

ENTWICKLUNG: Die Entwicklung durch KODAK ist im Kaufpreis des Filmes inbegriffen, der Film ist dementsprechend gekennzeichnet. Verwenden Sie den beiliegenden Versandbeutel und achten Sie bitte auf richtige Frankierung nach den gültigen Postbestimmungen.

These parallel texts are not actually a ST and a TT; rather, they are two different presentations of the same subject matter. The contrasts between them are informative in that they may suggest possible culture-specific differences between British and German 'instructions for use'.

We have recommended departures from literal translation in translating consumer-oriented STs, and have just illustrated substantial divergences in literal meaning between two parallel texts in German and English. However, this does not mean licence for indiscriminate distortion. The example of translating 'instructions for use' (or instruction manuals in general) aptly illustrates what we mean. The translator's prime responsibility to the manufacturer is to give a correct, unambiguous and comprehensible account of how the product is to be used. This places limits on possible departures from the substance of the ST. It does not, however, imply that the TT should be a carbon copy of the ST. First, as the Kodachrome example illustrates, textual cogency and the conventions by which information is presented are to some extent culture-specific. Consequently, readers from one culture might find the logic of presentation of a given text patronizingly over-explicit, whereas readers from another culture might find it over-economical and unclear. The literal exactitude of such corresponding texts is more a matter of neither text falsifying the technical details described than of a TT faithfully matching the form of the ST.

Second, it may be that, in certain fields, different pieces of background knowledge will be expected from SL consumers and TL consumers respectively. Thus the text in one of the languages may take for granted details which it is considered necessary to include in the text in the other language. For example, in the Kodachrome instance, any English consumer can be expected to know that the reel has come to an end when the word 'EXPOSED' appears on the film, whereas this is not a safe expectation in the case of German consumers. In other words, there will be points on which the TT needs to spell out more details than the ST, as well as, conversely, points on which it needs to be less explicit than the ST.

All this implies that when, for cultural reasons, a higher degree of sophistication is to be expected from either SL or TL consumers, the difference in sophistication needs to be reflected by formulating TTs in either more technical or less technical ways than the corresponding STs.

Closely related to these considerations is the question of register. The social and tonal registers of ST and TT may need to differ in ways reflecting different consumer expectations. Features of register in consumer-oriented texts tend to stereotype three things: first, the purveyor of the commodity; second, the targeted consumer; and third, the relationship between purveyor and consumer. (One feature that plays a major role in this stereotyping is the choice of alternative imperative forms: compare 'use daylight filter' with 'you should use a daylight filter', 'a daylight filter should be used', 'you must use a daylight filter', and so on. The choice between different imperative formulations is, if anything, even richer and more significant in German: compare 'verwenden Sie ein Tageslichtfilter' with 'Sie verwenden ein Tageslichtfilter', 'Tageslichtfilter verwenden', 'bitte Tageslichtfilter verwenden', 'Tageslichtfilter erforderlich', and so on. The issue of imperatives would repay discussion in Practical 14.)

It may be that in the ST the relationship between purveyor and consumer is stereotyped as being, for example, one of the expert addressing poorly informed non-experts, while, for cultural reasons, the relationship in the TT is more aptly stereotyped as one of expert to other experts, or of non-expert to non-experts. Recipe books are a case in point: it is probably a fair assumption that a British reader of a recipe book is less likely to feel insulted by being 'talked down to', but more likely to react adversely to terse directives, than most German readers. (There will be a chance to put this assumption to the test in Practical 14.)

Where the need arises for differences in stereotyping, it follows that the register of the TT will differ from that of the ST in terms of a number of features: vocabulary; grammatical/syntactic structure (for example, active and personal constructions may be preferable to passive and impersonal ones); sentential structure (for example, the presence or absence of parenthetical clauses; use or non-use of 'telegraphese'; colloquial or formal use of sentential markers, illocutionary particles and connectives); discourse structure (for example, marked or less marked use of devices signalling textual cohesion, more or less transparent textual layout); and so on. In principle, every level of textual variable may be drawn on to signal register.

In particular, features of tonal register may need to be altered between ST and TT in order to establish and maintain a certain desired relationship between TT and consumer which is different from that between ST and consumer. The genre-specific tendencies of the ST may, for instance, lead one to expect a text that addresses the SL consumer in a formal tonal register, whereas the chosen genre of the TT may lead one to expect a text that addresses the TL consumer in an informal tonal register. In a situation like this, the knock-on effects of a change of register may imply quite drastic departures from the framework of the ST, on any or all levels of textual variables discussed in Chapters 4–6.

Considerations of this sort will arise in Practical 14. It is important to remember, however, that changes in structure, vocabulary and register are as much subject to standard differences between languages as to genre-specific cross-cultural differences. For instance, compare these corresponding clauses from the section on daylight movies in the German and English Kodachrome blurbs:

...wenn die [...] Camera ausreichende Lichtverhältnisse anzeigt	...whenever the camera indicates there is enough light

Whatever the genre, if the German text were translated literally into English, the resulting grammatical structure ('if the camera indicates adequate lighting conditions') would sound pompous, and unidiomatic, since English has a lower tolerance for compound, adjectivally modified nominal constructions (of the 'ausreichende Lichtverhältnisse' type) favoured by German.

All other considerations apart, choosing a register for a consumer-oriented TT can be problematic for the simple reason that there may be little in common between the groups of consumers targeted by the ST and the TT respectively. In any case, any TL genre selected as a prototype for the TT will probably provide specimens in widely divergent styles and registers, leaving the translator with a number of possible models. We end this chapter with extracts from three different recipe books in English that amply illustrate these potential problems of choice. Thanks to their manifest consumer orientation, the extracts are also clear concluding reminders that every text – and therefore also every TT – is made for a specific *purpose* and a specific *audience*:

BOUILLABAISSE

NOTE: This, the most famous of all fish soups, is made chiefly in the South of France, different districts having particular recipes. It is a kind of thick stew of fish which should include a very wide mixture of different kinds of fish. The original French recipes use many fish not available in Great Britain. The following recipe is adapted to use the available fish. In order to get a wide enough variety a large quantity must be made.

[Ingredients listed]

Clean the fish, cut them into thick slices and sort them into 2 groups, the firm-fleshed kind and the soft kind. Chop the onion; slice the leek, crush the garlic; scald, skin and slice the tomatoes. In a deep pan make a bed of the sliced vegetables and the herbs, season this layer. Arrange on top the pieces of firm-fleshed fish; season them and pour over them the oil. [...]

(Beeton, 1962, p. 119)

155 ZUPPA DA PESCE

It doesn't matter whether you call it bouillabaisse, cippolini, zuppa da pesce, or just fish stew; whether it has lots of liquid, or, like this, is simmered in its own richly aromatic juices. It's not just good, it's wonderful. To put it in the oven is somewhat illegitimate, but you are less apt to overcook it. Serve with Spanish rice (for the hearty ones), tossed green salad, French bread to sop up the juices.

[Ingredients listed]

Put the olive oil and garlic in a warm, deep casserole and heat. Place the large fish on the bottom, then the mussels and shrimp. Season, and sprinkle the parsley over all. [...] Baste from time to time with the juices, using an oversized eyedropper called a baster. Serve in deep hot plates. Serves 6 generously. Time: 45 minutes.

(Tracy, 1965, n.p.)

FISH CAKES

[Ingredients listed]

1 Chop the parsley with both hands, one on the knife handle and one on the top of the knife blade. This chops the parsley smaller and keeps your fingers safely out of the way of the knife.
2 Put the potatoes on one plate and mash them up with the fork. Add the fish and mash it up too. Add the butter, parsley, salt and pepper. Mix them all together.
3 Turn the mixture out on to the board and make it into a roll with your hands like a big sausage. Cut off rounds with the knife.
[...]

(Anderson, 1972, p. 26)

PRACTICAL 14

14.1 Consumer-oriented texts

Assignment

(i) Compare and contrast the texts from the English and German versions of the Kodachrome blurb, given on pp. 158–9.
(ii) Determine what general conclusions can be drawn from the comparison.

14.2 Consumer-oriented texts

Assignment

(i) Compare and contrast the texts from different English recipe books given on pp. 161–2.
(ii) Compare and contrast the texts from the English and German versions of recipes for the same dish (Scheiterhaufen/bread and butter pudding).
(iii) Determine what general conclusions can be drawn from these contrasts.

Contextual information

The texts below are taken, respectively, from a German and two English recipe books chosen at random. The German text is from a supplement to the women's magazine *Brigitte* (*Was essen wir heute? Rezept-Sonderheft*) and comes with a glossy photograph; the English texts come from recipe books supplied with kitchen appliances.

Turn to p. 164

Scheiterhaufen

5 alte Brötchen, 1/2 l Milch, 100 g Butter oder Margarine, Schale 1/2 unbehandelten Zitrone, 2 Eier, 100 g Zucker, 500 g Äpfel, Fett für die Form, 100 g Rosinen, 50 g gehackte Mandeln.

Die Brötchen in Scheiben schneiden und in eine Schüssel schichten. Milch mit 50 Gramm Fett und der Zitronenschale aufkochen, handwarm abkühlen lassen. Die Zitronenschale herausnehmen. Eier mit dem Zucker verquirlen und nach und nach die Milch unterrühren. Über die Brötchen gießen, 15 Minuten ziehen lassen. Äpfel schälen, vierteln, vom Kerngehäuse befreien und in Scheiben schneiden. Die Hälfte der Brötchen in die gefettete feuerfeste Form schichten. Die Äpfel darauf verteilen. Mit gewaschenen Rosinen und Mandeln bestreuen. Die restlichen Brötchenscheiben dann schuppenartig darauflegen. Fettflöckchen darüber verteilen und den Auflauf im vorgeheizten Backofen bei 220 Grad/Gas Stufe 4 ca. 45 Minuten backen. (1 Stunde 20 Minuten)

Dieses Rezept ist für vier Personen berechnet und enthält (Beilagen nicht mitgerechnet): Eiweiß: 56 g, Fett: 146 g, Kohlenhydrate: 367 g. 12 980 Joule/3100 Kalorien, pro Person ca. 3240 Joule/775 Kalorien, Beilagen: Zimt-Zucker und Vanillesoße.

Bread and Butter Pudding

2oz	**56g**	**butter**
6		**slices of bread**
2oz	**56g**	**currants**
2oz	**56g**	**sultanas**
1oz	**28g**	**mixed nuts; chopped**
2		**eggs; lightly beaten**
2oz	**56g**	**caster sugar**
½ tsp		**vanilla essence**
½ pt	**250ml**	**milk**

Method

1 Butter bread, remove crusts and cut in half diagonally.

2 Place fruit and nuts between layers of bread in a suitable dish.

3 Mix eggs, sugar and essence together and add the milk gradually. Pour over the bread.

4 Bake until bread is crispy and golden brown.

servings:	4
small oven: PREHEATED	180° C – 50–60 minutes bottom shelf
fan oven: COLD START	170° C – 50–60 minutes

BREAD AND BUTTER PUDDING

Children love bread and butter pudding with sliced bananas between layers of bread.

6 slices white bread (buttered)
50 g (2oz) sultanas
50 g (2oz) caster sugar
568ml (1pt) milk
2 grade-3 eggs (beaten)
pinch nutmeg

1 Butter a deep pie dish.

2 Cut bread into triangles and place half over bottom of dish.

3 Sprinkle over the fruit half of sugar and cover with remaining bread. Heat milk and mix with eggs.

4 Pour milk mixture over bread and leave to soak for 30 minutes.

5 Sprinkle with remaining sugar and nutmeg and cook at 160° C, 325° F, Mark 3 for 45 minutes.

6 Serve with custard.

14.3 Consumer-oriented texts

Assignment

(i) Discuss the strategic decisions confronting the translator of the following text, and define your own strategy for translating it.
(ii) Translate the text into English.
(iii) Explain the main decisions of detail you made in producing your TT.

Contextual information
The text is taken from the same glossily illustrated supplement to the women's magazine *Brigitte* as the Scheiterhaufen recipe on p.164.

Text

Kräuterrührei

4 Scheiben Schweinebauch (400 g), Thymian, 1 Eßl. Senf, Salz, Pfeffer, 8 Eier, Rosenpaprika, je 1/2 Bund Petersilie, Schnittlauch und Dill oder 1 Päckchen Tiefkühlkräuter).

Schweinebauch mit Thymian, Senf, Salz und Pfeffer einreiben und in einer Pfanne zehn Minuten knusprig braun braten. Eier mit acht Eßlöffel Wasser verquirlen, salzen, pfeffern und mit Rosenpaprika würzen. Die Kräuter waschen, mit Küchenkrepp trockentupfen und fein hacken. Unter die Eier rühren. Schweinebauchscheiben warm stellen und im Bratfett das Rührei bereiten. Rührei und die halbierten Schweinebauchscheiben auf einer Platte anrichten. (25 Minuten)

Dieses Rezept ist für vier Personen berechnet und enthält (Beilagen nicht mitgerechnet): Eiweiß: 84 g, Fett 232 g, Kohlenhydrate: 4 g. 10 905 Joule/2605 Kalorien, pro Person ca. 2720 Joule/650 Kalorien. Beilagen: Bratkartoffeln und Kopfsalat mit Tomaten.

14.4 Consumer-oriented texts

Assignment

(i) Discuss the strategic decisions confronting the translator of the following text, and define your own strategy for translating it.
(ii) Translate the text into English.
(iii) Explain the main decisions of detail you made in producing your TT.

Contextual information
The text is the manufacturer's blurb included with the children's game sold in Germany under the name of 'Clown'.

Text

Clown

Ausgezeichnet mit dem Prädikat ‘spiel gut’ vom Arbeitsausschuß Gutes Spielzeug.
Ravensburger Spiele ® Nr. 00 360 0

Würfelspiel für 2–6 Personen ab 5 Jahren
von Edith Prentkowski

Spieldauer: 20–40 Minuten
Inhalt: 48 Karten, 1 Würfel

Bevor zum ersten Mal gespielt wird, werden die Karten sorgfältig voneinander getrennt. Es sind 48 Karten im Spiel, mit denen sich 6 Clown-Figuren legen lassen. Jede Figur besteht aus 8 Karten. Diese sind auf der linken Seite von 1–8 numeriert. Sechs Karten haben die Ziffer 1 (= sechs Schuhe), sechs Karten gibt es mit der Ziffer 2 (= sechs Beine) und so fort bis zu sechs Karten mit der Ziffer 8 (= sechs Hüte).
Rechts auf jeder Karte sind die Würfelpunkte angegeben, nach denen die Karten erwürfelt werden können.

Ziel des Spieles ist es, in acht Würfelrunden seine Clown-Figur aus 8 Karten von unten nach oben zu legen und am Schluß die größte Figur zu erlangen.
Je nachdem, ob man breite oder schmale Karten erwürfeln kann, entstehen größere oder kleinere, immer wieder neue, lustige Clown-Figuren.

Spielvorbereitung: Zu Beginn des Spiels werden die Karten nach den Ziffern sortiert auf 8 Häufchen gelegt.

Spielverlauf: In der ersten Würfelrunde wird reihum um die Karten mit der Ziffer 1 (= Schuhe des Clowns) gewürfelt. Jeder erhält die Karte, deren Würfelpunkte er würfelt. Ist eine Karte schon weg, weil ein Mitspieler die Punkte-Zahl schon vorher würfelte, darf man diese Karte dem Mitspieler rauben und damit seine eigene Figur beginnen. Es wird so lange reihum gewürfelt, bis jeder eine Karte mit der Ziffer 1 hat. Dann beginnt die zweite Runde.
In gleicher Weise wird nun um die 6 Karten mit der Ziffer 2 gewürfelt, danach in der dritten Runde um die Karten mit der Ziffer 3 und so weiter.
Nehmen 6 Personen am Spiel teil, so braucht der letzte Spieler, der noch keine Karte hat, nicht mehr um seine Karte zu würfeln.
Er erhält die übriggebliebene 6. Karte ohne zu würfeln.
Je höher die Punktezahl ist, die man würfelte, desto größer wird die Figur.

Ende des Spiels: Nach der 8. Würfelrunde hat jeder seine Figur vollendet. Gewinner ist, wer die größte Figur hat.

15

Stylistic editing

Throughout the course, we have considered translation sometimes as a process, and sometimes as a product (a TT). The assessment of existing TTs has been an important feature in practicals, even before we started discussing the question of genre. In this chapter, we turn our attention to the final stage of translation as a process, where the proposed TT is actually examined as a product. This stage is known as **editing**. A TT is only really complete after careful stylistic editing.

Any form of textual editing is intrinsically an operation carried out in writing on a pre-existent written text. (Even editing spoken dialogue is normally performed on a written transcript.) That is, the editor already has at least a tentative draft form of a text. Basic editing, of course, is concerned with eliminating outright errors – anything from incorrect spelling or punctuation, through ungrammatical constructions to obscure, ambiguous or misleading sentential configurations; all the linguistic levels of textual variables require checking for mistakes. When the object of editing is a TT, this process has to include checking back to the ST to make sure that its basic literal meaning has not been misrepresented in the TT. Nevertheless, much of this stage of textual editing is done on the TT as a TL text in its own right, without reference to the ST. In a sense, therefore, the transitional process of editing is a post-translational operation used for tidying up an almost complete TT, and is done with as little reference as possible to the ST.

In principle, no TT is ever finished and polished to the point where it could not be edited further. It is a practical question whether further editing will actually improve it. In practice there must, sooner or later (and for busy professional translators it is likely to be sooner), come a point where one has to stop tinkering with a TT. However, there is plenty of work to be done before that point is reached.

Just as basic editing presupposes at least a draft written text, so stylistic editing presupposes a text that is reasonably finished in such respects as literal meaning, grammar and spelling. This may turn out in practice to have been an unwarranted assumption, but it has to be the methodological starting-point. (A text might be rejected as unsuitable for stylistic editing if it were clearly not substantially correct.)

In the stylistic editing of a TT the translator considers only the alternative ways of expressing the literal meanings of parts of the text, rather than the possibility of altering the substance of what is expressed. This is admittedly a thin dividing line (as will be seen in Practical 15), because the way something is expressed is, to a great extent, part of what is expressed. Nevertheless, methodologically speaking, stylistic editing is purely a process of tinkering with stylistic effects in a TT. That is, it is not, in essence, a bilingual operation. It is perfectly possible for someone with no knowledge of, for example, Arabic to be called in to help with the stylistic editing of a TT translated from Arabic. As this observation suggests, the primary concern in editing is to enhance the quality of the TT, less as a translation than as a text produced in the TL for the use of a monolingual audience. Indeed, it is not uncommon for translations to be done by collaboration between one translator whose contribution is knowledge of the SL and another translator whose contribution is knowledge of the TL. With any luck, such collaboration would help in avoiding blunders like these classic captions:

HAMLET THE GREAT DANE

WHY KILL YOUR WIFE WITH HOUSEWORK?
LET ELECTRICITY DO IT FOR YOU!

Stylistic editing is most effective if the editor lays the ST aside and concentrates on assessing the probable effects of the TT on a putative TL audience. One of the biggest problems in translating is that it is hard to put oneself in the shoes of a TL reader looking at the TT with a fresh eye. This is why translations from German often have a Germanic flavour which immediately signals that the text is a translation. Even the translator who manages to avoid outright translationese is not best placed to judge how well the TT would convey particular meanings or nuances for a reader who did not know the ST. There is therefore a lot to be said for asking an independent TL-speaking observer, who does not know the ST, to help with the editing.

Perhaps the most central features for stylistic editing are connotative meanings, because they require to be triggered by the context of the TT alone. The translator, who cannot escape the influence of the ST context, is unlikely to be able to assess confidently whether a connotation that is crystal-clear in the context of the ST and the SL is equally clear to someone who only looks at the TT from the viewpoint of the TL culture. It is vital that this be checked. It is just as vital to check the converse – that there are no obtrusive unwanted connotations evoked by the TT. At best, such unwanted connotations show that the translator has failed to anticipate the stylistic effects the TT is liable to produce on its TL audience, and is not fully in control of its style. At worst, they may distort and subvert the overall content and impact of the TT, or they may create textual anomalies, contradictory connotations clashing either with one another or with the literal meaning.

Of course, it is easier for the independent editor to help with the second of these constraints than with the first. For instance, whatever the ST expression may be, the phrase 'the pictures were well hung' risks unfortunate innuendo, even if it appears in a newspaper review of an exhibition, and the editor may suggest that the translator think again. (Going back to the ST, the translator may then decide that the TT is an unfortunate rendering of 'die Bilder wurden gut angebracht', and opt for 'the pictures were well displayed' instead.) But, without knowing the ST, how can editors tell when connotations are *missing* from a TT? The best thing is to give them the ST and hope that they do not get so deeply immersed in it that they, too, cannot see the TT objectively. Otherwise, if there is time, the translator can put the TT away for a month and then look at it with fresh eyes; even so, there is no guarantee that missing connotations will be spotted.

The twin constraint of spotting both missing connotations and unwanted ones is best illustrated in cases of connotative clash. The elimination of connotative clashes is one of the principal aims of stylistic editing. Thus, for instance, only an unbiased reading of the TT may reveal that juxtaposed literally exact expressions in the TT convey conflicting attitudinal meanings which make the text anomalous by virtue of the clash between contradictory attitudes ascribed to the author or speaker. Such textual anomalies leave the TT audience in doubt as to how to take the attitudes connoted in the text. Attitudinal anomalies are exemplified in the first of the Dürrenmatt TTs on p. 136:

Sie sehen, Majestät, ich bin eiskalt.	You see, Your Majesty, I am as cold as ice.

The connotations of this TT sentence are likely to convey a pejorative attitudinal meaning, the sentence reading as an expression of self-deprecation, not cool determination. This clashes with the attitudes of the speaker conveyed elsewhere in the TT. Stylistic editing might produce a better suggestion: 'I must make it clear to you, Your Majesty, that I am adamant about this'.

Sie müssen mir ohne mit der Wimper zu zucken zugeben[...]	You must admit without batting an eyelid[...]

The idiom 'without batting an eyelid' has inappropriate attitudinal connotations suggesting neutrality on the part of the speaker and calm indifference on the part of the addressee, whereas the context demands a blustering expression forcing a grudging admission of defeat: 'look me in the eye and tell me I'm wrong' conveys exactly the right nuances, given the blackmailing nature of the situation.

Clashes like these tend to reduce the connotative content of the TT to absurdity and paradox. Where the ST is not itself deliberately enigmatic and paradoxical, this constitutes a distortion of its overall meaning. However, even where no outright clashes occur, translators should be careful not to let gratuitous attitudinal meanings insinuate themselves into the TT. These should be picked up and eliminated, as far as possible, at the stylistic editing stage.

Similar considerations apply for all other types of connotation. Thus, for instance, the loss of an allusive meaning with a subtle but thematically important role in the ST is a significant translation loss. Here is an example from Liliencron's 'Der Blitzzug', already mentioned in Chapter 6, p. 70. The third stanza opens with the line 'Dämmerung senkt sich allmählich wie Gaze', which clearly alludes to Goethe's well-known line 'Dämmrung senkte sich von oben' and creates irony by means of the contrasting moods of the two poems. A translation from which an appropriate allusion is missing would, therefore, be inadequate (although, as we have suggested, it is hard to see how an independent editor would pick this up, except by studying the ST). Provided that this can be reconciled with the prosodic patterns of the TT, a possible rendering, with allusion to the well-known English hymn 'Round me falls the night', is: 'Round us falls the night's enfolding muslin'.

Reflected meanings in a ST are also notoriously difficult to render adequately in a TT; and, conversely, unforeseen and potentially embarrassing reflected meanings can create translation loss by jeopardizing the seriousness of a TT through unwanted comic effects or innuendo, as in the example of the well-hung pictures given above.

As regards collocative meanings, the most obvious flaws to look out for are mis-collocations. These are a likely result of the translator's immersion in the ST and the SL at the earlier stages of translating. (Even where, strictly speaking, they do not trigger problems of collocative meaning as such, they are a common source of translation loss on the grammatical level. Our discussion here embraces mis-collocations in general, as well as collocative meaning.) Some mis-collocations may actually amount to outright grammatical errors, not merely stylistic ones. For example, the collocation of definite article and proper name is grammatical and idiomatic in German, but is ungrammatical as it stands in English; compare 'die Petra' with 'the Petra'. This kind of grammatical mistake will presumably be eliminated at an early editing stage. However, there may be collocations that are not categorically ungrammatical in the TL, yet introduce a jarring note into the TT. It is sometimes hard to pin down just what makes a certain collocation seem ungainly. At best, one can suggest that speakers of a language have a sense of 'euphonic order' by which they judge certain collocations to be more acceptable than others. For example, German 'rechts und links' is more felicitous than 'links und rechts', whereas, in general, English 'left and right' is more felicitous than 'right and left'. Similarly, German 'hin und her' may, in some contexts, need to be rendered as 'back and forth', but never as 'forth and back'.

When differences between felicitous collocations in one language and those in another are overlooked, a TT will often signal, by its clumsiness, the fact that it is a translation and not an indigenous text. Here are some examples of such translationese:

vor und zurück	forwards and backwards (*edit to*: backwards and forwards).
Sind noch Äpfel da?	Are there still apples there? (*edit to*: Are there any apples left?).

Hier steht's schwarz auf weiß.	Here it is in black on white (*edit to*: Here it is in black and white).
Ich weiß den Text nicht mehr.	I don't know/remember the words any more (*edit to*: I forget the words).
[*Colloquially*] Der Aufzug ist kaputt.	The lift is broken (*edit to*: The lift's not working).

Other things that often create collocational problems of a stylistic rather than grammatical nature are deictic and anaphoric elements. Deictic elements like 'this', 'that', 'the', and 'a' are often involved in subtle and complex collocational euphonics. So, for example, 'this England' seems to be felicitous, 'that England' is (depending on context) less so, while 'the England' is (as a complete noun phrase) downright ungrammatical. 'That which the butler saw' is ungainly, while 'what the butler saw' is felicitous. Anaphorics, too, show clearly that there are collocational choices to be made on the basis of felicity or infelicity in a given language. For example, 'die Petra, die spielt nicht' is usually better rendered as 'Petra isn't playing' than as 'Petra, she isn't playing'. The translation of deictics and anaphora is far from being a straightforward matter of literal translation. Here are some examples:

Hans Castorp blickte um *sich*...	Hans Castorp looked round *him*...
Und noch eins...	And there's one more *thing*...
...in *jenem* schicksalhaften Jahr, das seinem Aufbruch nach Paris voranging...	...in *the* fateful year which preceded his departure for Paris
Das Zusammentreffen *dieser* zwei Mannschaften lenkte *die* Aufmerksamkeit auf die Hauptstadt der Sowjetrepublik Armenien...	The encounter between *the* two teams focuses attention on the capital of the Soviet Republic of Armenia...
Kapitalismus ist Ausbeutung des Menschen durch den Menschen; im Kommunismus: umgekehrt.	Capitalism is the exploitation of man by his fellow-man; in communism, *it*'s the other way round.

Infelicity in anaphora and deictics may in some cases originate from a factor of tedious repetition. That is, collocational possibilities may be stylistically affected by some kind of textual 'boredom factor'. If this is the case, however, it must be said that different textual genres in different languages have very different tolerances to repetition. In an English novel, for example, there may be countless repetitions of 'he said', without this repetition being thought obtrusive or tedious. If the dialogue is translated into Hungarian, however, the translator soon feels the need to vary the formula through translating 'he said' by various verbs descriptive of the manner of utterance (the Hungarian counterparts of 'he replied', 'he queried', 'he whispered', 'he affirmed', and so on). Thus it would seem that, in certain genres at least, the English-speaking reader's tolerance to the 'boredom factor' caused by continual use of 'he said' is higher than the Hungarian reader's tolerance of repetitions of the corresponding formula in Hungarian.

In a similar vein, it is clear that German has in general a lower tolerance than English for the repetition of identical word-stems in parallel morphological compounds, as exemplified by the clear preference for 'Tarif- und Sozialpartner' (as opposed to 'Tarifpartner und Sozialpartner'), 'mittel- und unmittelbaren Bundesbeteiligungen' (as opposed to 'mittelbaren und unmittelbaren Bundesbeteiligungen'), 'Aus- und Weiterbildung' (as opposed to 'Ausbildung und Weiterbildung'), 'Hoch- und Tiefbau' (as opposed to 'Hochbau und Tiefbau'), and so on. These differential tolerances and preferences have obvious implications for translating and for stylistic editing:

unemployment benefit, housing benefit and child benefit	Arbeitslosengeld, Wohngeld und Kindergeld (*edit to*: Arbeitslosen-, Wohn- und Kindergeld)

and, conversely,

dunkel- oder hellblau	dark or light blue (*edit to*: dark blue or light blue)

It is clear from these examples that stylistic editing is in part an exercise in taste. Even if it means taking liberties with the literal faithfulness of TT to ST, rooting out unidiomatic collocations is a recommended editing process, except, of course, where the ST deliberately exploits them. This last proviso, however, highlights a vital point concerning all stylistic editing: while it is highly desirable to test the TT on SL speakers who do not know the ST, and to take careful account of their suggestions, *the ultimate editing decisions must always be taken by the translator, with reference to the ST.*

Rooting out unidiomatic collocations is one thing, but there is, of course, also the converse case to consider, where the TT collocation is idiomatic to the point of being clichéd. Clichés can be obtrusive in their own way, and are therefore capable of creating their own unwanted stylistic effects. In particular, if the ST typically avoids hackneyed expressions, their use in the corresponding TT amounts to significant translation loss, trivializing the text or even falsifying it. This effect is illustrated in an example from the Brecht text in Practical 8:

Und die Kälte der Wälder Wird in mir bis zu meinem Absterben sein.	And the chill of the forests Will be in me to my dying day. (*edit to:* Will be in me till my dying away).

As we have suggested, it should not be forgotten that collocative clashes may be used deliberately. In such cases it will usually be appropriate for the TT to coin equally deliberate mis-collocations. The main thing then is to make sure that the contrived mis-collocations in the TT are stylistically plausible in the light of the TL, and are clearly recognizable as deliberate ploys, not stylistic hitches. Here is a good example from the same text in Practical 8:

[...] schlafe beunruhigt ein	go unpeacefully to sleep (*edit to*: go to sleep with my mind at unrest)

For affective meanings, and stylistic uses of language varieties of all sorts, the same considerations hold as for the types of connotative meaning we have been discussing. These considerations can be summed up by calling attention to four problems: the problem of losing from the TT important connotations contextually triggered in the ST; the problem of accidentally creating unwanted connotative effects in the TT; the problem of bringing about connotative clashes in the TT; and the problem of deliberately introducing gratuitous connotations into the TT. These are the main points to look for in stylistic editing.

One other thing that should be reviewed at the stylistic editing stage is the textual effects of language variety – alternatives associated with different social registers, dialects, sociolects and tonal registers. Even though conscious choices have been made about these things at the drafting stage, stylistic editing offers one more chance to weigh up how successful the outcome of these choices is over the TT as a whole. The four problems outlined above are all likely to arise here as well, *mutatis mutandis*. It is also particularly important, when using a marked language variety in a TT, to avoid the two extremes of 'too little' and 'too much'. Editing offers the chance to make sure that the TT contains enough features of language variety to prevent its coming across as a neutral, standard sample of the TL, but not so many that it seems caricatural. The 'boredom factor' we referred to earlier can also be invoked here, and so can an 'irritation factor': over-using stylistic features all signalling the same language variety can very easily lead to tedium, embarrassment or exasperation (as witness some of the dialectal features of D.H. Lawrence's writing).

There is always a threat of connotative clash in the stylistic use of language variety. There is only one genuine excuse for mixing features from different registers, dialects and sociolects in a TT, and this is when the ST itself deliberately uses code-switching for specific thematic purposes, as for instance in the text from *Mathilde Möhring* used in Practical 9 (pp. 105–6). (If the mixture is accidental, then the ST will probably not be worth translating anyway, unless it is a potboiler that has sold a million copies and been turned into a television series with an all-star cast – in which case, the last thing the likely readership is going to be interested in is accuracy of language variety.)

Finally, here are two passages manifestly in need of stylistic editing, and which are well worth discussion in class:

(i) Long will machinery menace the whole of our treasure,
while it, unmindful of us, dares to a mind of its own.
Checking the glorious hand's flaunting of lovelier leisure,
now for some stubborner work sternlier it fashions the stone.

(ii) There is no doubt that with his capabilities he would have done better at smuggling, which the times made more profitable, than at soldiering. But he submitted without further ado when in 1917 his extreme shortsightedness was summarily ignored and he received a call to arms, as the phrase went. True, even while he was being trained in Fulda he did manage to wind up a tobacco business here and there, but soon enough he dropped everything. Not only because his military duties made him tired and inapt for other things.

PRACTICAL 15

15.1 Stylistic editing

Assignment
Discuss the two passages given immediately above and edit them to read better where you think they are stylistically or idiomatically defective. Earmark points where you think editing may be necessary but cannot be done without reference to the ST.

15.2 Stylistic editing

Assignment

(i) Working in groups, each taking roughly equal amounts of the text, edit the following English TT to read better where you think it is stylistically or idiomatically defective.
(ii) Earmark points where you think editing may be necessary but can only be done with reference to the ST.
(iii) After discussion of your provisional edited version, you will be given the ST and asked (a) to assess the accuracy of the TT and (b) to complete the editing of the TT.

Contextual information
Robert Musil (1880–1942) was a major novelist, best known for *Der Mann ohne Eigenschaften*. 'Grigia' (written in 1921/2) is an extremely densely textured short

story of about 26 pages in which, in the words of H. Sacker (Musil, 1970, p. 27), Musil 'attempts...not simply to record symbolic experience, but to embed it in an appropriate intellectual and social framework'. The extract comes early in the story and forms part of the description of the remote Fersenatal in South Tirol to which the central character has come and in which he will meet his death.

Target text

Also the landscape around this village was not without peculiarities. It consisted of a more than semicircular embankment of higher mountains, with their tops punctuated by crags, that fell steeply to a depression surrounding a smaller and forested cone standing in the middle, whereby the whole took on the appearance of a hollow world shaped like a kind of cake from which a small piece had been snipped off by the deep-flowing stream, so that it leaned gaping towards the high, opposite bank of the stream stretching along with it down towards the valley. It was there that the village lay perched. There were, all around below the snow, corries with dwarf-pine and some deer scattered here and there. On the wooded central summit the mating season of the blackcock was already in full swing, and in the meadows on the sunny side flowers were blooming, shaped like yellow, blue and white stars that were as big as if someone had shaken them out of a sack of gold coins. But if one climbed yet another hundred feet or so higher behind the village, then one came to a flat, not too wide plateau covered by cultivated fields, pastures, hay-barns and scattered houses, while from a bastion jutting out towards the valley the little church peeked out into a world that, on fine days, lay before the valley like the sea before an estuary. One could hardly discern what was still the distant golden yellow of the blessed lowlands, and where already the precarious cloud floor of the sky had begun.

Contrastive topics and practicals: introduction

The following four chapters will deal with a selection of topics from the 'contrastive linguistics' of German and English. While each of these chapters is self-contained, and can be used as the basis of a practical at whatever stage of the course it seems most useful, there is clearly a close link between Chapters 16 and 17, both of which concentrate on the topic of modal particles.

The ultimate aim of including these contrastive topics is to sharpen students' awareness of certain characteristic difficulties in translating particular types of construction from German to English, and to increase their awareness of the range of options open to them in translating these constructions.

In principle, a contrastive study of German and English – especially valuable as a component in a course on translation for the insight it offers into structural differences between German and English that constitute stumbling-blocks to literal translation – offers a vast number of systematic discrepancies between German and English usage. 'Compensation in kind', discussed in Chapter 3, is generally made necessary by one or more of these numerous differences between the two languages. Anaphora and deictics, which we looked at briefly in Chapter 15, offer good examples of such areas of interlingual contrast, to each of which a complete chapter could have been devoted. The common feature these contrasts display from the translator's point of view is the frequent need for **grammatical transposition**. By grammatical transposition we mean the replacement of a particular type of structure containing given parts of speech in the ST by some other type of structure containing different parts of speech in the TT (for instance, 'Ist er schon da?' into 'Has he arrived?'). Many other writers designate this phenomenon simply as 'transposition'; we have used the full term 'grammatical transposition' here in order to prevent confusion with 'cultural transposition' (see above, pp. 20–6). Chapters 18 and 19 explore aspects of two areas of grammatical transposition particularly characteristic of translation from German to English: the transposing of phrases containing an adverbial qualifier into phrases containing two verbs, and the reorganizing of predicative constructions necessitated by differences in German and English word order.

The choice of just four contrastive topics out of the many that we could have chosen was a difficult, and in the end rather arbitrary, one. We have picked out three of the most common and rich contrastive sources of translation difficulties between German and English, and illustrated each through a variety of classroom exercises. The topic of modal particles proved in fact to be too rich for just one chapter dealt with in a single practical: the material for this highly challenging topic has been divided over two chapters, one with a more general focus, the other with a more particular emphasis on a selection of commonly used German modal particles whose translation into English is problematic.

There are two ways in which the contrastive exercises differ from other practicals in the course. First, students will be translating sentences taken out of context, so that attention can be focused specifically on the contrastive problems themselves – problems that, in textual context, tend to be masked or blurred by considerations of style or genre. Naturally, we do not mean to imply that context is, after all, less important than we have insisted hitherto. However, the routine of strategic decisions we are suggesting depends on fostering a contrastive awareness of available translation options, to which strategic considerations involving context can be subsequently applied. The availability of options can only be properly assessed by taking sentences out of textual context.

Second, in the contrastive chapters we frequently reverse the direction of translation to translating from English to German. This is in order to bring into the open certain possibilities *in English* which one can easily overlook when translating *from German*. For many German sentences, the option of translating into English without significant grammatical transposition actually exists, but frequently at the cost of significant translation loss in terms of idiomaticity and appropriate register in the TT. Many of the English STs in the contrastive chapters contain constructions which cannot pass into German without (sometimes drastic) transposition. These are instances of precisely those idiomatic English constructions which it is easiest to overlook as possible options when one is translating a German ST, particularly one whose structure can be replicated in English. Our hope is that, having come across these constructions as stumbling-blocks in translation *into* German, students will remain aware of their availability as options in translating *from* German.

16

Contrastive topic and practical: the function of modal particles

This chapter constitutes the material for all or part of a practical. If possible, the following exercise should be handed in before the practical. It should in any case be completed before going on to the material in the rest of the chapter.

PRELIMINARY EXERCISE

Translate the following passage into German, using only a monolingual German dictionary.

The speakers are German soldiers during World War I.

'But what I would like to know,' says Albert, 'is whether there would not have been a war if the Kaiser had said No.'
'I'm sure there would,' I interject, 'he was against it from the first.'
'Well, if not him alone, then perhaps if twenty or thirty people in the world had said No.'
'That's probable,' I agree, 'but they damned well said Yes.'
'It's queer, when one thinks about it,' goes on Kropp, 'we are here to protect our fatherland. And the French are over there to protect their fatherland. Now, who's in the right?'
[...]
Tjaden reappears. He is still quite excited and again joins the conversation, wondering just how a war gets started.
'Mostly by one country badly offending another,' answers Albert with a slight air of superiority.
Then Tjaden pretends to be obtuse. 'A country? I don't follow. A mountain in

Germany cannot offend a mountain in France. Or a river, or a wood, or a field of wheat.'

This chapter deals with a practical problem which has very considerable implications for translation between German and English. The problem is more obvious in translating from German to English, because of the difficulties the translator may experience in finding appropriate ways of rendering certain sentential particles – we shall be referring to them as modal particles – that are evidently functional (that is, meaningful) in the German ST. On the other hand, the problem is more insidious in translating from English to German, mainly because the translator may overlook the need to supply additional sentential particles in a German TT where there are no such particles in the English ST. The result is often a TT that copies the propositional content of the sentences of the English ST, but fails to achieve 'normalcy' in German, owing to the lack of sentential particles. German sentences tend to contain a greater number and range of sentential particles than English. The cumulative effect of their absence from a German TT will be an impression of oddness, even foreignness. There is also a risk of quite serious errors in the register of the TT, particularly tonal register.

The passage supplied in the preliminary exercise is itself from a published translation of Erich Maria Remarque's novel *Im Westen nichts Neues.* In context it may be assumed that the translator was seeking to suggest natural dialogue between ordinary serving soldiers. Of the problems involved in translating the passage either way, the one to be focused on here is the difference between the two languages with regard to the use of modal particles, sentential markers whose function is to nuance the illocutionary meanings of sentences. A first illustration can be supplied by the English text: the difference between (simply) '... but they said Yes' and (the actual wording): '... but they damned well said Yes'. However, the dimensions of the potential translation problem become clear only when the TTs produced by the preliminary exercise are compared with the German original as a whole. Here is the German text:

'Eins möchte ich aber doch wissen,' sagte Albert, 'ob es Krieg gegeben hätte, wenn der Kaiser nein gesagt hätte.'
'Das glaube ich sicher,' werfe ich ein, – 'er soll *ja sowieso* erst gar nicht gewollt haben.'
'Na, wenn er allein nicht, dann vielleicht doch, wenn so zwanzig, dreißig Leute in der Welt Nein gesagt hätten.'
'Das wohl,' gebe ich zu, 'aber die haben *ja gerade* gewollt.'
'Es ist komisch, wenn man sich das überlegt,' fährt Kropp fort, 'wir sind *doch* hier, um unser Vaterland zu verteidigen. Aber die Franzosen sind *doch* auch da, um ihr Vaterland zu verteidigen. Wer hat *nun* recht?'

[...]
Tjaden erscheint wieder. Er ist noch immer angeregt und greift sofort wieder in das Gespräch ein, indem er sich erkundigt, wie *eigentlich überhaupt* ein Krieg entstehe.
'Meistens so, daß ein Land ein anderes schwer beleidigt,' gibt Albert mit einer gewissen Überlegenheit zur Antwort.
Doch Tjaden stellt sich dickfellig. 'Ein Land? Das verstehe ich nicht. Ein Berg in Deutschland kann *doch* einen Berg in Frankreich nicht beleidigen. Oder ein Fluß oder ein Wald oder ein Weizenfeld.'

Reprinted by kind permission from *Im Westen nichts Neues*, by Erich Maria Remarque (Berlin: Propyläen-Verlag, 1929, pp. 202–4), copyright © 1959, 1984, 1987 by Verlag Kiepenheuer & Witsch, Köln. [The italics are ours.]

Except in the hands of a very experienced translator, a 'back-translation' of the excerpt from English to German is not likely to reproduce more than one or two of the original German modal particles italicized above, for the translator will tend to be reluctant to 'invent' modal particles not explicitly present in the English text. As always, the translator's choices must be weighed against strategic considerations of context, idiomaticity, register and other stylistic features. But the colloquial raciness evident in the Remarque ST is not so explicitly marked in English; and a 'back-translation' to German will hardly recover this feature fully, if only because of the dearth of nuancing markers in 'normal' written English.

It is interesting to trace how the inflections carried by the italicized modal particles have been rendered (if at all) in the published TT. Apart from the question of whether 'erst' is accurately translated by '*from the* first' (as opposed to '*at* first'), the 'ja sowieso' disappears. A few lines later, 'ja gerade' is forcefully translated as 'damned well'. Twice in the following sentence (and once again in the last paragraph of the extract), 'doch' disappears. 'Wer hat nun recht?' becomes 'Now, who's in the right?', signalling (correctly) that the 'nun' is not a temporal adverb ('Who's right now?') but something else, an illocutionary particle. Further on, 'wie eigentlich überhaupt ein Krieg entstehe' is rendered as 'just how a war gets started'.

After completion of the preliminary exercise, close study of the sentential particles and the published renderings will prove rewarding. Does the 'ja sowieso' convey a note of confident appeal to common knowledge? Does the TT's 'damned well' convey vigour (and perhaps approval/disapproval) while losing the notion 'It was these twenty–thirty people that really counted'? Does the ST in fact imply such a notion, and, if so, how is it suggested? Is the 'gerade' really a sentential particle, or is it an adverb? Was the translator right not to include an explicit translation for 'doch' (three times in all)? If not, what did he miss, and what could he have done? The 'nun' clearly relates not to real time but to the little rhetorical edifice that Kropp has constructed: he is asking his mates to survey and resolve the paradox he has just outlined. How successful is 'just how' for the notably heavy 'wie eigentlich überhaupt'? Here the TT suggests serious – rather than idle – interest, which is surely appropriate, but also particular precision, which is more disputable; and, again disputably, it does not render the strong 'first principles' colouring which is imparted to the question by 'überhaupt'.

German particles of this type often simply disappear when their surrounding text is translated into English. (The Remarque text's examples with 'doch' are a case in point.) This at least is routine practice, a readily understandable practice in view of the elusive, variable and sometimes faint semantic content of true modal particles. In turn, while there can often be no quarrel with an individual translation decision not to attempt an English counterpart for a given modal particle, the very frequency with which the 'no counterpart' option is taken up is itself a reason for the high degree of uncertainty, among English-speaking learners of German, about the nature and function of German modal particles. Consider the following examples of spoken language, attempting to define how far each is individually coloured by the MPs (this abbreviation will be generally used from here on):

Kommen Sie doch herein!	Come in!
Wie heißt du denn?	What's your name?
Sagen S' mal...	Tell me...
Ich komm' doch schon!	I'm coming!
Das ist ja fein.	That's great/lovely.

The fact that many MPs are communicatively learnt and used, because they belong to the most recurrent social niceties, makes no difference to the generic uncertainty. If 'Wie heißt du denn?' and 'Kommen Sie doch herein!' are found to be communicative equivalents of 'What's your name?' and 'Come *in*!' – and most learners do have this experience – then it is understandable that MPs tend to be regarded as dispensable for purposes of German–English translation.

This chapter and the next have a threefold aim: to contradict that assumption, to suggest some *patterns* discernible within the shimmering wealth of practical usage, and to identify some translation tactics appropriate for particular circumstances.

As a first step towards the first broad aim – of demonstrating that MPs are functional – consider the following examples, examining in particular the appropriateness of the TTs offered:

ST 1	Kommen Sie rein!	TT 1	Come in!
ST 2	Kommen Sie mal rein!	TT 2	Would you come in for a minute?
ST 3	Kommen Sie doch rein!	TT 3	(Do) come in! / Come on in!
ST 4	Kommen Sie ruhig rein!	TT 4	Come on in!
ST 5	Kommen Sie bloß endlich rein!	TT 5	*Will* you come in!/For goodness' sake come in!
ST 6	Was wollen Sie denn von mir?	TT 6	What can I do for you?
ST 7	Was wollen Sie eigentlich von mir?	TT 7	What are you after?
ST 8	Was wollen Sie überhaupt von mir?	TT 8	I wish you'd leave me alone.

ST 9	Das geht zu weit.	TT 9	That's going too far.
ST 10	Das geht doch wohl zu weit.	TT 10	I think that's going a bit far.
ST 11	Das geht eigentlich zu weit.	TT 11	That's going too far, you know.
ST 12	Das geht denn doch zu weit.	TT 12	(No,) that's going *too* far.
ST 13	Wir müssen jetzt *langsam* fahren.	TT 13	We'll need to go slow here.
ST 14	Wir müssen jetzt langsam *gehen*.	TT 14	It's about time we were going.

The Remarque ST may already have suggested that MPs in sustained dialogue (or indeed in any sustained text) call for a strategic approach in translation, and to this point we will return later. Analysis of the short examples leaves no doubt that even when shorn of context these normally unobtrusive particles may influence the communication decisively. In requests/commands, they modulate the 'Do this!' message on an emotive range from gentle coaxing to peremptory and even angry orders. In yes/no questions *(Entscheidungsfragen)*, they can suggest innocence or incredulity. In questions requiring an expository answer, such as the set used above *(Ergänzungsfragen* or *WH-questions)*, they can likewise suggest innocence – or a readiness for serious confrontation. In statements, what is said can be nuanced by MPs in any of a vast number of ways, and with widely varying *degrees* of impact. It is beyond the scope of the chapter, let alone of the fifteen or so short examples quoted, to do more than merely suggest the potential expressive contribution of MPs to those areas of German discourse where they are used. Two further short observations should be made on the basis of the above sets of examples. The first is that where in German a MP *can* be used, its non-use will be significant. The second is the point made by the last pair of examples above. ST 13 introduces an adverb lookalike – or, to put it more fairly, ST 13 and ST 14 introduce adverb and MP lookalikes. Most MPs are in fact adverb homonyms. The example is chosen as a striking one to illustrate how the MP characteristically has (a) sentential function and (b) a meaning which is both related to its adverb lookalike and yet also significantly different. The translator has to be relatively green to translate 'langsam' in ST 14 as 'slowly'; later examples will show the greater risk of mistaking *adverbial* use of (say) 'schon' or 'mal' for MP use.

At this point it seems appropriate to offer a generalizing description of German MPs and their function, and a note on their habitat. What class of signifiers is it that can include, at one extreme, a 'vielleicht' capable of provoking an ordinary German to fury, and at the other extreme a whole range of usages which make it into modern monolingual dictionaries, only to be glossed as 'ohne eigentliche Bedeutung'?

MPs, whether derived from adverbs or not, have, like the so-called 'sentence adverbs' ('leider', 'glücklicherweise'), the function of modalizing the whole sentence and not the verb alone. Thus they may indeed be called sentential particles. They individually *or collectively, even through their very frequency or infrequency*, indicate the tenor, atmosphere, climate of the communicative interaction in progress. MPs are in fact indissolubly identified with the idea of communicative interaction – as opposed to one-way communication. In this they are true illocutionary particles.

In genuinely impersonal communications (for example, scientific, legal, official) the frequency of MPs approaches nil. The same, of course, applies if the communicator has a reason to *seem* objective or non-committal. These observations point to the essential function of MPs as lying outside the factual content of what is said: they 'nuance' the message, not directly like an adverb ('These problems proved *rather* difficult to solve'), but indirectly, perhaps by indicating the speaker's attitude to what is said, and/or by conveying to the listener a hint on the type of response expected. Particles such as 'denn', 'ja', 'mal', 'doch' and 'eben' are in fact like a simultaneous commentary or decoding instruction which tells the recipient how to read the basic factual communication. Consider the following examples, identifying the particular 'spin' imparted by the italicized MP.

Er weiß *ja,* wie es bei dir aussieht.
Er weiß *doch*, wie es bei dir aussieht.

[*identifying someone passing down the street*]
Das ist *ja* Harry!
Das ist *doch* Harry!

Das hast du *aber* fein gemacht!
Das hast du *eigentlich* fein gemacht.

Ich will nur eben *mal* raus.
Ich will nur *überhaupt* raus.
(Note that here the MPs respectively suit very different propositional contents, hence they signal that as well.)

Wollen Sie *eigentlich* behaupten, wir hätten das nicht richtig angefaßt?
Wollen Sie *etwa* behaupten, wir hätten das nicht richtig angefaßt?

Ist das *nun* dein Ernst?
Ist das *vielleicht* dein Ernst?

MPs generally mark the speaker's attitude not just to the content of the discourse but also to the interlocutor(s). In particular instances, examination will suggest, indeed, that MP choice is related to the *response* of the person(s) addressed. Where such a relationship exists, it is a complex one: part diagnosis, part prognosis, part manipulation. The point may be illustrated by the following simple examples:

Ich weiß ja, daß du nichts dafür konntest.	I know you couldn't do anything about it.

Characteristically (though not always) a 'consensus' particle, the 'ja' forestalls the defensive response by establishing common ground – sympathy – between speaker and listener. Similarly:

Fahr doch selber hin!	(Why don't you) go yourself!/ Why not go yourself?

The tone of the ST here is almost inescapably rude – a point, incidentally, which can be made about at most one of the three TTs offered. The adversative particle 'doch' diagnoses and challenges the (perceived) contrary intention, that is, the unwillingness to make the trip. By contrast:

Fahr doch mal selber hin!	(Why don't you) go yourself!/ Why not pop over yourself?

In commands, 'mal' is always disarming, and consequently the 'doch' in this example says no more than that the idea proposed is a fresh one. The illocutionary approach is therefore much less confrontational.

MPs may be said to have their natural role, their home, in spoken dialogue. The evidence for this lies in the frequency of 'lookalike' and near-'lookalike' sentences in the examples provided so far in this chapter. In many cases voice inflection and pitch are crucial to correct understanding. By the same token a third component, body language, must be taken into account. The point may be illustrated through one of the rare cases where English appears to have a MP usage closely analogous to a German one. In German it is standard among children and young people to ask: 'Wie heißt du denn?'. The 'denn' is the MP that goes with the most open, innocuous type of question. English does not have a counterpart – *except* perhaps in such a situation as a crowded airport lounge where someone else's four-year-old comes to stare at me: 'What's *your* name then?' is a fairly stock response. Similarly: 'Was hast du denn?' translates as: 'What's the matter with you (then)?' The 'then' has no temporal connotation, and only a very distant logical one. Facial expression, eye contact, body distance, and so forth may, and speech melody certainly will, help convey not only the basic question but also the illocutionary data which may well play the *major* role in influencing the recipient to fraternize, fight or flee. These generalizations apply to both languages (though of course there are differences in detail). In this area, the interesting difference between German and English from the translator's point of view is that speech melody and body language, the two physical components of the core message's 'packaging' (or one might say 'sub-text'), are in German very much more richly supplemented by textual data, particularly those sentential particles which are the subject of this chapter. In practice, MPs and other particles do not *necessarily* play a much larger role, relative to acoustic and visual signals, in German dialogue than in English, but they are certainly capable of doing so – for instance, given the right circumstances, the 'vielleicht' of 'Ist das vielleicht dein Ernst?' will sting like a bee – and in general they can be said to constitute a very substantial commentary on attitudes and perceptions underlying any text in which there is an element of real or implicit dialogue.

The implications for *written* texts, whether reporting or suggesting dialogue, are obvious: the nuancing of the text is readable from the printed page on the basis of much more copious evidence than is afforded by English or French. Regular use of MPs is by no means confined either to explicit dialogue or to texts of informal register. Colloquial dialogue is indeed almost always heavily laced with MPs even when otherwise terse: 'Nee, sag' bloß!' – 'Det is man so'. While in written STs of neutral or formal register the incidence of MPs is usually much lower, those that are used may be correspondingly significant. Local variations within a text may alert the translator to a change of tone, MPs acting collectively to signal by their presence that the communication is personalized – or, more precisely, response-oriented. Globally, to take a concrete instance, the relatively liberal use of MPs in the *linking narrative* sections of the novels of Theodor Fontane marks him as a writer whose preferred narrative stance is conversational rather than distant or clinical.

The implications, in turn, for *translation* of written texts are likewise obvious: the translator from German to English basically has to choose between close matching, omission and compensation. The first option, where possible at all, risks over-marking the English TT; omission, in the long run, under-marks; compensation may require a well-planned strategic approach. In translation into German, the 'understating' tendency of English written STs means that the translator must be not only alive to the inflections and implications latent in the English text, but also familiar with the rich possibilities of German MP usage. The problem is that the MP system is not readily transparent to the non-native learner and cannot be tackled as readily as standard lexical items on a word-by-word basis. The best approach is the long-term one of familiarization with the routine MPs of everyday speech through modern communicative language-teaching and native-speaker contact. Only this general familiarity and competence can provide the basis and continuing background for specialist studies.

(Taught in some detail by Trevor Jones at Cambridge as early as the late 1950s (under the more telling name of 'emotive particles'), modal particles appear to have had little attention in UK teaching publications for a quarter-century after that, but with the rise of German studies in general and communicative language-teaching in particular they have now come into their own and are the subject of extensive treatment in some good recent publications aimed at the British learner (see for example Lockwood, 1987, Hammer (2nd ed.), 1991, and for translation purposes especially Durrell, 1992). For a detailed analytical survey it is still necessary to go to a good German source such as Helbig and Buscha (1991) or Weydt *et al.* (1983).)

CONCLUDING EXERCISE

Identify, review and discuss the modal particles used in the texts from *Des Teufels General* (Practical 10.1) and *Mathilde Möhring* (Practical 9.2), focusing in particular on (i) the distribution of MPs in continuous dialogue text and (ii) the relative frequency of MPs as between the two texts named.

17

Contrastive topic and practical: translating modal particles

A chapter designed to provide material for a practical class cannot, of course, cover its topic in exhaustive detail. There are, in any case, advantages in getting away from an alphabetic A–Z of MPs and suggesting, instead, the rudiments of an approach that groups and categorizes the varied problems posed by German MPs. Working with a representative sample, we shall in what follows suggest broad functional categories to which a number of familiar MPs may be assigned, and consider translation problems in relation to this essentially pragmatic categorization.

Any categorization of MPs by function must initially make distinctions under the major headings of 'imperative', 'interrogative' and 'statement'. In view of the often elusive meanings of MPs, it is interesting to note that their usage is very sharply differentiated between commands/requests, questions and statements (for an overview see Helbig and Buscha, 1991).

MPs cannot be treated in the same way as other items of vocabulary. Whether in first language acquisition or in second language learning, they are more resistant to analysis in their own right than, probably, any other lexical category. The meaning of a 'modalized' sentence is conveyed by the utterance as a whole; hence MP meaning is acquired pragmatically. This is different from being taught that, say, the word 'house' has both a literal and a figurative sense, or that 'form' has a whole host of meanings, literal and figurative. MPs differ from lexical items such as these in having no fixed reference at all, existing only as expressions of mood and attitude underlying communication. It is true that they have developed patterns of usage so strong that many contextless sentences can be sharply differentiated on the basis of MP marking alone, for instance:

Der gehört doch nicht zu uns. (with unstressed 'doch')	He's not one of ours. (*that is, you are wrong to think we are responsible for him*)
Der gehört auch nicht zu uns. (with unstressed 'auch')	He's not one of ours anyway. (*as already suggested by his behaviour*)

But where an individual MP can reasonably be said to have a *single* sense, this is still extremely generalized. For instance, 'doch' can be seen always to have an *adversative* sense; but compare for instance 'Fahr doch mal selber hin' and 'Das ist doch schön geworden' ('Oh, that's turned out very nice!') on the one hand with 'Er ist doch dein Bruder' (whose force, with unstressed 'doch', may be as strong as 'He's your brother, for goodness' sake!') and 'Er ist *doch* dein Bruder' (which, with stressed 'doch', has the force of an outright contradiction) on the other. There is in fact no reason why any given MP should be tied down to a single invariant sense, and many have in practice widely differing import according to context. Compare for instance:

Hast du auch alles verstanden?	Now, are you quite sure you've got all that?
Wozu soll er auch herkommen?	Anyway, why *should* he come?
Wie heißt der Typ schon?	What was the guy's name (again)?
Wer bist du schon?	Who do you think you are?
Keine Angst, ich pass' schon auf.	Don't worry, I'll keep my eyes open all right.
Und das will schon was heißen!	And that's (really) saying something!

Given the variability of the illocutionary meaning attaching to MPs, there is a case for basing a contrastive approach on an informal grouping of MP usage according to affective value, very broadly conceived. This groups like with like, makes it possible to set up scales of forcefulness (one of the few useful parameters available), and also, in focusing first on overall force and then on the details of a range of expressive possibilities, accords with our general principle that analysis of translation problems should start from strategic considerations and progress from them to points of detail. Indeed, given the 'commenting/modalizing' function of MPs, few other types of textual variable could illustrate the principle so well.

The material in the rest of this chapter is arranged on the basis of the above considerations. While the need for separate treatment of interrogatives, imperatives and statements is established, the subgroupings suggested within these categories should be regarded as informal, aiming simply to organize and facilitate discussion in the practical.

1 IMPERATIVES

1.1 Playing down

1.1.1 *mal*

Könnten Sie schnell mal Verbandzeug holen? (*standard polite request using question form*)	Could you fetch some bandages quickly, please?
Gib mal her! (*Compared with* Gib her! *this is just as forceful, but less rude.*)	Let's have it./Hand it over.
Thomas, lauf mal schnell zu Oma und sag ihr,...	Thomas, (will you) run quickly over to Grandma's and tell her...

In the minds of many German learners of English, and of some translators, the MP 'mal' is identified rather too uncritically with English 'just'. In statements this indeed often works, with 'Ich geh kurz mal raus' being rendered as 'I'm just going out for a minute'. But in commands the terms diverge. 'Mal' is so automatic with simple commands in German ('Guck mal!'; 'Kommen Sie mal!') as to signify little more than casualness, and is in part a mere prosodic filler. That is precisely where 'just' will not do in English. For the last two brief examples, neither 'Just look' nor 'Just come' can be even remotely accurate in English without further modalization. The translator can opt for either 'Look!' and 'Come over here!', or for alternatives such as '(Just) Take a look at this'! and 'Can you (just) come here a minute?'.

1.1.2 *doch mal*

Mach doch mal Rühreier, es soll ja schnell gehen!	Why not make scrambled eggs? We're in a hurry.

Here, 'doch' at most blends in the nuance of a new thought. Cf. 1.2.1 below.

1.2 Insisting or contradicting

1.2.1 *doch*

Mach doch Rühreier, es soll ja schnell gehen!	Just make scrambled eggs, we're in a hurry!
[*sharply*] Warten Sie doch!	Will you *please* wait/be patient!/ Here, hang on a minute!

[*child, plaintively, to schoolmates running ahead*] Wartet doch mal!	Wait for *me!*

As in statements, 'doch' is a reliable marker of at least some *adversative* element: perhaps as mild as a change of tack on the speaker's part (cf. 'doch mal' in 1.1.2 above), but perhaps as strong as a perceived clash of wills over the command. English characteristically does not mark this group specifically; most TTs are straight imperatives. However, the first example of the set is a little sharper than its counterpart at 1.1.2 and so suggests a suspicion that the cook's intentions are already formed.

1.2.2 *nur;* (regional) *man*

Nur Ruhe, nur Ruhe!	Let's have some peace and quiet!
Bleiben S' nur hübsch zu Hause und warten S' ab.	Just you stay put at home and wait.
Geh du man hin. Red man nicht so viel.	(You can) just go yourself. Oh, don't keep on about it.

These two MPs are used to press a request, but, in general, in a low-key way, without the note of sharpness or irritation signalled by some uses of 'doch' and by most uses of 'schon', 'bloß' and 'endlich' (see below). Suggested renderings here may involve 'just' or 'just you' or a complete rephrasing:

1.2.3 *schon; endlich*; *bloß*; stressed *ja*

Nun, mach schon!	Come on, get a move on!
Nun, komm schon, wir kaufen dir eine neue Puppe.	Come on, calm down, we'll buy you a new doll.
Sag ihm *ja* nicht, daß ich auch dabei war!	For goodness' sake don't tell him I was there too.
Geht mir *ja* nicht zu nah ans Wasser ran!	Whatever you do, don't go near the water!
Ja, Kinder, hört endlich auf!	Come on, children, pack it in!

These four MPs are at the top end of the scale of forcefulness in commands, but the associated situations differ. 'Schon' implies resistance, and may be coaxing – or simply impatient. 'Endlich' connotes impatience. 'Bloß' may in appropriate situations express impatience – but elsewhere is synonymous with stressed 'ja' (and the top end of the 'nur' range), i.e. simply a strong adjuration as to future conduct. English TT possibilities for the stronger particles include 'Whatever you do...', 'Above all', 'Make sure you...', 'For goodness' (etc.) sake...' and a simple strong emphasis on the operative verb or phrase.

EXERCISE: ***Propose and discuss appropriate translations for the following sentences, paying special attention to the role of modal particles.***

1 Why don't you try getting up a little earlier?
2 Throw discretion to the winds and be your own person!
3 Whatever you do, don't ask after his health.
4 Please replace your handset.
5 Komm, gib schon her!
6 Waren Sie diesen Monat schon im Haxen-Grill? Wenn nicht, dann besuchen Sie uns doch mal!
7 Jetzt, hört doch endlich zu!
8 Hör doch bloß endlich auf mit deiner ewigen Quengelei!
9 Nun hör'n Sie mal, was Sie da sagen, das gefällt mir aber gar nicht.
10 Laß dir ja nichts von dem weismachen!

2 INTERROGATIVES

It should be noted that MPs are by no means an automatic garnish for questions in German. The informal categories below suggest conditions in which given MPs tend to be used. If the conditions do not apply, no MP is used. Even where they do apply, successive sentences are rarely marked in the same way (cf. 3.3.2 below).

2.1 Innocent

(*The tone suggests that the person asked has all the answers.*)

2.1.1 *denn*

[*hotelier to guest*] Was wollen Sie denn morgen tun?	What are your plans for tomorrow?
[*landlady to guest*] Was möchten Sie denn zum Frühstück?	What would you like for breakfast?
[*one friend to another*] Warum ist deine Mutti nicht mitgekommen?	Why didn't your Mum come?

Even within the main category of interrogatives, 'denn' can be observed to have distinct functions depending on the type of question. Compare the examples given in the 'innocent' subgroup (all WH-questions) with those given in the following ('analytical') subgroup. WH-questions lacking the 'denn' sound more purposive, businesslike; with it they sound more chatty and relaxed. In the set of three examples given above, the use or non-use of 'denn' will mark register or circumstances or both. If the landlady is short-staffed, and late with the orders, the breakfast-menu question is less likely to have a 'denn'. The third question, however, being inherently of a more intimate and searching nature, is likely to take either no particle, or an 'analytical' one, probably 'eigentlich'. (It is true that length of sentence is probably also a factor in MP choice, but the illocutionary point remains valid.)

The implications for the translator are (as pointed out in the preamble to Chapter 16) difficult because they are subtle. Ingenious periphrasis ('And what have you got in mind for tomorrow?') can be tried, but must be used extremely sparingly. Totally bald (unmodalized) translations will serve in the short and even medium term; but something will be lost unless other ways can be found to indicate the conversational temperature. For the translator working into German, the challenge is to read that temperature from dialogue and linking narrative and transpose it into a German TT in which the textual markers harmonize with the mood.

2.2 Analytical

2.2.1 *denn* (in Yes/No questions)

Haben Sie unser Zimmer eigentlich schon vergeben? – Nein. Wollen Sie denn noch etwas länger bleiben?	Has anyone else taken our room for tonight? – No. Do you want to stay on?

The function of 'denn' is included in the loose grouping called 'analytical' because, when attached to a yes/no question, it tends strongly to signal a 'follow-up', as opposed to an opening gambit. The follow-up may, of course, be to no more than a facial expression.

2.2.2 *eigentlich*

Wie lange arbeiten Sie eigentlich schon bei Großmanns?	How long have you been working for Grossmanns'?
Ist da eigentlich was draus geworden?	Did it ever come to anything?
Was willst du denn eigentlich werden?	What do you want to be when you grow up?

Wie übersetzt man eigentlich *eigentlich*? [*title of article by Jörn Albrecht*]	How *does* one translate 'eigentlich'?

The MP 'eigentlich' is not far in sense from the English modal particle 'actually', but neither is a reliable translation for the other. The German MP is used far more frequently than its English counterpart. It is unstressed, used almost as an unconscious linguistic reflex, and in questions suggests that the enquiry (however trivial) is *not* perfunctory, that there is an interest in getting to the heart of the matter. Yet, as the third of the above examples suggests, it can be used alongside 'denn' without any sense of clash.

2.2.3 *auch*

Und bist du auch glücklich?	And are you really happy?
Wirst du auch bestimmt hingehen?	You really will go, won't you?
Und ist er auch gekommen?	And *did* he come in the end?

In questions 'auch' seems to relate to the function of '(denn) auch' in statements, which itself marks a sense of expectation duly fulfilled. The force it has in questions tends to be one of anxious enquiry. The translator needs to be aware of these rather elusive MP uses of 'auch', if only to avoid confusions with the adverbial homonym meaning 'also'.

2.2.4 *überhaupt*

Ich habe noch gar nicht gefragt, mögen Sie überhaupt klassische Musik?	I'm sorry, I never asked you, you do like classical music, don't you?
Wer sind Sie denn überhaupt?	May I ask who you are exactly?
Ist das überhaupt wahr?	(But) Is that true?
Wie kann sowas überhaupt passieren?	(But) how could it *happen*?

The MP 'überhaupt' – again a MP with a closely related adverb homonym – betokens a sense of sweeping details aside in favour of first principles or overriding general considerations. English renderings to consider include 'at all', 'anyway', verbs of judgement and simple emphasis for intensity.

2.2.5 *doch wohl, doch hoffentlich (used in questions with a statement form)*

Die Arbeit werden Sie doch wohl inzwischen abgeschlossen haben?	I take it you have finished the paper by now?
Dein Mann ist doch hoffentlich nicht krank?	I do hope your husband's not ill or anything?

These combinations belong to the more deliberate MP usages, expressing an assumption subject to some doubt, and as questions (in statement form) are often used ironically. The most useful stock translation is probably verb plus noun clause: 'I take it (that)...', 'I hope (that)...'.

2.3 Playing up/rhetorical

2.3.1 *bloß, nur*

Was ist denn bloß passiert?	What (can have) happened?
Was kann ihm bloß zugestoßen sein?	What (on earth) can have happened to him?
Was hat er bloß?	Whatever's the matter with him?
Was sollen wir nur tun?	What *are* we to do?

These correspond fairly straightforwardly to English formulations such as 'Whatever happened?', 'What on earth...', 'What *can* have...? ' or (simply) very strong emphasis (for instance, on the two words 'What happened?').

2.3.2 *schon*

Wer braucht mich schon?	What use am I anyway?
Was kann *ich* denn schon dagegen tun?	There's nothing *I* can do about it.

This use of 'schon' dramatizes and heightens certain questions. Here there is no close adverbial cognate at all; English may use strong speech inflection or an approximating communicative translation.

2.4 Tentative/mock tentative

2.4.1 *etwa*; *vielleicht*

Sind Sie etwa der Herr, der vorhin Frau Meyer sprechen wollte?	Are you the gentleman who was looking for Frau Meyer?
War das etwa Ihr Mann, der eben verunglückte?	That wasn't your husband in the accident, was it?
Könnten Sie mir vielleicht Feuer geben?	Could you give me a light?

Both these MPs are used frequently as an apologetic formula to accompany an enquiry which may prove to be misdirected or sensitive. While English marks these situations with formulae such as 'Are you by any chance...?', 'I say, that wasn't your husband...?', the translator needs to bear in mind that in German the same two MPs are often used ironically or tauntingly and then allow a rather wider range of translations in English.

Soll das vielleicht witzig sein?	Was that meant to be funny?
Ist das vielleicht dein Ernst?	Are you serious?/You can't be serious.

EXERCISE: ***Propose and discuss appropriate translations for the following sentences, paying special attention to the role of modal particles.***

1 Gentlemen, you've heard the arguments. Who is for the proposal?
2 Did he marry her in the end?
3 Before you invite him on your chalet party, find out if he can ski!
4 Why do you want to do Medicine?
5 What on earth's he up to?
6 You need to think seriously about where you're going to live.
7 Hast du vielleicht zehn Mark bei dir?
8 War's schön? – Gut! – Wo wollt ihr denn morgen hin?
9 Sie räumte Tassen aus dem Schrank und sah mich fragend an. 'Wie viele sind wir eigentlich?'
10 Was soll denn das überhaupt?
11 O Gott, das war doch nicht etwa dein Chef vorhin?
12 [*from Lessing's* Nathan der Weise, *1779*] Nun, wo ist es denn? Es ist doch wohl nicht etwa gar gestorben?

3 STATEMENTS

3.1 Playing down

(*Acknowledges the commonplace or obvious, the agreed; in dialogue placatory.)*

3.1.1 *ja*

[*as visitors arrive*] Da sind sie ja!	There they are!
Gehen wir lieber zu Fuß, wir haben ja Zeit.	Let's walk, we've got time.
Wollen Sie nicht lieber so lange warten, er kann ja jeden Augenblick kommen.	Wouldn't you like to wait? He should be here any minute.
Das ist ja gut und schön, aber...	That's all very well, but...
Sie wissen ja alle, um was es geht.	You all know why we are here.

The MP 'ja' and (more emphatically) 'schließlich' and 'ja schließlich' are all used to accompany statements of the obvious. In this sense 'ja' is one of the most frequently and unthinkingly used MPs of all, much more so than its English near-equivalent 'of course'; so it is a curiosity that it is also sometimes used in exclamatory statements (see next subgroup). At its weakest, as in the first example above, 'ja' finds no direct English rendering. Like English 'of course', but less obtrusively, 'ja' may be used ironically.

3.2 Playing up

('*This is something exceptional.*')

3.2.1 *ja*

Das ist ja herrlich!	Oh, that's wonderful!
Das ist ja wunderschöne Arbeit!	But that's *lovely*!

3.2.2 *doch*

[*sudden, unexpected recognition*] Das ist doch dein Bruder!	Look! It's your brother!

3.2.3 *schon*

Du wirst schon sehen.	You'll see (all right/in due course).
Du kriegst von mir schon einen Denkzettel.	I'll give you something to remember me by/think about.
Das bringt schon was ein.	It's quite a good earner./It pays off.
Wenn schon, denn schon.	In for a penny, in for a pound./Don't spoil the ship...

Even as a MP, 'schon' has widely varying senses. The one we focus on here is that of a strong assurance. (This should be distinguished from the possibly related use of 'schon' in the coupling 'schon... aber', which is close to 'zwar... aber'.) Affirmative 'schon' is a natural particle in (but not exclusive to) statements about the future (see the first two examples above).

3.2.4 *aber*; *vielleicht*

[*adult to child*] Du bist aber ge*wachs*en!	I say! (How) you've grown!
Das hast du aber fein gemacht!	That's beautifully done!
Das war vielleicht ein Reinfall!	What a disaster!/That was a disaster and no mistake!
Der ist vielleicht gefahren, sag ich dir.	He didn't half drive!/That was some drive!

These two MPs are used in similar ways to lend illocutionary force to exclamations, each amounting to something like an audible exclamation-mark. However, there are register differences (social and arguably tonal). 'Aber' belongs on the whole to genteel usage, 'vielleicht' is earthier.

3.3 Adversative

(*'There is a difference of perception between us on this issue.'/ 'I have just had a fresh thought.'*)

3.3.1 *eigentlich*

Ich würde das eigentlich lieber so ausdrücken...	I'd prefer to put it like this...

As a basically 'analytical' particle, 'eigentlich' can be used adversatively with demurring or tempering effect, that is, as a tactfully disguised contradiction. Apart from this, 'eigentlich' in statements seems to have little independent status as an MP, its sense never departing far from English 'actually' or 'really'.

3.3.2 *doch*

Da hat doch der Arzt gewohnt.	[*revisiting town*] Oh! That's where the doctor used to live!
	[*arguing*] No, it was the doctor who lived there. (*i.e. not the solicitor)*
Er weiß doch sehr gut, daß...	He knows perfectly well that...
Wo ist denn die Karin? Sie wollte doch kommen.	Where's Karin? I thought she was coming.
Es tut mir leid, ich kann wirklich nicht noch eine halbe Stunde dableiben, ich muß doch für die Kinder das Essen kochen.	I'm sorry, I really can't stay another half-hour, I have to see to the children's supper.

The 'adversative' subgroup is dominated by 'doch', certainly one of the three or four most frequently used MPs of all. The salient point is simply that 'doch' is triggered extremely readily and will be found marking statements which have only the faintest trace of (for instance) surprise, irony or argumentative value – as well as those which are strongly loaded. As indicated in the general introduction to this chapter, it has a correspondingly wide range of nuance.

A balanced study of 'doch' as of other particles is only possible on the basis of discourse extended over several sentences. Like others, it is used to nuance a point or convey an attitude and is then typically not used again in the next two or three sentences. (The translator into German needs to take care not to over-mark MPs.) In German STs, the frequency of 'doch' correlates closely with the degree of agitation, argumentativeness or hostility of the speaker. The following example from Plenzdorf's *Die neuen Leiden des jungen W.* is an extreme case, strongly enough marked to suggest a particularly disputatious state of mind. The eponymous hero remarks about Goethe's Werther:

Das war noch lange kein Grund, sich zu durchlöchern. Er hatte doch ein Pferd! Da wär ich doch wie nichts in die Wälder. Davon gab's doch damals noch genug.	That was no sort of a reason to blow his brains out. He'd got a horse, hadn't he? I'd have cleared off into the woods, straight off. Plenty of those around then, weren't there?

3.4 Analytical/reflective

3.4.1 *ja*; *(ja) schließlich*; *nun einmal*; *eben*; *halt*

Nein, wo Ihr Schirm geblieben ist, weiß ich nicht. Das Haus ist schließlich kein Fundbüro.	No, I don't know where your umbrella is. I'm not running a lost-property office.
Nein, diesmal bin ich dran. Ich will schließlich auch mal ausspannen.	No, it's my turn. I want some time off too.
Ihr Vater ist nun einmal über achtzig Jahre alt. Sie dürfen nicht zu viel von ihm verlangen.	Remember, your father is over eighty. Don't expect too much of him.
Frauen, die Feuerwehrwagen fahren, Schlauchtrommeln bedienen und Feuer niedermachen, das sind eben keine Frauen.	Women who drive fire-engines, handle hoses and put out fires just aren't women.
Du, per Bahn kostet die Reise 200 Mark pro Person! – Gut, dann fahren wir eben mit dem Bus.	It's going to cost 200 marks if we go by train! – O.K., then we'll just go by coach.

Any of the above MPs can have an explanatory nuance. 'Ja' is easily the least obtrusive; the others usually impose a fairly explicit nuance of generalization or truism to support and underline a contention.

The MP 'nun einmal' (colloquially 'nun mal') likewise goes with statements of the obvious, differing from '(ja) schließlich' perhaps in tending more strongly to go with truisms delivered in a sententious or even didactic tone. English may use voice inflection only, or a tagged-on 'you know', or even something as obtrusive as 'the fact is that...'.

As a MP, 'eben' has two related but distinct functions. First, it is a near-synonym for 'schließlich' and 'nun einmal', marking a truism, if rather less pompously. In its 'summing up' character, it also marks a much more limited, pragmatic and practical conclusion, as in the train/bus example above. Regionally, 'halt' is used similarly in both respects.

3.4.2 *auch*

Der hat auch nie was getaugt.	He was never any good.
[Die Sondermarken sind leider schon ausverkauft.] – Die wollen wir auch nicht.	That's O.K., it's not them we want.

In statements, MP 'auch' is like its adverb counterpart in referring back to something mentioned already. The sense is not so much of an *additional* point as of a rejoinder which matches and fulfils an expectation implicit in the prompt. Hence it features frequently in dialogue, but (particularly in the expanded form 'denn auch') is also a feature of certain types of traditional fictional narrative, where surmise and expectation are followed by the event.

3.4.3 *langsam*

Wir müssen langsam gehen.	It's about time we were going.
Das wird langsam unerträglich.	This is getting unbearable.
Der fällt mir langsam auf den Wecker.	He's beginning to get on my wick.

'Langsam' is analytical in that it comments on an observed process. Its true reference is back to the speaker. It makes a formal show of polite temporizing/modalizing, and often it means no more than that. But it can also be used in a palpably 'understating', ironic way, so that the illocutionary effect is to lend force by suggesting that the proposition's validity is steadily rising. It is also a good example of the often indistinct boundary between MPs and their homonymic adverbial counterparts. The English translation typically requires a present participle or a communicative rephrasing.

3.5 Attitudinal/permissive

3.5.1 *ruhig*

Wir möchten ein paar Freunde einladen, habt ihr was dagegen? – Könnt ihr ruhig machen.	We want to ask a few friends in, is that O.K.? – Yes, go ahead.
Du hättest ihr ruhig schreiben können.	It wouldn't have hurt you to write.
Sie sollen ruhig warten.	Let them wait/It won't hurt them to wait.

As an MP 'ruhig' is *untypical* only in having a unique function and in being relatively easily described and delimited. It is typical in having an adverbial cognate, in conveying information about mood, and in needing a communicative rather than a literal translation. Attached to permissions, it actively suggests a relaxed and tolerant attitude. Linked with modal verbs, and with a subtly different (rising) sentence inflection, 'ruhig' yields interesting variations: it can then underline a reproof, or (as in the third example) suggest the speaker's indifference to other people's discontent.

To remain within the scope of the practical, the two exercises which follow may need to be treated as alternatives. Ideally, both should be attempted.

EXERCISE A: *Propose and discuss appropriate translations for the following sentences, paying special attention to the role of modal particles.*

1. Boys will be boys. – That's no excuse!
2. You know, this is starting to look serious.
3. What counts at the end of the day is customer satisfaction.
4. He's asking a bit much when you come to think about it.
5. Is that all you have? I'd have liked a seat nearer the front.
6. Wir sind doch keine Untertanen mehr, wir sind Demokraten.
7. Das konnte ich doch nicht wissen! Du hättest es mir eigentlich sagen können.
8. [*book title, collection of light humorous essays by H. Spoerl*] Man kann ruhig darüber sprechen.
9. Aber der Peter kann ja doch bei uns übernachten!
10. Guckt euch *das* mal an! Die Elke hat eine Eins! Die wird sich aber freuen!

EXERCISE B: *Propose and discuss appropriate English translations for the following dialogue, paying special attention to the role of modal particles.*

KUNDE:	Das ist aber eine interessante kleine Porzellanfigur.
HÄNDLER:	Gefällt sie Ihnen? Ich kann sie Ihnen für dreißig Pfund lassen.
KUNDE:	Aber ich habe doch gerade gehört, wie Sie dem anderen Kunden da gesagt haben, Sie wollten sechzig Pfund.
HÄNDLER:	Da haben Sie eben einen guten Tag, ne?
KUNDE:	Was ist denn los? Auf einmal etwa Winter-Schlußverkauf?
HÄNDLER:	Schon eher Ausverkauf. Im Februar kauft doch kein Mensch Antiquitäten.
KUNDE:	Sie verkaufen also alles zum halben Preis?
HÄNDLER:	Um Gottes willen, nein! Ich kann es mir doch nicht leisten, Porzellanfiguren wie die da zu dreißig Pfund anzubieten. Da wäre ich ja sofort pleite.
KUNDE:	Aber Sie haben doch vorhin gesagt, ich könnte sie für dreißig Pfund haben.
HÄNDLER:	Sie *wollen* sie aber nicht – oder?
KUNDE:	Eigentlich nicht, das können Sie aber doch nicht wissen.
HÄNDLER:	Doch. Sobald jemand ins Geschäft kommt, kann ich so ungefähr drauf tippen, worauf er aus ist. Sie zum Beispiel interessieren sich eigentlich überhaupt nicht für Porzellan, oder?
KUNDE:	Nein, nicht besonders.
HÄNDLER:	Überhaupt nicht – die Uhr dahinten aber, die gefällt Ihnen, nicht wahr?
KUNDE:	Doch, ja. Aber wie *kommen* Sie darauf?

18

Contrastive topic and practical: concision and the adverb in German

This chapter constitutes the material for all or part of a practical. If possible, the following exercise should be handed in before the practical. It should in any case be completed before going on to the material in the rest of the chapter.

PRELIMINARY EXERCISE

Translate the following sentences, using only a monolingual German dictionary.

1. Meanwhile, I continued occasionally to see something of Quiggin, though I came no nearer to deciding which of the various views held about him were true.
2. He has come to appreciate that money alone is not the answer to his problems.
3. It would interest me to know whether he got his information in-house.
4. There, without bothering to light the lamp which stood ready with its box of matches, I tried one key after another in the door until I had found the right one.
5. Signs of tension were beginning to show.
6. But that wasn't how he went about it. What he did was to write to Mr Smith asking for more time.
7. What he really enjoyed was drinking cups of coffee at odd times of day.
8. It was in the light of these considerations that your Board decided to terminate the discussions with the X Group.
9. It was all they could do to shift the boulder.
10. Er bestellte nur noch Kaffee.
11. Du siehst deine Zukunft ja ganz positiv.

12 ...die Paradiesvögel... hatten ihn anfangs an die Chinoiserien auf frühen Meißener Kannen erinnert, bis allmählich die Liebenden des 'Yun Yu' aus den Seidengründen dämmerten...

18.1 INTRODUCTION

Alongside a chapter illustrating the relatively explicit marking of German texts by sentential particles, it may seem odd that the present chapter argues German to be, in a different respect, more concise than English. There is in fact no paradox. Good modern written German is syntactically much simpler than popular myth will have it, indeed simpler in some important respects than English; and its relative syntactic simplicity relates to – among other things – the strength of adverbial and particle function.

That German syntax tends to be more concise – and perhaps inherently more forceful – than English is due in part to differences between the two languages in the ways they articulate clauses: differences which for present purposes are most conveniently approached by focusing on certain English constructions with verbs. Certain types of translation work are instrumental in illustrating the point. For instance, to attempt to render *Times* or *Guardian* leading articles into German is to find that native English, particularly but not only in this register, is unsuspectedly rich in hypotactic constructions (that is, complex syntactic structures such as the immediately following example, in which an 'if' clause is embedded in a 'that' clause). The middlebrow British public is used to being offered such formulae as:

> Mrs Thatcher used to promise that if the nation would only work harder the balance of payments would improve and all other problems would then resolve themselves.

Translation exercises in this kind of material, however, have a way of showing rapidly that there are problems of adjustment between such 'nesting' clauses and the conventions of German syntax. It may even be that word-order constraints in formal German have encouraged a certain economy, relative to English, in the use of subordinating verbs. A number of factors are involved. For instance, in newspaper-type reports and commentary – to stay near the initial example – subjunctive markers can replace verbs denoting verbal communication. A significant further contribution to simpler clause construction (relative to English) is made by formulae such as 'nach Ansicht Frau Thatchers' or 'laut Thatcher' (adverbial), or 'so Thatcher' (interjection). It needs to be said at once that such formulae belong either to relatively formal written language or to the spoken language peculiar to broadcasting and debate. Informal language is less shy of simple successions of noun clauses, and finds its own ways of dealing with the type of complexity marked in English by 'She said that, if...'.

The contrastive concern of this chapter is with the preference of more formal German for compactness of utterance. The tendency is attested to by such features as the familiar – or to non-Germans notorious – encapsulated participial phrases preceding the noun, which are by no means confined to serious expository texts. Then there is the morphological precision which in the last four words of the following example permits an impressive density of information (even if an English TT reduces the previous five words to two):

> Alles begann bei uns 1979: ein Ehepaar, beide Partner mit abgeschlossenem Hochschulstudium, er promoviert, sie promovierend.

The chapter's specific focus is on comparisons of verb–adverb constructions on the German side with syntactically more complex verb-on-verb constructions and a range of other constructions in English including so-called 'cleft structures' (for example, 'It's the tobacco that counts') and 'pseudo-cleft structures' ('What counts is the tobacco'). In as far as German tends to prefer verb–adverb constructions, while English tends to prefer verb-on-verb constructions, 'cleft' structures and subordinate clauses, there is a discrepancy between the two languages which is of some significance to translators. Yet for those working into English this is not a discrepancy that regularly calls attention to itself. There is usually little or no sense of 'translation resistance' as one translates a verb–adverb combination from German into the same structure in English. Consider sentence 12 in the preliminary exercise, and a parallel, simpler example:

ST12	....bis allmählich die Liebenden... aus den Seidengründen dämmerten.
TT12(a)	...until the lovers... gradually became visible in the silken depths.
ST13	Seine Besuche wurden allmählich seltener und hörten zuletzt ganz auf.
TT13(a)	His visits gradually grew less frequent and eventually stopped altogether.

While these TTs individually are not particularly 'strange' in English, they do not take up an option which in practice is very readily and very often used in English: the double verb construction. Is it less good? Or just less imitative of the ST's structure?

TT12(b)	...until the lovers... began to take on shape in the silken depths.
TT13(b)	His visits began to grow fewer, and eventually stopped altogether.

There is a possible danger here for the translator working into English, and we shall return to it. But first it needs to be demonstrated that in the area under discussion there is a substantial discrepancy between the two languages. We shall do this first through a further illustration of an 'easy' German–English translation, then through illustrations of English–German translations which seem 'difficult', that is, require grammatical transpositions.

On an individual level, not all adverbial uses of 'allmählich' will allow the translator equal freedom. In the following sentence, for instance, 'gradually' is not automatically possible; should it be allowed to determine the choice of verb?

ST14 Eine neue Gefahr zeichnete sich allmählich ab.
TT14(a) Gradually, a fresh danger became apparent.
TT14(b) A fresh danger began to loom.

The constraints on the use of 'allmählich' in this example suggest that, in certain adverbs, apparent 'equivalences' should not be taken for granted. The reason for avoidance of 'begin' in translating 'allmählich' may be euphony in some cases (for instance, avoidance of '*be*gin to *be*come'), or it may be unconscious retention of ST structures; but there is clearly at least a risk that a translator working fast may unintentionally favour the verb–adverb structure in English simply because it is closest to the German ST structure, at the expense of TT alternatives.

That there is indeed a disparity between the two languages, with English favouring many more two-verb structures, is sharply apparent to translators working *into* German. Here, certain frequently used English structures resist literal translation into German; solutions involving grammatical transposition have to be found. Some of the most frequent of these English constructions are illustrated by the following examples drawn from the preliminary exercise:

ST6 But that wasn't how he went about it. What he did was to write to Mr Smith asking for more time.
ST2 He has come to appreciate that money alone is not the answer to his problems.
ST4 There, without bothering to light the lamp which stood ready with its box of matches, I tried one key after another in the door until I had found the right one.

In ST6, it is hard to envisage a remotely literal translation for 'What he did...'. It would be more appropriate to simplify the syntax and introduce a cohesion marker, corresponding to the actual function of the ST's opening phrase:

TT6 Er schrieb vielmehr an Herrn Smith und verlangte eine Terminverzögerung.

ST2 poses difficulties in combining the verbs 'come' and 'appreciate'. The most straightforward solution is to report, not the completed 'journey' ('has come...'), but the new position arrived at ('now appreciates...').

TT2 Er sieht inzwischen ein, daß seinen Problemen nicht mit Geld allein beizukommen ist.

This translation points to the significant potential of adverbs of time, such as 'schon', 'noch', 'nicht mehr', to convey ideas of change and continuation often covered in English by verbs such as 'begin', 'go on', 'give up'.

ST4 would present distinct problems in literal translation. The sentence is already complex, and translations involving 'sich die Mühe geben' are not merely unwieldy, but miss the point that 'without bothering to' is a stock formulation which modalizes the factual point similarly to a German modal particle, and does not require a literal translation. Hence:

TT4 Die samt Streichholzschachtel bereitstehende Lampe zündete ich gar nicht erst an, sondern probierte einen Schlüssel nach dem anderen im Türschloß aus, bis ich den richtigen gefunden hatte.

Sentence 1 in the preliminary exercise presents two separate verb–verb combinations, 'continued... to see' and 'came no nearer to deciding'. The first finds a grammatical counterpart in German ('fuhr fort... zu sehen') and thus tempts the translator towards a stylistically infelicitous TT. The second is patently resistant to literal translation, and thus may guide the translator towards the underlying principle: namely that in German this is adverb territory. A solution to the two problems might be:

TT1 Mittlerweile hatte ich gelegentlich noch Kontakt zu Quiggin, nur stand ich so ratlos vor der Frage wie eh und je, welche der verschiedenen Ansichten über ihn denn eigentlich zuträfen.

Further examples for discussion are provided in the later part of the practical. But it should already be becoming clear that there is a submerged problem, in German–English translation, in the general SL preference for verb–adverb structures over the English alternatives. Thought needs to be given to the *collective* impact, in an extended English TT, of adverbial patterning which too closely matches that of the German text and is thus subtly deficient in the characteristic English structures involving verb-on-verb, or other complex syntactic alternatives.

18.2 TRANSPOSITION TO ENGLISH CONSTRUCTIONS INVOLVING TWO VERBS

18.2.1 Expressions of starting, continuing and ceasing

In this subsection we shall look at English double-verb constructions in which the (actual or implied) grammatical subject is the same for both verbs. These are usually infinitive or gerund constructions. The examples we shall focus on are concerned with the starting, continuing and ceasing of activities. On the German side – the exercise should be thought of as contrastive, not directional – we shall look, in each of the three subsections of 18.2, both at literal equivalents (that is, verb constructions) and at adverbial formulations.

None of the first set of English examples below present any serious difficulties in translation. In general a case exists for a literal translation with, say, 'anfangen', 'fortfahren', 'aufhören', though its appropriateness may vary sharply from case to case. Here, as later in the practical, it can be instructive to compare the two-verb TTs with others built on adverbs. For instance, to use 'fortfahren' with ST16 seems quaintly old-fashioned. For ST5, 'Signs of tension were beginning to show', a translation with 'allmählich' could be considered. The further examples below offer scope to explore the adverbial uses of 'schon', 'weiter(hin)', 'noch', 'nicht' and 'nicht mehr', in some cases amplified by further adverbs such as 'unverdrossen', 'unbeirrt'.

ST15 It's beginning to get dark.
ST16 He just went on sawing.
ST17 The baby continued to cry.
ST18 He failed to understand.
ST19 It has stopped raining.
ST20 He has stopped writing to us.

The next three examples point the question: how far does the choice of construction depend on register, and how far on the collocational possibilities of (in these cases) 'aufhören' and 'fortfahren'?

ST21 Poetry ceased to concern itself with serious things.
ST22 May we continue to count on your support?
ST23 He continued to manipulate events to his own advantage.

18.2.2 Expressions of perception, cognition and volition

This subsection deals with verb-pairs on the English side, in expressions of perception, cognition and volition. These are often, but not always, cases where the two verbs have *different* grammatical subjects. English constructions vary (for instance, 'I believe it to be true', 'I believe that it is true').

In the first pair of examples (ST24 and ST25), there is a clear choice between using 'gern' and finding a more particularizing TT. While 'gern' is more readily thought of in ST25 (explicit liking), the stronger case for it is in ST24.

ST24 He tends to stray from the point.
TT24 Er schweift gern ab.
ST25 He was keen on meeting people he felt were important.
TT25 Er war erpicht darauf, gesellschaftlich mit jenen Menschen zu verkehren, die er für wichtig hielt.

ST26 and ST27 both involve German modal verbs but have little else in common. ST26 again illustrates the need for lateral rather than literal thinking in translation. ST27 needs context: the speaker is referring to a projected trip which still lies ahead. On that basis, 'Perhaps we want...' is translationese, and the assessment of probability is better rendered by 'We might want...'. In sentence 3 of the preliminary exercise, working from English to German, the apparently literal equivalents 'to interest' and 'interessieren' prove not to match exactly:

ST3	It would interest me to know whether he got his information in-house.
TT3(a)	Mich interessiert, ob er das hier im Hause erfuhr.
TT3(b)	Ich möchte gern wissen, ob er das hier im Hause erfuhr.
ST26	I meant it to hurt.
TT26	Es sollte auch verletzen.
ST27	Vielleicht wollen wir auch ein Jahr drüben bleiben.
TT27	We might want to stay over there for a year.

Still in the field of perception and cognition, German has a whole range of adverbs, for instance, 'bekanntlich', 'vermutlich', 'wohl', 'voraussichtlich', 'hoffentlich', which in some cases have direct equivalents in the form of English adverbs – 'hopefully' may now be said to have arrived – but which also offer the forms illustrated below (ST28).

ST28	Die Gespräche werden voraussichtlich zwei Tage dauern.
TT28(a)	The talks are expected to last two days.
TT28(b)	It's expected that the talks will last two days.

Parallel examples may be identified, and alternative solutions found, for 'schätzungsweise', 'lieber', 'wissentlich' and 'geflissentlich'. As a surprised rejoinder to a statement, 'Im Ernst?' may be translated either communicatively ('Do you mean that?') or with a straightforward adverb. The group denoting expressions of opinion (such as 'laut', 'nach Ansicht... + *genitive*' and 'meines Erachtens') are regularly used to by-pass 'daß' clauses, especially where a degree of terseness is to be conveyed. In many cases English offers a similar choice: for instance, between 'I consider (that)...' and 'in my view'. But, as suggested early in this chapter, such parallels can be specious: depending on register, English is usually more ready than German to use the 'I think' form.

18.2.3 German adverbials and English hypotaxis

The material in this subsection is more heterogeneous than that of 18.2.1 and 18.2.2, being intended to show something of the wide range of English TT constructions which may correlate with a 'concise' adverbial construction in German. The common factor in the English versions is a degree of hypotaxis: that is, a syntactically complex formulation is often felicitous in English whether or not a simpler adverbial construction is available.

For focus or emphasis, English often uses a construction of the type:

ST29	What annoys me most is that they never even say hello.
TT29(a)	Am meisten ärgert mich, daß sie niemals grüßen.

While German most often uses the syntactically simpler structure shown in TT29(a), it is not debarred from using the English-type emphasis:

TT29(b) Was mich am meisten ärgert, ist, daß sie niemals grüßen.

However legitimate, this German construction is probably more frequent in translations from English than in native texts. The 'pseudo-cleft' WH-construction is not only very frequent in English but sometimes very emphatic, as in sentence 7 of the preliminary exercise:

ST7 What he really enjoyed was drinking cups of coffee at odd times of day.

Even here, it needs to be considered whether significant translation loss is incurred by rendering the emphasis adverbially: 'Am liebsten trank er...'.

German compactness is well illustrated in the next two examples, of which the first is from a newspaper report and the second is literary.

ST30 ... sagte George Bush dann in einer der wohl stärksten Reden, die ein amerikanischer Präsident über den Nahen Osten gehalten hat.

ST31 [*about the Danube region*] Der Raum Norditaliens, Südpolens bereichert durch geistige Impulse die ohnehin satte Mischung.

In ST30, 'wohl' can hardly be translated without expansion: '... what was probably one of the toughest...' In ST31, the option of a single-word literal translation of the adverb is open: 'the already rich mixture'. But how often in a text can this structure be translated literally without introducing a note of foreignness into the TT?

The following examples may be used for discussion of the treatment of emphasis in the two languages, including the role of cleft and pseudo-cleft structures in English. ST32 includes sentence 10 of the preliminary exercise.

ST32 Später setzte man sich zu andern, die ihn nicht kannten; vielleicht wurde er deswegen still. Er bestellte nur noch Kaffee.

ST33 The most you could say was that it was an honourable defeat.

ST34 The first thing they did was to tie him to a chair.

ST35 It was in underestimating his opponent's ability that he made his one serious error.

Finally, in order to consolidate the chapter's central theme of German adverb use and its English renderings, it is helpful to evaluate the translations offered for the following miscellaneous sentences and consider the respective cases for grammatical transposition. (The first two examples come from a newspaper interview with a young shop girl, the last is based on sentence 9 in the preliminary exercise.)

ST11 Du siehst deine Zukunft ja ganz positiv.
TT11 You view your future very positively, don't you?
ST36 Auf jeden Fall will ich Geld verdienen.
TT36(a) In any case I want to make some money.
TT36(b) I definitely want to make some money.
TT36(c) Whatever happens I want to make some money.
ST37 Erst nach wiederholten Kraftanstrengungen konnten sie den Felsbrocken wegrollen.
TT37(a) They had to heave and strain for a long time before they could shift/ succeeded in shifting the boulder.
TT37(b) It took a lot of heaving to shift the boulder.
TT37(c) It was all they could do to shift the boulder.

18.3 CONCLUSION

The main thrust of Chapter 18 has been to suggest that in a number of ways English usage (all registers) embodies constructions which, in literal translation into German, would lead to TTs unacceptably cluttered with verbs; and that German on the other hand tends much more strongly to concentrate meaning in a single arch or span. The bridge metaphor, though not exactly new, is helpful: the image is of a single large span, perhaps heavily loaded with adverbial qualifiers, rather than of a series of spans between supports. If this tendency is indeed marked in German, then it may be inferred that literal translation of German STs into English, while seldom presenting *obvious* structural difficulties, will in the long run result in TTs which lack the characteristic English diffusion of meaning between verbs, and are thus subtly foreign. To point out the ready availability of adverbs and adverbial phrases in English, and the (albeit more restricted) availability of two-verb combinations in German, far from showing that there is no translation problem, is to show rather that the problem has teeth.

19

Contrastive topic and practical: word order and emphasis in German

This chapter constitutes the material for all or part of a practical. If possible, the following exercise should be handed in before the practical. It should in any case be completed before going on to the material in the rest of the chapter.

PRELIMINARY EXERCISE

Translate the following texts into German, paying attention particularly to the syntax of your TT.

1 [*After an earthquake, a young girl has rescued her baby from a convent*]
The Abbess was there, clasping her hands above her head, and Josephe was about to collapse into her arms when a falling gable-end of the building, most dreadfully, struck and killed the Abbess and almost all of her nuns.

2 [*A boy at boarding-school is writing to his new girl-friend*]
'Beloved!' – I kept on in that kind of style.
'Van Tast is to come out for a minute!' – A kitchen tap was dripping.
Flattered, I worked at it for a couple of hours and then followed the others to bed.
I found my fountain pen the next morning where I had left it – but not the letter I'd started.
Then a notice appeared on the wooden post-box where we left our letters for posting. It said: 'Outgoing letters are subject to censorship. Envelopes must be left unsealed.'
I was livid.

3 He was the general who had defeated the cream of the French army and

> scattered the untamed Turkish hordes; he was the statesman who had contrived to bring the war in the West to an honourable conclusion, that in the East to a glorious one; and all Europe was united in its admiration for this man.

The main aims of this chapter are: first, from the standpoint of the native speaker of English, to illustrate some distinctive characteristics of German syntax; second, to investigate the handling of emphasis in German; third, to look more specifically at some examples of 'inversion' in German; and fourth, concurrently with the first three, to take note of the implications for translators of the syntactic differences discussed.

In modern descriptions of German word-order, for instance Martin Durrell's revision of *Hammer's German Grammar and Usage* (2nd edition, 1991) and Durrell's more recent *Using German* (1992), it is demonstrated that German word-order has on the one hand a flexibility unachievable in English, and on the other certain fixed structural features. This combination of flexibility and patterning is one of the features that gives the German language, written and spoken, its highly distinctive character.

In what follows we shall use some of the terminology of Durrell's (1992) basic sentence analysis, adding the two useful concise German terms 'Vorfeld' and 'Mittelfeld'. We shall in particular consider two features known collectively in English as the verbal bracket (hereinafter simply 'bracket') and their role in the management of sequential focus (see Chapter 6, p. 65). Following Durrell (1992) and others, we may define the 'bracket' as consisting of either:

(a) the finite verb (opening bracket) and any remaining part of the verb (closing bracket), – or:
(b) a conjunction or preposition (opening bracket) and the complete verb (closing bracket).

The bracket structure so fundamental to German discourse – and so foreign to English or French – has interesting implications for the dynamics of reading and listening to German, implications which the translator in either direction needs to understand. To keep the discussion focused, we shall neglect imperatives and interrogatives, even though they too essentially conform to the bracket pattern. We shall be concentrating on (a) complete constructions containing subject and verb (such as ST1–3 below); and (b) subordinate clauses with finite verb (such as ST4), and non-finite clauses with participle or *zu + infinitive* (ST5). Here are some examples:

	Initial element ('Vorfeld')	**Opening bracket**	**Central elements ('Mittelfeld')**	**Closing bracket**
ST1	Wir	sind	extra seinetwegen nach Rom	gefahren.
ST2	In seiner Antwort	wich	er meinen Fragen	aus.
ST3	Der Donnerstag	war	trüb und neblig.	
ST4		daß	er sofort damit	aufhören solle.
ST5		um	ungestört	arbeiten zu können.

The advantage of the bracket model is that it allows one to give an account of how sequential focus works in German. Except for the opening and closing brackets themselves, which occupy second and last places respectively, there is considerable flexibility in the placing of the elements of a statement. While the grammatical subject is most often placed first (that is, in the 'Vorfeld'), it may for emphasis be replaced in that position by almost any other element. Indeed, even the conventional 'closing bracket' itself may for purposes of emphasis be uprooted and moved to the 'Vorfeld': for instance, the sentence 'Du kannst erst morgen schlafen' would fit the 'neutral' bracket pattern, but the idea it conveys is more plausibly expressed in the form: 'Schlafen kannst du erst morgen'. We shall look at this later in the context of 'optional' emphasis.

This analytical presentation of the 'bracket structure' may now be illustrated with some very simple examples. Reading or listening to German, we encounter a finite form of 'haben' or 'sein' which points to a past participle or infinitive to come. A form of 'lassen', 'können' or other modal verb points to an infinitive to come. A finite verb may not point beyond itself – but it will if, say, it is a verb of indeterminate motion. For instance, 'bewegte sich' or 'rollte' or 'schritt' can only signal a generalized alert to the reader until the *anticipated* directional expression is provided: say, '... die Straße hinunter auf uns zu'. The same logic applies when the reader encounters a conjunction such as 'wenn' or 'daß', or a relative pronoun. Opening bracket implies closing bracket; and until the waited-for 'end marker' is reached, the reader remains in suspense. There is a certain tautness in the syntactic structure, a stretched line which is quite alien to most forms of English. For this reason the grammatical 'bracket' concept might well be complemented by a more pragmatic metaphor involving tension, such as 'bridge' or 'arch'. It is failure to supply this tension that underlies the curiously limp effect created by many otherwise competent English–German translations. Consider the following examples:

ST6 You still get bears in the Pyrenees.

ST7 I had a good day yesterday.

ST8 Swiss French, even with the best will in the world, find the language problem difficult.

Here, ST6 and ST7 could in theory be translated with their elements retaining the ST order. Such translations would in theory be acceptable as simple statements on the pattern of ST3, lacking a closing bracket. But these adverbial elements, particularly 'gestern', are so weak, and German so strongly requires a substitute for the missing bracket – in the form of a firm accented end to the sentence – that 'in den Pyrenäen' and 'gestern' are unthinkable in final position except as an explicit afterthought. ST8 illustrates another English speech-habit which runs counter to the 'sprung' German sentence. Here a word-for-word translation into German fails to put the opening bracket in place, and the sentence hangs fire instead of taking its momentum from the verb. In all three of these examples, the adverbial can fit naturally in the 'Vorfeld'. In TT7 and TT8 it can also easily fit in the 'Mittelfeld'. Among the translation possibilities are:

TT6 In den Pyrenäen gibt's noch Bären.

TT7 Ich hatte gestern einen guten Tag.

TT8 Auch beim besten Willen haben die Welschschweizer mit dem Sprachproblem einen schweren Stand.

The perspective needs to be widened, for a moment, beyond the limits of the individual sentence. What has been described here as the 'tautness' or 'sprung' nature of German syntax is seen also in the wealth (relative to English) of cohesion markers, both intra- and inter-sententially: not only 'zwar' (signalling an 'aber' to come), but, in formal texts, elaborate concessive constructions with 'während' or 'mögen'. When a *Times* theatre reviewer claimed some years ago that German actors were no good at improvisation because the verb had to come at the end of the sentence, he was not strictly right, but still could be said to have identified the typically more tightly organized nature of German discourse. Here is a compact illustration:

ST9 Das macht zwar nichts ungeschehen, hat aber viele von ihnen veranlaßt, sich dem friedlichen Gebiet der Biophysik und Molekularbiologie zuzuwenden.

TT9 That can't undo what was done, but it did persuade many of them to turn to peaceful research in biophysics or molecular biology.

For translators working into German, the difference illustrated in ST9 and TT9 highlights an acute problem. Logical links left implicit in the reasoning of an English ST need to be explicitly marked in German, and the syntactic organization normally needs to be tight, as in ST9. A rendering as 'Das macht nichts ungeschehen, aber es hat viele...' would be felt to be relatively ill-considered, even sloppy. In the patterning of the German sentence, the correspondence between opening bracket and closing bracket (or analogue) seems to provide an acoustic parallel to the overt logical linking. Working into English, the translator will have no difficulty in losing the 'bracket' structures but needs to consider whether some or even most of the cohesion markers of the German ST should disappear too.

A last comment on the topic of internal linking and 'anticipation' is provided by the first text of the preliminary exercise. All three English texts used there are themselves translations of original German STs, which are reproduced in the course of this discussion so that their syntactic organization can be studied alongside the translations produced in the exercise. The original ST for sentence 1 in the preliminary exercise runs as follows:

> Sie wollte der Äbtissin, welche die Hände über ihr Haupt zusammenschlug, eben in die Arme sinken, als diese, mit fast allen ihren Klosterfrauen, von einem herabfallenden Giebel des Hauses, auf eine schmähliche Art erschlagen ward.

This text, from Kleist's *Das Erdbeben in Chili* (c. 1806), illustrates how the structural feature of the closing bracket could be used for dramatic suspense. This device is of course still available in modern German, but would clearly require compensation of some kind if the TT is to be idiomatic. While syntactically simpler (as argued in Chapter 18), modern German – even in relatively 'reader-friendly' genres such as tourist literature – tends to pack a considerable amount of material into a single bracket structure.

In the syntax of German statements, the relationship between anticipation, emphasis and inversion is a close one, but not straightforward. One reason for this is that there are three points in the sentence at which the question of emphasis has to be considered: the 'Vorfeld', the 'Mittelfeld' and the closing bracket. We shall not concern ourselves here in detail with the arrangement of the elements in the 'Mittelfeld', which is dealt with extensively and helpfully by existing sources. The essential point is a clear tendency *in German* for the focal elements to gravitate to the end of the 'Mittelfeld':

ST10	Uwe ist gestern mit der neuen Maschine leider *zu tief* geflogen.
TT10	Unfortunately, Uwe flew too low yesterday in the new machine.

While a given German construction *may* be dominated by an emphasis of this kind within the 'Mittelfeld', our concern here is with the importance of the concept of the closing bracket. Even when the position of the closing bracket is not formally filled (by a verb or verb part), the need for it is felt, and German speakers tend to provide an accented end to the sentence. The bracket patterning of German is so pervasive as to create a regular focal point at the end of each bracket structure. The German writer or speaker can thus reliably reckon on emphasis conferred by *anticipation*: that is, emphasis derived from positioning at the anticipated close of the bracket. This type of emphasis in particular is distinctively German. Like the recognized ascending order of elements within the 'Mittelfeld', it might be called 'structural' emphasis. As we have seen, there is a requirement here which translators from English (with its often anticlimactic sentence endings) ignore at their peril.

The term 'inversion' needs to be handled with a little caution. As an inflected language, German is, like Latin, understood analytically, so that the grammatical form of the leading word – 'ich', 'dir', 'gefahren' – and the awareness of predictable fixed points to come will give the listener the necessary broad orientation. While the simplest and probably most useful definition of inversion in statements is that it places the subject after the verb and replaces it before the verb with another element, the facility is so much an unthinking part of the language that it is often not perceived as 'inversion' in the sense of a stylistic feature. Goethe's Werther (1774) reports being criticized for the 'Inversionen, die mir manchmal entfahren', but even his pettifogging employer will hardly have been thinking of sentences like 'Jetzt lacht sie wieder'. Inversions (in the narrow syntactic sense as above) are found on every point of a scale from negligible to very striking. The challenge to the German–English translator is clear. While there can be no clear categorization of scale, our discussion will move gradually from the everyday to the most arresting examples.

If we turn now to the 'Vorfeld', what we are dealing with is the emphasis associated with the main area of flexibility within the overall patterning of German. This is the 'topic' position at the beginning of the statement. This too is 'structural' emphasis, that is, emphasis through positioning. But it is of course by no means exclusive to German. Still at the same point in the sentence, an additional emphasis, which we shall call 'optional' emphasis, may be provided. The writer/speaker regulates the strength of this 'optional' emphasis principally through choice of syntactic element to occupy the topic position. The more unusual the choice (in purely statistical terms), the stronger the emphasis will be.

Emphasis depends on referential content as well as on syntactic and stylistic factors. The immediately following examples illustrate how, with fairly evenly balanced sentence elements, mild emphasis can be conferred through 'Vorfeld' position:

ST11 Über zehntausend Mark spendete unsere Gemeinde zu Weihnachten für Wohltätigkeitszwecke.

ST12 Für Wohltätigkeitszwecke spendete unsere Gemeinde zu Weihnachten über zehntausend Mark.

ST13 Zu Weihnachten spendete unsere Gemeinde für Wohltätigkeitszwecke über zehntausend Mark.

These present some translation difficulties, partly because of limitations in the TT on what can occupy the initial position, partly because the emphases are not particularly strong. Possible renderings:

TT11 A total of over 10000 marks was donated by...

TT12 Charity donations in our community at Christmas totalled...

TT13 Last Christmas our community donated...

In sentences of this length and type, English seems to give mild emphasis likewise through initial position. More interesting, perhaps, is the German use of initial position in short sentences in dialogue:

ST14 [*The boy has pleaded to be given milk rather than water. The mother replies:*]
Milch kriegst du in den Kaffee.

ST15 A: Du hast geträumt.
B: Kann mich nicht erinnern. Geträumt... kann sein.
A: Laut geschrien hast du.

These two cases are quite different. The clear inversion in the first is sentential marking, and illustrates a standard German dialogue pattern in which the reply uses the 'Vorfeld' position to indicate the point of focus selected from the triggering remark. It is not necessarily informal in register, though it is here. In English this response is usually (as here) handled through voice inflection, a procedure so standard that the written form would have no special marking:

TT14 You'll get milk in your coffee.

The second of the two examples is not sentential, but a more strongly marked emphasis, one perhaps found more in an informal register. A is very interested in B's nightmare, highlights the unusual feature and lingers over the words. In grammatical terms he has led with the closing bracket. As suggested earlier, the impact of this 'inversion' is directly related to its unusualness and that in turn can only be assessed on the basis of experience of the language. Here the translation raises some interesting issues. 'Yelling, you were' is possible – but not as natural as the ST. 'You were yelling' could be inflected to convey the interest behind the ST emphasis. But probably the best TT reinforces in another way: 'You weren't half yelling'.

Another pair of examples related to the last one will illustrate the variety of emphasis marking in English:

ST16 Paß auf, in der Schachtel sind doch Eier!
TT16(a) Look out, there's eggs in that box!
TT16(b) Look out, that box's got eggs in it!

In both the above TTs, 'eggs' is in middle position yet clearly highlighted. German as always has the emphasis points at start and end. In the next variation a very minor wording change in the German ST produces a new formulation in English, one which, extended by a verb as in TT18, becomes the familiar cleft structure:

ST17 Paß auf, in der Schachtel sind doch die Eier!
TT17 Look out, that's the box with the eggs in.
ST18 Und in dem Haus da wohnen meine Schwiegereltern.
TT18 And that's the house where my parents-in-law live.

Yet a further English option, much used in both short and long sentences, is the passive. German often uses a passive to give topic-position emphasis, but is almost as likely to lead with an accusative or dative object:

ST19 Ihnen blieb nicht erspart, was für den Reisenden mit der Fähre die Regel ist.
TT19 Nor were they spared the procedure that ferry passengers have to undergo.

In short sentences, then, it may be helpful to distinguish between two communicative situations tending to trigger conspicuous inversion in German: the picking up of a 'Stichwort' in dialogue and a sense of strong emphasis. The former situation is perhaps most often covered in English translation by voice inflection only (for instance, 'I haven't *got* your scissors'); the latter may, depending on its form, require any of a range of approaches: voice inflection only; cleft and pseudo-cleft structures; passive constructions; and constructions which change the relation of the elements, such as:

ST20 In dem Fleisch sind ja Maden!
TT20 This meat's got maggots in it!

To end the present section, here is the original German text of which the second passage in the preliminary exercise is a translation. It illustrates the natural use – unexceptional in any register – of simple inversions in sentence linking.

...'Geliebte!' – In diesem Sinne fuhr ich fort.
...'van Tast soll mal rauskommen!' – In der Küche ging ein Wasserkran nicht mehr zu. Geschmeichelt bastelte ich zwei Stunden und folgte den anderen ins Bett.

Meinen Füllfederhalter fand ich am nächsten Morgen noch auf demselben Platz. Den angefangenen Brief aber nicht!

Und dann hing an unserem hölzernen Postkasten, in den wir unsere Briefe warfen, eine Papptafel:

'Abgehende Briefe stehen unter Zensur.'
'Die Briefumschläge sind offen zu lassen.'
Ich kochte.

In the remainder of the chapter we shall look briefly at some relatively deliberate and striking uses of inversion, of a type found in relatively formal expository and literary texts. First, from literary criticism, a short sentence inverting subject and *sein*-predicate:

ST21 Eine ausschließlich politische Tragödie ist das Drama nirgendwo.

To reproduce the force of this statement, an English TT would have to use its own inversion, a different one, and possibly emphasis:

TT21 At no point can the play be described as a purely *political* tragedy.

Second, and strictly speaking an inversion only from the English-speaker's point of view, is the macrocephalic 'daß' clause subject favoured by academics:

ST22 Daß alle diese Deutungen in die Zeit einer idealistisch orientierten Germanistik fielen, relativiert allein schon ihre Aussagekraft.

ST23 Daß diese Auffassung den tatsächlichen Funktionen des Staates [...] nicht entspricht und [...] vermutlich noch nie entsprochen hat, wird dabei verkannt.

While technically there is no grammatical inversion here, a sense of logical inversion is created by the fact that relatively complicated analytical findings precede the principal statement. German could, and English usually would, remove the inversion. For example:

TT23 They fail to realize that this view does not describe the true functions of the State, [...] and [...] probably never has.

Third, a true inversion may occasionally be – so to speak – given added value by a process of delaying the subject (which thus becomes an unusually strongly marked substitute for the closing bracket). From a description of the Berolina figure in Berlin:

ST24 Den Oberkörper umschmiegt, bis zu den Hüften, knapp anliegend, ein Schuppenpanzerhemd.

Here it might be felt that the stylistic means are out of proportion to the end, and translation via an English passive presents no serious problems. But the delayed subject has a pedigree in serious poetic diction. Hölderlin in particular uses expectation and delayed fulfilment to achieve emotional charge. In the following quotation from the second version of his *Der Tod des Empedokles,* the subject of the verb 'umfängt' is 'Natur'.

ST25

Mit Ruhe wirken soll der Mensch,
Der sinnende, soll entfaltend
Das Leben um ihn fördern und heitern
denn hoher Bedeutung voll,
voll schweigender Kraft umfängt
Den ahnenden, daß er bilde die Welt,
die große Natur [...]

Fourth, the relatively high-profile tactic of placing the past participle first (and incidentally thus creating a new point of attention at the *end* of the sentence) can be found in a range of contexts ranging from consumer information through feature journalism to serious expository texts. A number of sentences in this category are grouped together for translation and discussion in the closing exercise. Given that these constructions owe their impact to their relative infrequency, it is striking stylistically that the last three sentences in the exercise occur within a few lines of each other in four paragraphs of the same piece of upmarket journalism. These three sentences should therefore be regarded as linked: the translator has to decide whether this is intentional structuring or an unconscious foible.

Fifth, against standard preferences and accordingly heavy in impact, is the positioning of 'nicht' in Feuchtwanger's account of a carefully manipulated court hearing:

ST26 [...] da griff Dr. Hartl ein, da war eine Mauer. Nicht erfuhr das Gericht, wie Ratzenberger zuerst ganz unbestimmt ausgesagt hatte [...]. Nicht erfuhr man, wie da Fäden gingen von der Polizei zu den Justizbehörden, von den Justizbehörden zum Kultusministerium.

A published translation recognizes the weight of these inversions with the formulations: 'The court was not to learn [...] They were not to learn...'.

Sixth and last, and the original of text no. 3 in the preliminary exercise, is a representative example of a historian's carefully measured analytical style:

ST27 Dem Feldherrn, der das französische Eliteheer überwunden und die ungestümen türkischen Massen zertrümmert hatte, dem Staatsmann, der es verstanden hatte, den Krieg im Westen zu einem ehrenvollen und den im Osten zu einem glorreichen Abschluß zu bringen, gehörte die Bewunderung Europas.

It is debatable whether an English TT can successfully reproduce the 'periodic' style of the ST without reversing the order of the ideas (i.e. putting subject and main verb first); lacking the precise grammatical control announced in the German ST from the start ('Dem...'), English makes heavier weather of controlling the syntax, and that in turn makes it difficult to translate the last four words of the ST without underlining the bathos. As an alternative to the spaced-out English version offered for back-translation in the preliminary exercise, one could consider a more imitative translation such as TT27(a). But yet a third possibility might be more congenial to an English-speaking audience, because less deliberate in structure: a recasting of the sentence, as indicated in TT27(b), so that it leads with the idea of Europe's admiration. The choices faced here are among those that the translator of the book would face at the strategic level.

TT27(a) As the general who had defeated the cream of the French army and scattered the untamed Turkish hordes, as the statesman who had contrived to bring the war in the West to an honourable conclusion, that in the East to a glorious one, he was the focus of Europe's admiration.

TT27(b) All Europe admired him as the general who had...

EXERCISE: *Assess the position and strength of emphasis in the following sentences and suggest suitable English translations. (Note that the last three sentences featured in a single 500-word article.)*

1 [*fares brochure, after explaining first introduction of off-peak fares*] Erreicht werden soll damit, daß es im Berufsverkehr etwas mehr Platz gibt.
2 Gekonnt sein will auch das Auftragen von Speisen. [...] Beim Abräumen trägt ein Butler nie mehr als zwei Teller auf einmal: gefragt ist Souveränität, nicht Akrobatik.
3 In der Vergangenheit blockierten sich die fünf ständigen Mitglieder des Sicherheitsrates durch Ihr Veto meist gegenseitig. Gewählt wurde dann regelmäßig ein Verlegenheitskandidat, der sich allerdings in der Folge durchaus als starke Persönlichkeit entpuppen konnte.
4 Zu diesen Verhältnissen beigetragen hat eine Linke, die hilflos die alten Antifa-Rituale der 30er Jahre wiederbelebte, energischen Widerspruch gegen Le Pens These, die Immigrantenflut werde die französische Identität ruinieren, aber nicht aufbrachte.
5 Unterstützt wird diese Argumentation von Politologen, die die sozialen Probleme der Immigration in einen bloß politischen Konflikt umdeuten, dessen Ursache sie in Rassismus und Ausländerfeindlichkeit sehen.
6 Beachtet werden muß endlich, daß das In-Szene-Setzen traditioneller Antifa-Rituale, so echt die Wut der Beteiligten auch sein mag, auch unbeabsichtigte Auswirkungen hat.

20

Summary and conclusion

The idea of translators as active and responsible agents of the translation process has played a constant and central part throughout this course. Indeed, the personal responsibilities of translators are, in our view, of paramount importance. Although loyalties may genuinely be divided between responsibilities to the author of the ST, to the manifest properties and features of the ST (in particular, with a view to what is there in black and white in a written ST, as opposed to what its author may have intended), to the 'paymaster' by whom a TT has been commissioned, and to a putative public for whom the TT is meant, it is, in the end, the translator alone who is responsible for submitting a particular TT. Responsibility entails decisions, and it is with this in mind that we have insisted at every juncture on the key notions of *strategy* and *decisions of detail,* stressing the idea that decisions of detail should be rationally linked to the prior formulation of overall strategy for translating a particular text in a particular set of circumstances.

The adoption of an appropriate translation strategy implicitly means 'ranking' the cultural, formal, semantic, stylistic and genre-related properties of the ST according to their relative textual *relevance* and the amount of attention these properties should receive in the process of translation. The aim is to deal with translation loss (see especially Chapter 2), and the attendant necessities of compromise and compensation (see the discussion in Chapter 3), in a relatively rational and systematic way: in short, by sanctioning the loss of features that have a low degree of textual relevance, sacrificing less relevant textual details to more relevant ones, and using techniques of compensation to convey features of high textual relevance that cannot be more directly rendered.

To return briefly to the idea of 'textual relevance', this is a qualitative measure of the degree to which, in the translator's judgement, particular properties of a text are held responsible for the overall impact carried in and by that text. In a sense, textually relevant features are those that stand out as features that make the text what it is. This is not as trivial and circular as it might sound. On the contrary, it is the basis for the only reasonably reliable test of textual relevance. No such test can, of course, escape a degree of subjectivity, but the most objective test of textual relevance is to imagine that a particular textual property is omitted from the text and to assess what difference this omission would make to the overall impact of the text as a whole. If the answer is 'little or none', we may take it that the property in question has a very low degree of textual relevance. If, on the other hand, omission of a textual property would mean a palpable loss in either the genre-typical or the individual (perhaps even deliberately idiosyncratic) character of the text, we may attribute a high degree of relevance to the textual property in question.

Ideally, developing a translation strategy by way of assessing textual relevance in a ST entails scanning the text for every *kind* of textual feature that might conceivably be relevant to formulating an appropriate TT. For such scanning to be systematic yet speedy, it is vital to have in mind a concrete 'check-list' of the *kinds* of textual feature one needs to look out for. It is with this in view that we suggest the schema of textual 'filters' sketched out on p. 227. The overall schema summarizes practically the entire framework of the course, and, for the most part, follows the order of presentation in the main body of the text. The only exception to this is in the inclusion of 'grammatical transposition' among the options listed in the 'cultural' filter, where it occupies a position between 'calque' and 'communicative translation'. It can be argued that grammatical transposition is, indeed, a cultural matter and has important implications in the presentation of different world-views favoured by SL and TL respectively (for instance, the tendency for German to express the inception of an action by an adverbially qualified verb, as against the tendency in English to express the same message by a verb-on-verb construction, cf. 'Die Kinder fragen *schon*' versus 'The children are *starting to ask* questions'). It can also be argued that as an option grammatical transposition is intermediate between the rather more SL-oriented creation of calqued expressions (which retain much of the cultural flavour of their SL models) and the considerably more TL-oriented choice of communicative translations (which retain none of the cultural flavour of their SL counterparts). Consequently, the position accorded to grammatical transposition in our schema of textual 'filters' is fully justified. The reason why this does not match our presentation in the main body of the course is a tactical one: grammatical transposition forms the subject matter of four contrastive chapters (Chapters 16–19), which we have chosen to use as moveable course components, and which, by sheer size alone, could not be incorporated in the chapter on cultural issues (Chapter 3) without disrupting the modular structure of the course. For reasons of practical usefulness, grammatical transposition has been taken out of its logical place in Chapter 3 and given extended treatment in the form of contrastive exercises. The schema of textual 'filters' restores this issue to its logical place.

For the rest, the contents of the 'cultural' filter correspond to issues discussed in Chapter 3. This component calls attention to textual features that present choices between 'extra-cultural' and 'indigenous' elements (see the discussion in Chapter 3). As such, it invites the translator to assess – when considering a ST in this light – the degree to which features of the ST are detachable from their cultural matrix, that is to say, the extent to which their culture-specificity is textually relevant.

The 'formal' filter corresponds in content and organization to Chapters 4–6 – with the proviso that it is to be read from bottom to top (see the discussion at the beginning of our Introduction) – and constitutes a component for scanning the formal properties of texts, which are discussed in detail in these chapters.

The 'semantic' filter summarizes the contents of Chapters 7 and 8, focusing the translator's attention on the important decisions relating to the translating of literal meaning, as well as of textually relevant features of connotative meaning.

The 'varietal' filter sums up the stylistic aspects inherent in the use of different language varieties, and invites the translator to pay due attention to the textual effects of sociolinguistic variation. The contents of this filter correspond to Chapters 9 and 10 in the course.

Finally, the 'genre' filter serves as a brief and necessarily sketchy reminder of the vital importance of assessing the genre-membership of texts, and discovering their genre-related characteristics. This filter corresponds to the entire contents of Chapters 11–15.

Although analogies can be misleading when used in explanation, we risk an analogy by suggesting that the schema visualizes the methodological framework of translation as a 'battery of filters' through which texts can be passed in a systematic attempt to determine their translation-worthy properties. In terms of this analogy, textually relevant properties find their level by being 'collected' in the appropriate filter; the importance of the various levels can be ranked according to the nature of the text (for example, the prosodic level will probably rank as minimally important in scientific texts, but as maximally important in some poetic genres); and certain filters or levels will be found to contribute no textually relevant features (for example, a particular text may contain no detectable allusive meanings).

It should also be said that STs are not the only texts that can be passed through the elements of the proposed battery of filters: both tentative and published TTs can be similarly processed before they are finalized, and their features compared with those of the ST, as a means of evaluating their success.

The analogy of filters is a mechanical one, and in this lies a serious danger of misunderstanding. We do not wish to imply that our schema is intended as a means of mechanizing the process of translation; on the contrary, we believe this process to be an intelligent and 'humanistic' one involving personal, and in the final analysis subjective, choices made by the translator. The schema of filters is not a mechanical device but a mnemonic one: it reminds the working translator of what features to look for in a ST, as well as of the need to rank these features in order of relative textual relevance, as part and parcel of working out a strategy for translating the ST. It also serves to remind translators of options and choices when tinkering with the details of editing a provisional TT. But the decision and choices remain entirely non-mechanical: they are for the translator to make.

A further point to be made about the schema of textual filters concerns the time element. Scanning a text in the kind of detail that a full use of the filters would seem to imply is unrealistic when the translator is working against a time limit. In such cases, a more perfunctory use of the schema is still useful in speeding up the process of adopting a translation strategy, and in spotting and handling particular problems of detail. It is worth remembering that the usefulness of the schema is not dependent on making a full and exhaustive use of its scanning potential: it performs a useful function even in speed translation. The translator simply has to make as much, or as little, use of it as time will allow.

Finally, it is worth noting that, through practice, the scanning of texts in the manner suggested by the schema quickly becomes habitual, so that the translator comes to perform the process automatically and rapidly, without having to consult the check-list contained in the schema.

SCHEMA OF TEXTUAL FILTERS

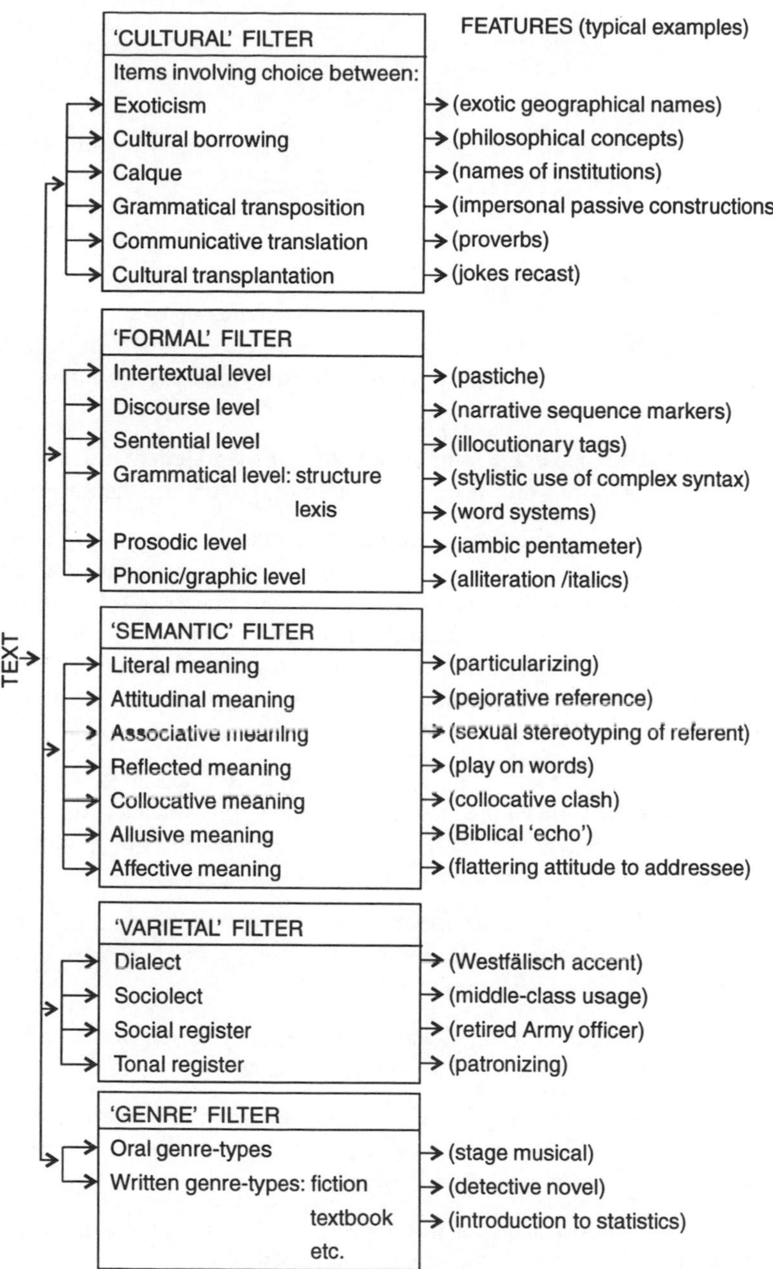

Figure 20.1

Glossary

affective meaning the emotive effect worked on the addressee by the choice of a particular **linguistic expression**, in contrast with others that might have been used to express the same literal message; affective meaning is a type of **connotative meaning**.

alliteration the recurrence of the same sound/letter or sound/letter cluster at the beginning of two or more words occurring near or next to one another in a **text**.

allusive meaning the **connotative meaning** of a **linguistic expression** which takes the form of evoking the meaning of an entire saying or quotation of which that expression is a part. (NB If a saying or quotation appears in full within a **text**, that is a case of citation; we speak of allusive meaning where only a recognizable segment of the saying or quotation occurs in the text, but that segment implicitly carries the meaning of the entire 'reconstructed' saying or quotation.)

anaphora in *grammar*, the replacement of previously used **linguistic expressions** in a **text** by simpler and less specific expressions (such as pronouns) having the same contextual referent; in *rhetoric*, the repetition of a word or phrase at the beginning of successive clauses.

associative meaning the **connotative meaning** of a **linguistic expression** which takes the form of attributing to the referent certain stereotypically expected properties culturally associated with that referent.

assonance the recurrence of a sound/letter or sound/letter cluster in the middle of words occurring near or next to one another in a **text.**

attitudinal meaning the **connotative meaning** of a **linguistic expression** which takes the form of implicitly conveying a commonly held attitude or value judgement towards the referent of the expression.

calque a form of **cultural transposition** whereby a TT expression is modelled on the grammatical structure of the corresponding ST expression.

code-switching the alternating use of two or more recognizably different language variants (varieties of the same language, or different languages) within the same **text.**

cogency the 'thread' of intellectual interrelatedness of ideas running through a **text**.

coherence the tacit, yet intellectually discernible, thematic development that characterizes a **cogent** text, as distinct from a random sequence of unrelated sentences.

cohesion the explicit and transparent linking of sentences and larger sections of text by the use of overt linguistic devices that act as 'signposts' for the **cogency** of a **text**.

collocative meaning the **connotative meaning** lent to a **linguistic expression** by the meaning of some other expression with which it frequently or typically collocates in a grammatical context; that is, collocative meaning is an echo of the meanings of expressions that partner a given expression in commonly used phrases.

communicative translation a style of **free translation** involving the rendering of ST expressions by their contextually/situationally appropriate cultural counterparts in the TL; that is, the TT uses situationally apt target culture counterparts in preference to **literal translation**.

compensation the technique of making up for the **translation loss** of important ST features by approximating their effects in the TT through means other than those used in the ST – that is, making up for ST effects achieved by one means through using other means in the TT.

compensation by merging condensing the features carried over a relatively longer stretch of the ST into a relatively shorter stretch of TT.

compensation by splitting distributing the features carried in a relatively shorter stretch of the ST over a relatively longer stretch of the TT.

compensation in kind compensating for a particular type of textual effect in the ST by using a textual effect of a different type in the TT (for instance, compensating for **assonance** in the ST by **alliteration** in the TT).

compensation in place compensating for the loss of a particular textual effect occurring at a given place in the ST by creating a corresponding effect at a different place in the TT.

connotative meaning the implicit overtones and nuances that **linguistic expressions** tend to carry over and above their **literal meanings**. (NB The overall meaning of an expression in context is compounded of the literal meaning of the expression plus its contextually relevant connotative overtones.)

crossover the conversion of a written **text** into a corresponding oral text, or, conversely, of an oral text into a corresponding written text. (NB The correspondences are a matter of degree, and are never more than approximate.)

cultural borrowing the process of taking over a SL expression verbatim from the ST into the TT (and, ultimately, into the TL as a whole). The borrowed term may remain unaltered in form or may undergo minor alteration or **transliteration**.

cultural transplantation the highest degree of **cultural transposition**, involving the replacement of source-cultural details mentioned in the ST with cultural details drawn from the target culture in the TT – that is, cultural transplantation deletes from the TT items specific to the source culture, replacing them with items specific to the target culture.

cultural transposition any degree of departure from a maximally **literal translation** – that is, the replacement in a TT of SL-specific features with TL-specific ones; cultural transposition entails a certain degree of TL orientation.

decisions of detail in translating a given **text,** the decisions taken in respect of specific problems of grammar, lexis, and so on; decisions of detail are ideally taken in the light of previously taken **strategic decisions**.

deictic a **linguistic expression** (for instance, a demonstrative, a pronoun, a temporal expression) designating a specific referent which the hearer/reader is required to identify relative to context of situation.

dialect a language variety with non-standard features of accent, vocabulary, syntax and sentence formation (for example, **illocutionary particles**, intonation) characteristic, and therefore indicative, of the regional provenance of its users.

discourse level the textual level on which whole **texts** (or sections of whole texts) are considered as self-contained, **coherent** and **cohesive** entities; the ultimate discourse structure of texts consists of a number of interrelated sentences, these being the lowest analytic units on the discourse level.

editing the last stage of the translation process, consisting in checking over the draft of a written TT with a view to correcting errors and polishing up stylistic details.

exegetic translation a style of translation in which the TT expresses and explains additional details that are not explicitly conveyed in the ST; that is, the TT is, at the same time, an expansion and explanation of the contents of the ST.

exoticism the lowest degree of **cultural transposition** of a ST feature, whereby that feature (having its roots exclusively in the SL and source culture) is taken over verbatim into the TT; that is, the transposed term is an ostensibly 'foreign' element in the TT.

free translation a style of translation in which there is only a global correspondence between units of the ST and units of the TT – for example, a rough sentence-to-sentence correspondence, or a still looser correspondence in terms of even larger sections of text.

generalizing translation rendering a ST expression by a TL **hyperonym** – that is, the **literal meaning** of the TT expression is wider and less specific than that of the corresponding ST expression; a generalizing translation omits details that are explicitly present in the literal meaning of the ST.

gist translation a style of translation in which the TT purposely expresses a condensed version of the contents of the ST; that is, the TT is, at the same time, a synopsis of the ST.

grammatical level the level of linguistic structure concerned with words, the decomposition of complex (inflected, derived, or compound) words into their meaningful constituent parts, and the patterned syntactic arrangement of words into phrases, and phrases into yet more complex phrases.

grammatical transposition the technique of translating a ST expression having a given grammatical structure by a TT expression with a different grammatical structure containing different parts of speech in a different arrangement.

hyperonym a **linguistic expression** whose **literal meaning** is inclusive of, but wider and less specific than, the range of literal meaning of another expression: for instance, 'parent' is a hyperonym of 'mother'.

hyponym a **linguistic expression** whose **literal meaning** is included in, but is narrower and more specific than, the range of literal meaning of another expression; for example, 'younger sister' is a hyponym of 'sibling'.

illocutionary particle a discrete element which, when added to the syntactic material of a sentence, informs the listener/reader of the affective force the utterance is intended to have – for example, 'alas', 'dammit!', 'doch mal', 'nicht wahr?'.

interlineal translation a style of translation in which the TT provides a literal rendering for each successive meaningful unit of the ST (including affixes) and arranges these units in their order of occurrence in the ST, regardless of the conventional grammatical order of units in the TL.

inter-semiotic translation translating from one semiotic system (that is, system for communication) into another. For a translation to be inter-semiotic, either the ST, or the TT, but not both, may be a human natural language.

intertextual level the level of shared culture on which texts are viewed as bearing significant external relationships to other texts (for example, by allusion, by imitation, by virtue of genre membership).

intralingual translation the re-expression of a message conveyed in a particular form of words in a given language by means of *another* form of words in the *same* language.

linguistic expression a self-contained and meaningful item in a given language, such as a word, a phrase, a sentence.

literal meaning the conventional range of referential meaning attributed to a linguistic expression (as abstracted from its **connotative** overtones and contextual nuances).

literal translation a word-for-word translation, giving maximally accurate literal rendering to all the words in the ST as far as the grammatical conventions of the TL will allow; that is, literal translation is SL-oriented, and departs from ST sequence of words only where the TL grammar makes this inevitable.

partially overlapping translation rendering a ST expression by a TL expression whose range of **literal meaning** partially overlaps with that of the ST expression – that is, the literal meaning of the TT expression both *adds* some detail *not* explicit in the literal meaning of the corresponding ST expression, and *omits* some other detail that *is* explicit in the literal meaning of the ST expression; in this sense, partially overlapping translation simultaneously combines elements of **particularizing** and of **generalizing**.

particularizing translation rendering a ST expression by a TL **hyponym**, that is, making the **literal meaning** of the TT narrower and more specific than that of the corresponding ST; a particularizing translation adds details to the TT that are not explicitly expressed in the ST.

phonemic translation a technique of translation that consists in an attempt to replicate in the TT the sound sequence of the ST, while allowing the sense to remain, at best, a vague and suggested impression.

phonic/graphic level the level of linguistic structure concerned with the patterned organization of sound-segments (phonemes) in speech, or of letters (graphemes) in writing.

prosodic level the level of linguistic structure concerned with metrically patterned stretches of speech within which syllables have varying degrees of *prominence* (in terms of such properties as stress- and vowel-differentiation), varying degrees of *pace* (in terms of such properties as length and tempo) and varying qualities of *pitch*.

reflected meaning the **connotative meaning** lent to a **linguistic expression** by the fact that its *form* (phonic, graphic, or both) is reminiscent of a homonymic or near-homonymic expression with a different **literal meaning**; that is, reflected meaning is an echo of the literal meaning of some other expression that sounds or is spelled the same, or nearly the same, as a given expression.

rephrasing the exact rendering of the message content of a given ST in a TT that is radically different in form, but neither adds nor omits details explicitly conveyed in the ST.

script a written **text** intended as a basis for the performance of an oral text realized in spontaneous (or apparently spontaneous) form.

sentence markers linguistic devices that, over and above the syntactic basis of words and phrases, endow sentences with a specific type of communicative purpose and intent; the principal types of sentence marker are intonation or punctuation, sequential focusing (that is, word order) and **illocutionary particles**.

sentential level the level of linguistic structure concerned with the formation of sentences as complete, self-contained linguistic units ready-made to act as vehicles of oral or written communication. (NB Over and above the basic grammatical units – which may be elliptical – that it contains, a sentence must be endowed with sense-conferring properties of intonation or punctuation, and may in addition contain features of word order, and/or **illocutionary particles**, all of which contribute to the overall meaning, or 'force', of the sentence.)

social register a style of speaking/writing that gives grounds for inferring relatively detailed stereotypical information about the social identity of the speaker/writer. (NB 'Social identity' refers to the stereotypical labelling that is a constant feature of social intercourse.)

sociolect a language variety with features of accent, vocabulary, syntax and sentence-formation (for example, intonation, **illocutionary particles**) characteristic, and therefore indicative, of the class affiliations of its users

source language (SL) the language in which the **text** requiring translation is expressed.

source text (ST) the **text** requiring translation.

strategic decisions the general decisions taken, in the light of the nature of the ST and the requirements of the TT, as to what ST properties should have priority in translation; **decisions of detail** are ideally taken on the basis of these strategic decisions (though, conversely, decisions of detail may have an effect on altering initial strategic decisions).

synonymy the highest degree of semantic equivalence between two or more different linguistic expressions having exactly identical ranges of **literal meaning**. (NB Synonymous expressions usually differ in **connotative**, and therefore in 'overall', meaning; that is, they are unlikely to have perfectly identical meanings in textual contexts – compare 'automobile' and 'jalopy', for instance.)

target language (TL) the language into which a given **text** is to be translated.

target text (TT) the **text** proffered as a translation (that is, a proposed TL rendering) of the ST. (NB 'Publishing' a target text is a decisive act that overrides the necessarily relative and tentative success of the target text.)

text any given stretch of speech or writing produced in a given language (or 'mixture of languages' – see **code-switching**) and assumed to make a self-contained, **coherent** whole on the **discourse level**.

textual variables all the ostensible features in a **text**, and which *could* (in another text) have been different; that is, each textual variable constitutes a genuine *option* in the text.

tonal register a style of speaking/writing adopted as a means of conveying affective attitudes of speakers/writers to their addressees. (NB The **connotative meaning** of features of tonal register is an **affective meaning**. This connotative meaning is, strictly speaking, conveyed by the *choice* of one out of a range of expressions capable of conveying a particular literal message; for example, 'Give me the money, please.' versus 'Chuck us the dosh, will you?'.)

transcript a written text intended to represent and record (with a relative degree of accuracy) a particular oral text.

translation loss any feature of inexact correspondence between ST and TT. (NB Where a TT has properties, effects or meanings that are *not* represented in the ST, the addition of these counts as a translation loss. That is to say, translation loss is not limited to the omission from a TT of properties, effects or meanings present in the corresponding ST.)

transposition see **grammatical transposition**.

transliteration the use of TL orthographic conventions for the written representation of SL expressions; for example, Russian 'спутник' transliterated as English 'sputnik'.

word system a pattern of words (distributed over a text) formed by an associative common denominator and having a demonstrable function of enhancing the theme and message of the text (for example, an alliterative pattern emphasizing a particular mood).

References

Altmann, M. und Kittelberger, R. 1979. 'Gramicidin-S-Synthetase: Kinetik der Aktivierungsreaktionen', in *Hoppe-Seyler's Zeitschrift für physiologische Chemie,* Vol. 360, 1.

Andersch, A. 1971. 'Mit dem Chef nach Chenonceaux', in *Gesammelte Erzählungen.* Zürich: Diogenes Verlag AG.

Anderson, V. 1972. *The Brownie Cookbook.* London: Hodder & Stoughton.

Aphek E. and Tobin, Y. 1988. *Word Systems: Implications and Applications.* Leiden: E.J. Brill.

Arbeitstexte für den Unterricht. Fach- und Sondersprachen. 1974, Feinäugle, N. (ed.). Stuttgart: Philipp Reclam jun.

Baker, M. 1992. *In Other Words: A Coursebook on Translation.* London: Routledge.

Beeton, M. 1962. *Mrs Beeton's Family Cookery.* London: Ward, Lock & Company.

Biermann, W. 1977. 'Kunststück', in *Wolf Biermann: Poems and Ballads*, translated by Steve Gooch. London: Pluto Press.

Binding, R. 1954. 'Unsterblichkeit', in *Gesammeltes Werk, Band I.* Hamburg: Hans Dulk Verlag.

Brecht, B. 1958. 'Vom armen B.B.', in *Gedichte und Lieder.* Frankfurt: Suhrkamp Verlag.

Brecht, B. 1967. 'Die Seeräuber-Jenny', in *Gesammelte Werke. Band 2.* Frankfurt: Suhrkamp Verlag.

Brecht, B. 1967. 'Großer Dankchoral', in *Gesammelte Werke 8. Gedichte I.* Frankfurt: Suhrkamp Verlag.

Brecht, B. 1993. 'Surabaya-Johnny', in *Bertolt Brecht Gedichte 3. Gedichte und Gedichtfragmente 1913–1927. Bertolt Brecht Werke.* Vol. 13. Berlin and Weimar: Aufbau-Verlag, Frankfurt am Main: Suhrkamp Verlag.

Bridie, J. 1936. *Storm in a Teacup: An Anglo-Scottish Version of* Sturm im Wasserglas. London: Constable.

Carter, F. 1975. *Quer durch Deutschland.* Oxford: OUP.

Catullus, 1969. *Gai Valeri Catulli Veronensis Liber*, Zukovsky, C. and L. (trans.). London: Cape Goliard.

Celan, P. 1975. *Gedichte.* Frankfurt: Suhrkamp Verlag.

Cross, T. (ed.) 1988. *The Lost Voices of World War I.* London: Bloomsbury.

Deutsche Dialekte. Kultureller Tonbanddienst, Bonn: Inter Nationes.

Durrell, M. 1992. *Using German: A Guide to Contemporary Usage.* Cambridge: CUP.

Dürrenmatt, F. 1957. *Romulus der Große*, in *Komödien I.* Zürich: Peter Schifferli Verlags AG 'Die Arche'.

Fontane, T. 1966. *Frau Jenny Treibel.* München: Wilhelm Goldmann Verlag.

Fontane, T. 1969. *Mathilde Möhring.* Frankfurt/M–Berlin: Verlag Ullstein GmbH.

Frank, B. 1930. *Sturm im Wasserglas.* München: Drei Masken.

Gast, W. (ed.) 1975. *Parodie.* Stuttgart: Philipp Reclam jun.

Goethe, W. 1957. *The Sufferings of Young Werther*. Morgan, B.Q. (trans.). London: Calder.

Goethe, W. 1962. *The Sorrows of Young Werther*, Hutter, C. (trans.). New York: The American Library of World Literature, Inc., Signet Classic Series.

Goller, F. 1987. 'Der Gesang der Tannenmeise (*Parus ater*): Beschreibung und kommunikative Funktion', in: *J. Orn.*, 128, p. 306.

Goscinny, R. and Uderzo, A. 1965. *Astérix et Cléopâtre*. Neuilly-sur-Seine: Dargaud Editeur.

Goscinny, R. and Uderzo, A. 1966. *Astérix chez les Bretons*. Neuilly-sur-Seine: Dargaud Editeur.

Goscinny, R. and Uderzo, A. 1971. *Astérix bei den Briten*. Penndorf, G. (trans.). Stuttgart: Epaha-Verlag.

Halliday, M.A.K. and Hasan, R. 1976. *Cohesion in English*. London: Longman English Language Series.

Hamburger, M. and Middleton, C. (eds) 1962. *Modern German Poetry 1910–1960: An Anthology with Verse Translations edited and with an introduction by Michael Hamburger and Christopher Middleton*. London: MacGibbon & Kee.

Hammer, A. 1991. *Hammer's German Grammar and Usage*. (ed. M. Durrell; 2nd ed.) London: Arnold.

Heine, H. 1978. *Werke, Band II*, Atkins, S. (ed.) München: Verlag C.H. Beck.

Helbig, G. and Buscha, J. 1991. *Deutsche Grammatik. Ein Handbuch für den Ausländerunterricht*. Leipzig: Verlag Enzyklopädie/Langenscheidt.

Hervey, S. and Higgins, I. 1992. *Thinking Translation: A Course in Translation Method: French–English*. London: Routledge.

Hulme, J. 1981. *Mörder Guss Reims*. London: Angus and Robertson.

Jakobson, R. 1971. *Selected Writings*, Vol. II. The Hague: Mouton.

Kafka, F. 1989. 'Der neue Advokat', in *Gesammelte Werke*: *Band 1*. Frankfurt: S. Fischer Verlag.

Killy, W. 1962. *Deutscher Kitsch*. Göttingen: Vandenhoeck & Ruprecht.

Kleiner, G. 1969. 'Die Bäume des Herrn', in J. Stenzel (ed.) *Epochen der deutschen Lyrik 5 (1700–1770)*. München: Deutscher Taschenbuch Verlag.

Leech, G. 1974. *Semantics*. Harmondsworth: Pelican Books.

Liliencron, D. von. 1911. 'Der Blitzzug', in *Gesammelte Werke*. Vol. 3. Berlin: Schuster & Loeffler.

Lockwood, W.B. 1987. *German Today*. Oxford: Clarendon Press.

Malof, J. 1970. *A Manual of English Meters*. Bloomington (Ind.): Indiana University Press.

Mann, Th. 1954. *Der Tod in Venedig*. Fischer-Bücherei, Frankfurt: Lizenzausgabe des S. Fischer-Verlages.

Mann, Th. 1955. *Death in Venice*, Lowe-Porter, H.T. (trans.). Harmondsworth: Penguin.

Mann, Th. 1981. *Die Bekenntnisse des Hochstaplers Felix Krull*. Fischer Taschenbuch Verlag, Frankfurt: Lizenzausgabe des S. Fischer-Verlages.

McCluskey, B. 1987. 'The chinks in the armour: problems encountered by language graduates entering a large translation department', in Keith, H. and Mason, I. (eds.) *Translation in the Modern Languages Degree*. London: Information on Language Teaching and Research.

Musil, R. 1957. 'Grigia', in *Sämtliche Erzählungen*. Hamburg: Rowohlt.

Musil, R. 1970. *Three Short Stories*. Sacker, H. (ed.) Oxford: OUP.

Newmark, P. 1982. *Approaches to Translation*. Oxford: Pergamon.

Perkins, J. 1978. *Joyce and Hauptmann. Before Sunrise. James Joyce's Translation, with an Introduction and Notes by Jill Perkins*. [San Marino]: The Huntington Library.

Plenzdorf, U. 1973. *Die neuen Leiden des jungen W*. Rostock: VEB Hinstorff Verlag.

Remarque, E.M. 1929. *Im Westen nichts Neues*. Berlin: Propyläen-Verlag.

Remarque, E.M. 1929. *All Quiet on the Western Front*, Wheen, A.W. (trans.). London: Putnam & Co.

Rommel, B. 1987. 'Market-orientated translation training', in Keith, H. and Mason, I. (eds.). *Translation in the Modern Languages Degree*. London: Information on Language Teaching and Research.

Ryan, L. 1967. *Friedrich Hölderlin*. 2. Auflage. Stuttgart: J.B. Metzlersche Verlagsbuchhandlung.

Spoerl, H. 1961. 'Mädchen ohne Singular', in *Man kann ruhig darüber sprechen*. Hamburg: Rowohlt.

Tracy, M. 1965. *Modern Casserole Cookery*. London: Studio Vista.

Wagenknecht, C. 1981. *Deutsche Metrik. Eine historische Einführung*. München: Beck.

Weydt, H. *et al.* 1983. *Kleine deutsche Partikellehre*. Stuttgart: Klett.

'Wort der Bischöfe', *Amtsblatt des Erzbistums Köln*. 15.9.1980.

Zuckmayer, C. 1954. *Des Teufels General*. Frankfurt: S. Fischer-Verlag.

Index